Inside *Gilligan's Island*

Inside
Gilligan's Island

by
Sherwood Schwartz

St. Martin's Griffin ❧ New York

www.stmartins.com

Library of Congress Cataloging-in-Publication Data

Schwartz, Sherwood.
    Inside Gilligan's Island / Sherwood Schwartz.
        p. cm.
    Originally published : Jefferson, N.C. : McFarland, c1988.
    Includes index.
    ISBN 0-312-10482-0
    EAN 978-0312-10482-5
    1. Gilligan's Island (Television program) I. Title.

    PN1992.77.G53S37 1994
    791.45'72—dc20

                                                            93-43394
                                                            CIP

First published in the United States by McFarland & Company, Inc., Jefferson, North Carolina

First St. Martin's Griffin Edition: April 1994

10 9 8 7 6 5 4 3

Dedication

This book is dedicated to Bob Denver, Alan Hale, Jim Backus, Natalie Schafer, Tina Louise, Russell Johnson, and Dawn Wells, who, as Gilligan, the Skipper, Mr. and Mrs. Thurston Howell III, Ginger, the Professor, and Mary Ann, have brought, and continue to bring, laughter and entertainment into the homes of millions of people all over the world.

This book is also dedicated to television viewers, that resolute body that continues to ignore the suggestions of critics, the blandishments of networks, the promotions of producers. They create their own favorites, their own heroes and heroines, by turning the dial, pressing a button, or simply switching off their TV sets.

In a very special way, this book is dedicated to my brother Al, with whom I often worked, and without whom I may never have become a writer at all.

And last, but most of all, it is dedicated to my wife, Mildred. It was her constant help, encouragement and reassurance that enabled me to endure the experiences you're about to read.

Acknowledgments

This book could not have been written without the invaluable help of my assistant and private secretary, Darlene Dickinson.

Thanks to Ms. Dickinson's efforts in collating memos, messages, letters, newspaper and magazine clippings of yesteryear, I was able to verify my own recollections of meetings and events as to substance and chronology.

In addition, in recent personal meetings and/or phone conferences, I was also able to substantiate this information with many of the people who worked with me during my many years on *Gilligan's Island*.

I herewith acknowledge my thanks, alphabetically, for their help in adding many details to my own memory about specific conversations and events: Berle Adams, Rod Amateau, Jack Arnold, James T. Aubrey, Jim Backus, Bob Broder, Hal Cooper, Michael Dann, Bill Davenport, Guy Della Cioppa, Bob Denver, Dr. and Mrs. Richard Diroll, Richard Donner, Alan Hale, David P. Harmon, Larry Heath, Barry Hirsch, Dr. Fordyce Johnson, Russell Johnson, Ed Jurist, Oscar Katz, Perry Lafferty, David Lawrence, Perry Leff, Alan Levine, Bob Lewine, Tina Louise, Larry Marks, Betty Lou Peterson, Jack Petry, Charles Pomerantz, John Rich, Mike Rollens, Sol Saks, Natalie Schafer, Lou Scheimer, Al Schwartz, Lloyd J. Schwartz, Mel Shavelson, Hunt Stromberg, Jr., Pat Weaver, Dawn Wells, Ethel Winant, George Wyle.

Also, my thanks to C.B.S. and N.B.C. for their generous help with the many photographs of the Castaways and the various guest stars, visitors who managed to arrive on the island and then leave — something the shipwrecked seven were never able to do. In specific, at C.B.S. Publicity, Martin Silverstein, Gail Plautz, and Maureen Kaplan, and at N.B.C., Leona Blair.

Table of Contents

x

Table of Contents

Preface

Would you like to know how to create, write, and produce a comedy cult classic television series? Just read this book. It's as easy as falling off a log — into a sea of quicksand filled with alligators, piranhas, rattlesnakes, network executives, agents, studio executives, stars, critics, and other deadly creatures.

Go ahead and try, but don't say I didn't warn you!

Forewords

For 25 years, fans of *Gilligan's Island* have come up to me, and they're always smiling. So Sherwood, we must have done something right. As a writer and producer, you've given me the greatest of gifts. You've let me try to be funny, and I thank you. I think everyone is going to love this book, and I believe they'll learn from it, too. I know I did. Oh, and one last thank you. Thank you for showing me Kauai so I could show it to my wife, Dreama.

Bob Denver

They say that "imagination is the playground of the mind." Sherwood Schwartz benefited a multitude of viewers by using his imagination in creating *Gilligan's Island*. Maybe it was broad comedy. Maybe it was farce. Maybe it was even slapstick. But all seven of us were dead serious about the nonsense which we portrayed.

Inside Gilligan's Island is a mirthful collection of nonfiction! Thank you, Sherwood Schwartz, for our great fun in doing the show, and for giving me the best friend I ever had, the Skipper.

P.S. Move over, John Gunther, *Inside Gilligan's Island* is on the book shelves.

Alan Hale

I first met the man with the Arthurian name of Sherwood Schwartz, known to some of us as "Robin Hood's Rabbi," about forty years ago on the Alan Young radio show. I played the part of Hubert Updyke, a man so wealthy he had one chauffeur for left-hand turns and one for right-hand turns.

But there were even richer things in store. From Sherwood's fertile brow came a gossamer bit of fluff called *Gilligan's Island*. I was Thurston Howell III, a billionaire so wealthy he made Hubert Updyke look like an escapee from debtor's prison. I told my wife, Lovey, not to worry when we were shipwrecked, because if Thurston Howell couldn't take it with him he simply wouldn't go.

I enjoyed this book so much. Every page brought back memories of the best three years of my life. Thank you, Sherwood. You can always bank on me—Chase National, of course.

Jim Backus

Until I read this book I never realized the extent of Sherwood's trials and tribulations in bringing *Gilligan's Island* to the screen. In the pilot film it was frightfully simple for the actors. We got on a boat; it sank; and there we were on a lovely tropical island! But you can read for yourself about the labor pains involved — how the series was born, and why it remains such a success.

If ever again I find myself marooned on another one of those quaint, charming, romantic, adorable little islands, I hope I have this book with me.

Natalie Schafer

Inside Gilligan's Island is a hilarious unbelievable story of what really goes on behind-the-scenes in Hollywood. Bravo Sherwood! Against incredible odds your persistence made *Gilligan's Island* a star.

Tina Louise

I have read this Encyclopedia Schwartzica and I've made a discovery about my friend Sherwood Schwartz. I knew from working with him that he was a fine, honorable, and loving person. But now I know that he is also one tough son of a bitch. It's a fascinating story.

Russell Johnson

Here's to the man who, with vision, talent, love, fortitude, optimism, kindness and sensitivity created, for so many people, so many hours of fun! What a joy to be a part of it and television history! Sherwood, I salute you with love, gratitude and admiration.

Dawn Wells

Introduction

The episodes of *Gilligan's Island* have been repeated more often in more places than any other television series in history. Yes, even more than *I Love Lucy*. Yet, compared to the trip of the S.S. *Minnow* through network waters, the maiden voyage of the *Titanic* was a pleasure cruise.

The battles and struggles in getting *Gilligan's Island* on the air, and keeping it there, were monumental. John Rich, the director of many of the early episodes, suggested I call my company "Lazarus Productions," because it had come back from the dead so often.

In spite of all the difficulties, *Gilligan's Island* went on to become a major television hit. It fathered—or mothered, depending on the sex of that island—two Saturday morning animated series. It also spawned three prime-time television films, one of which, *Rescue from Gilligan's Island,* remains one of the highest rated film specials in television history.

The year 1988 marks a memorable anniversary in the life of *Gilligan's Island:* the twenty-fifth year since the pilot film in 1963. This book deals with that history, starting with the incredible meetings I had with C.B.S. executives: Mr. William Paley, Chairman of the Board, C.B.S.; Dr. Frank Stanton, President of C.B.S.; James T. Aubrey, President of C.B.S. TV; Robert Lewine, Vice-President West Coast C.B.S. TV; Hunt Stromberg, Jr., Vice-President Program Development West Coast C.B.S.; Larry White, Vice-President Program Development East Coast, C.B.S. A network has vice presidents like a dog has fleas. And they are just as maddening.

The year was 1963, and the three networks were already beginning to use the dictatorial power Newton Minow, Chairman of the Federal Communications Commission, had handed to them. Mr. Minow's famous "vast wasteland" speech, in 1961, at the N.A.B. convention, was brought on by the quiz show scandals, payola investigations, and the general low esteem in which television was held. Unintentionally, probably, that speech had a far more devastating impact than the conditions he was criticizing.

In effect, the chairman of the F.C.C., speaking for the government, took the position that the networks were responsible for everything they broadcast. The shocking aftermath of that designation of responsibility by Mr. Minow and the F.C.C. gave A.B.C., C.B.S., and N.B.C. absolute authority over everything that comes into your living room on network television.

The networks have become the de facto producers of all prime-time programs on their channels, with creative controls over writing, casting, directing, editing, and even the musical score. In fact, more often than not these days, the network is responsible for the actual concepts of the programs on their airwaves.

Lord Acton said, "Power tends to corrupt, and absolute power corrupts absolutely."

However, I'm not a historian or a philosopher. I'm basically a comedy writer. And comedy writers, by nature, view the glass as half full rather than half empty.

So, looking back over those times of turmoil, some of the valleys of deepest despair have become the highest peaks of comic recollection.

So sit back and get ready for a tale of a fateful trip. . . .

"No man is an *Island,* entire of it self."
—John Donne, *Devotions*

On the other hand, John Donne never heard of Gilligan.

The Importance of Being Illiterate

"A social microcosm?" asked Mr. Paley incredulously. "But I thought *Gilligan's Island* was a comedy!"

"It's a *funny* microcosm!" I replied in desperate haste.

Mr. William Paley, Chairman of the Board of the Columbia Broadcasting System, was visibly relieved by my assurance. As for me, I made a mental note never again to use a literary phrase to describe a comedy series in a network meeting. In drama it's okay. In fact, it's desirable. But in a comedy, it leaves the wrong impression.

That particular meeting took place in Television City, the C.B.S. headquarters in Hollywood, California, in June of 1963.

C.B.S. Television City is located at Beverly Boulevard and Fairfax Avenue. It's a three-story building set well back from both streets, as though reluctant to come in direct contact with them. The building is a block square that houses all these executives, and it's painted stark white. As the months went by it was to remind me more and more of Mount Olympus, the home of the Greek gods.

About twelve of us were gathered in the sort of handsome wood-paneled conference room you see in the movies, where high-level executives make important decisions.

This meeting was exactly that: high-level executives gathered to make an important corporate decision. C.B.S. top brass, East Coast and West Coast, were meeting to determine which projects in development as potential TV series were to be given the green light to proceed to final script. Then, hopefully, to a hit, to syndication, and then to the bank.

When I entered the room that day, I had no idea Mr. Paley and Dr. Frank Stanton would be attending that meeting. I expected James T. Aubrey and Michael H. Dann to be present because Mr. Aubrey was President of the C.B.S television network and in actual charge of programming, and Mr. Dann was next in command. It never occurred to me that the Chairman of the Board and the President of C.B.S. would be involved at this level, the beginnings of an idea for a new series.

At that time, Mr. Paley and Dr. Stanton were the Supermen of telecommunications, simply names I read in the paper, usually involved with planning groups for the Federal Communications Commission, or at the White House in discussion about the broadcasting industry. They were giants in the entertainment world, not only in television, but from the early days of radio.

Nevertheless, here I was, sitting across from them at the beautiful mahogany conference table. Mr. Paley was directly in front of me, and Dr. Stanton was seated to his left. Representing New York at the meeting were Mr. Aubrey, Mr. Dann, and several vice-presidents in programming from the East Coast. Representing Hollywood were Hunt Stromberg, Jr., Robert Lewine, John Reynolds, and several matching vice-presidents from the West Coast.

Somehow I had to convince both coasts to make *Gilligan's Island* part of their fall schedule the following year.

At that point in history, *Gilligan's Island* was simply an eight-page presentation and "bible."

The term "presentation," in television parlance, refers to a brief description of the projected series—the concept, the major roles, and sample storylines. Together, they form the blueprint, the framework on which the series will be built.

The term "bible" refers to the character analysis of the major roles and the way in which these characters interrelate. In crass commercial terms, the "presentation" and the "bible" are the sales pitch, to whet the network appetite for a new hit show.

"It's a *very* funny microcosm, Mr. Paley," I continued, "because the seven Castaways are all comic characters. The situations they get into are hilarious, as they try to rescue themselves from that desert island."

Trying to rectify my unfortunate use of the phrase "social microcosm," I leaned heavily on the comedy aspects.

"All the characters are painted with a very broad brush. Like Gilligan," I said. "He's so incompetent, if he had been born an owl, he would have said 'what' instead of 'who'." I remembered a phrase from my presentation. "Every week Gilligan manages to snatch defeat from the very jaws of victory."

There were a few smiles and chuckles in the room at this description of Gilligan.

"And the character of Thurston Howell III is just as broad," I continued, "but in a completely different way. Mr. Howell is so rich he buys a new car as soon as the ash trays are full."

That was an old joke I had remembered from a previous series, but it certainly fit Mr. Howell. "He doesn't even pay taxes," I added. "He just asks the government how much they need every year."

This got a bigger laugh. I'm sure several men present could identify with that kind of wealth.

"Ginger," I continued, "is the kind of woman every man dreams about—then he wakes up with his own wife."

As I described the various characters, my attention was focused almost exclusively on the two men seated across the conference table, Mr. Paley and

Dr. Stanton. They both communicated confidence and power, although in very different ways.

Mr. Paley was forceful and dynamic, and asked me many questions about the concept and the characters. Dr. Stanton was quiet and more reserved.

"When does this show take place?" asked Mr. Paley, "Is it present day?"

"Yes," I answered. I thought I saw the point of Mr. Paley's question. "The storm has driven the little boat far off course. 'Gilligan's Island' is such a tiny uncharted island it remains unnoticed."

"Even by planes?"

"It's a little south of no place and a little west of nowhere. So it's really hard to find."

Mr. Paley smiled. "South Seas? Caribbean? Where?"

"That depends on location problems, Mr. Paley. In any case, it's a tropical setting. Palm trees, flowers, lovely lagoons." I knew Mr. Paley spent a lot of time in the Bahamas, so that background should appeal to him. (In fact, in the years after *Gilligan's Island*, other C.B.S. series would use tropical backgrounds with great success, shows like *Hawaii 5-0* and *Magnum P.I.*)

Meanwhile, Dr. Stanton asked no questions. He was much less intense than Mr. Paley. He sat back, smoking his pipe. He appeared very thoughtful as I responded to Mr. Paley's questions, and continued describing *Gilligan's Island*.

Was he thinking about my project, I wondered? I knew Dr. Stanton was a brilliant research analyst. That's why Mr. Paley had brought him to C.B.S. many years earlier. Was that famous computer in his head evaluating my show as I outlined it? Or was he preoccupied with other thoughts? It was hard to say from that twenty minutes we spent together. I just remember Dr. Stanton listening politely, puffing his pipe without comment.

Aside from Mr. Paley and Dr. Stanton, who would ultimately have final say on every new C.B.S. project, the only two men in the room whose vote I needed were James T. Aubrey, Jr., and Hunt Stromberg, Jr.

Jim Aubrey was President of C.B.S Programming, and his support was absolutely essential. His tall, lean frame was relaxed in a conference chair to my left toward the end of the long table. He had been nicknamed "the smiling cobra" by many people in the industry because, they said, Jim derived pleasure in firing stars, executives, or producers without any warning. Whether that was true or not, it had a tendency to keep you alert when you were with him in a meeting.

Hunt Stromberg, Jr., was medium in height and build, with none of Jim's cool, detached, casual manner. Although Hunt was relatively quiet in this meeting with several important supervisors, he was usually hyper and nervous in meetings in his own office. He was the only man I ever knew who could puff a cigarette and chew his fingernails at the same time.

Hunt was Aubrey's link on the West Coast, and he could help your project with Jim or he could kill it. Hunt had liked *Gilligan's Island* from the start, and

Gilligan (Bob Denver), facing the future with his customary confidence and poise.

he was probably more responsible than anyone else for my appearance in the room that day.

As I started outlining the interrelationships of the various Castaways, I noticed a small paper airplane taking flight from the conference table to my left. It was a page from one of the memo pads that were in front of each of us, folded in the traditional concorde-like shape. A quick glance in that direction told me the source. It was James T. Aubrey, President of C.B.S. Television.

This might seem like bizarre behavior on the part of a major executive, particularly in the presence of his C.B.S. superiors, Mr. Paley and Dr. Stanton. But perhaps Mr. Aubrey was entitled to bizarre behavior. Under his programming leadership, the C.B.S. prime-time schedule during the prior season, 1962/63, was the greatest victory by a network in the history of television to that date, or since. That year, C.B.S., thanks to Mr. Aubrey's brilliant programming strategy, had fourteen of the top fifteen television shows, according to the National Nielsen ratings. With the single exception of N.B.C.'s *Bonanza,* C.B.S. had a clean sweep. No network has ever been able to duplicate that feat. Certainly one could overlook a little eccentricity on the part of the man responsible for that achievement.

Another paper airplane took off. Was it simple eccentricity, or was Mr. Aubrey trying to tell me something? Although this was Mr. Paley and Dr. Stanton's first exposure to the concept of *Gilligan's Island,* Mr. Aubrey and I had discussed the show many times. And we had a major disagreement. Mr. Aubrey loved the idea of Gilligan, the Skipper, and their little charter boat, but he wanted me to call the series *Gilligan's Travels.* In Mr. Aubrey's view of the series, the shipwreck, the Castaways, and the deserted island were simply the first episode. In succeeding episodes of the show, Gilligan, the Skipper, and the rebuilt S.S. *Minnow* would take other passengers on other trips to other places.

In *my* series, Gilligan, the Skipper, and the Castaways would remain on the island. The episodes would detail their adventures and misadventures in forming a new little community. The various characters learning to live together because they *had* to live together was the core of the series. It was precisely when I got to this part of my presentation that Mr. Aubrey's airstrip became active.

Mr. Aubrey had explained his objection to my version in previous meetings. Several times. In his opinion, my concept of the show would need an enormous amount of explanation each week, expository scenes to explain why this group of people was marooned on the island. Exposition is the most deadly obstacle to entertainment, whether it's a comedy show or a dramatic show.

Each time Mr. Aubrey and I argued this point, I assured him that a theme song at the beginning of the show would obviate that problem. There would be no need for exposition because the opening song would tell the story in an entertaining way. In 1963, however, few TV themes had ever been used for this purpose.

In spite of our disagreement, Mr. Aubrey was sufficiently intrigued by the idea of Gilligan, the Skipper, and their little charter boat to encourage development of the project. He hoped, I presume, that he could persuade me to do it his way.

In 1963, before networks fully exercised their authoritarian powers granted by Newton Minow, it was possible to argue with network executives, champion a cause, and win some battles. That knowledge alone was enough to encourage producers with conviction to stand their ground.

Now it's infinitely more difficult. Today I would have been summarily dismissed from *Gilligan's Island* after this meeting, or any of the other meetings you will be reading about.

But it was 1963, and there was still some network respect for producers. It was not yet necessary to kneel and kiss the ring of the head of programming. Or kiss anything else either. You could fight for something you believed in. And sometimes you could win.

I left that meeting with Mr. Paley, Dr. Stanton, James T. Aubrey, Jr., and the rest of the C.B.S. brass at the end of my allotted twenty minutes. The producer who preceded me had been given his twenty minutes, and I had had mine. Another producer was waiting his turn now.

It somehow seemed unfair to me that months—or, in some cases, years—of work had to be condensed into a twenty-minute period. This *Reader's Digest* version of all your thoughts and plans for your project had to be distilled into less time than it takes to get a haircut.

My mind kept going back to Dr. Stanton, puffing on his pipe, saying virtually nothing. Had he even been listening to me? I wouldn't find out the answer to that question until some months later.

As I left the conference room, I wondered whether I had spent my time wisely. I didn't really know. Meetings are like icebergs. You only see the tip. Ninety percent of the iceberg is below the surface, and that's the part that sinks your ship.

The Home Front

"How did the meeting go?" asked Mildred.

That's a question millions of wives ask millions of husbands every day when they get home from millions of offices. Our marriage was no different from others in that respect. In other ways, it's quite different. Mildred and I had been married for twenty-two years at that time. We are now married forty-six. That's no record, but on the other hand, it's a good beginning.

By 1964, Mildred had been my wife through my years with *The Bob Hope Radio Show,* the Armed Forces Radio Service, *The Adventures of Ozzie and Harriet, I Married Joan, The Red Skelton Show,* and *My Favorite Martian.* Any woman who has lived through all of that with a writer, and has also raised four terrific kids, deserves to be in the Hall of Femme. Especially if she has to listen to bilingual puns like that.

When we were first married, I used to try out new jokes on Mildred, and she used to try out new recipes on me. It's a miracle either one of us survived. Actually, I began to like her cooking, and she began to like my shows.

Mildred has that rare combination; common sense and uncommon intelligence. And she's pretty, too.

We met in 1940 in Far Rockaway, a seashore resort on Long Island, New York. Mildred was on the boardwalk, sitting on a railing, wearing blue slacks, a red cardigan sweater, and an honest smile. I decided to marry her after about five minutes, but it took me a whole year to arrange it. I was working for Bob Hope in those days and it wasn't easy to get time off.

"What about the meeting, honey? What happened?"

"Oh," I answered as casually as I could, "it was just a run-of-the-mill-meeting, with Mr. Paley, the Chairman of the Board of C.B.S., Frank Stanton, President of C.B.S. Television, and so forth."

"What a meeting!" Mildred exclaimed. "That's enough to make anybody nervous."

"Actually, they seemed perfectly calm to me," I joked.

Mildred pretended to throw a pillow. I pretended to duck. There's a lot of situation comedy in our home.

Then I tried to tell Mildred about the meeting. It wasn't easy. Not with her preparing dinner, and four children, ranging in age from eighteen to six, running in and out. Our first three were boys, Don, Lloyd, and Ross. Our youngest was a girl. Finally. For obvious reasons, we named her Hope.

However, when Hope was born, I was writing *The Red Skelton Show*. When Red, who knew I had written for Bob Hope, learned what I had named my daughter, he sent me a telegram: "WHAT'S WRONG WITH SKELTON SCHWARTZ?"

At the table, all the kids wanted to know about the meeting, too. They were always interested in any new project in which I was involved. They asked a million questions: "Who's going to be in it?" "Where are you going to film it?" "Can I be in it?" etc., etc.

As Longfellow said, "The thoughts of youth are long long thoughts." My kids had the show on the air already. They had no inkling of what lay ahead.

For that matter, neither did I.

Later that night, when the tumult of dinner and questions died down, and the kids had either gone to sleep or were doing their homework, Mildred and I had our first chance to be really alone. It's the kind of scene they do in a movie with a man and woman having a quiet drink in the den, puffing on cigarettes as they muse about an important event. Mildred and I don't smoke, and we don't drink much either. But we're very good at musing.

"How did it really feel?" she wanted to know. "What were William Paley and Frank Stanton really like?"

I knew what Mildred meant. I had had many meetings with important people before, both stars and executives. But those important people came and went. William Paley and Frank Stanton were permanently important figures. Like television's Mount Rushmore.

"I was a little in awe," I confessed. "Like a buck private meeting General Eisenhower. I felt like saluting."

"If they're so wonderful," Mildred wanted to know, "why did they let Jim Aubrey sail those silly paper airplanes?"

"First of all, you're assuming they saw those little airplanes," I answered. "Maybe they didn't."

"Maybe they did," said Mildred, a lady who doesn't like to be dismissed.

"Even if they did, they certainly weren't going to stop the meeting to reprimand the head of programming."

"Didn't those airplanes get you flustered?"

"Don't be silly, I was too nervous to get flustered."

"I mean it. That was a terrible thing to do. Was he just being mean? You know what they call Jim Aubrey in the tradepapers and the magazines," she reminded me. "The smiling cobra."

"Of course I know," I answered. "But until today we've had a very good relationship."

"You can't have a good relationship with a cobra," Mildred said, "You never know when someone's going to play the flute."

I reminded Mildred that Jim Aubrey had phoned me from New York two years earlier and asked me to remain on *The Red Skelton Show* as a personal favor to him. I stayed on for another year, and Jim's Tuesday night winning streak continued.

I also reminded her that Hunt and Jim were delighted when I answered their cry for help on *My Favorite Martian,* which was having first-year problems. *Favorite Martian* became a hit, and Hunt and Jim had congratulated me openly for that success.

After I reminded her about those times I had been of service to Jim, Mildred said, "I never remember reading that cobras had great memories. Or loyalties, either."

I decided to put the shoe on the other foot. "Okay, honey, suppose you were the one giving the presentation in that room. And suppose someone started sailing paper airplanes while you were speaking. What would you have done?"

"I would have taken the easy way out," Mildred answered. "I would have dropped dead."

Then she kissed me.

"Honey, I don't know how you do what you do. It's hard enough to think up new ideas for series. Then you write the scripts. And then you go to these impossible meetings to sell them. How do you do all this?"

"I'll tell you," I answered. "When I was a kid in grammar school, I used to get very good grades. And every time I came home with another exam marked '100,' my father would say to me, 'What's the big deal? Some day come home with 110, that'll be something.' Maybe I'm still trying to get 110."

"You can't get 110," Mildred said.

"I know," I admitted. "But I can try."

"What do you think's going to happen?" she asked. "Is C.B.S. going to buy the show?"

"I have no idea. I know Hunt Stromberg loves it. He loved it the first time he heard about it from Perry Leff. Hunt put it in development at once. And Hunt is closer to Jim Aubrey than anyone. Maybe he can get Jim to see the show my way."

Then suddenly I had second thoughts. "Honey, what if Jim's right about *Gilligan's Island?* Maybe it can't be done my way. Maybe Paley and Stanton didn't even like it. Especially after I said 'social microcosm.' That was a big mistake. And Stanton didn't say anything at all."

"You were so sure about this idea," Mildred reminded me.

"You thought it was ridiculous when I first told it to you," I reminded Mildred. "'Seven people on the same island every week. Who's going to watch?' you asked me."

"And you said, 'everybody.' You said it's important to show that all sorts of people can learn to live together. You said it's a very important idea. Because it applies to nations as well as to the Castaways. You said it was comedy on top and allegory underneath."

"I'm glad I didn't say 'allegory' in the meeting," I said. Then I shuddered as something else occurred to me. "And I'm glad I didn't say the Castaways were symbolic of the seven deadly sins."

"They probably would have made Billy Graham your technical advisor," said Mildred, who had an answer for everything. "Remember what you told me, honey," she added. "You even told me, 'with broad comedy it's easier to get messages across.'"

"I'm not so sure I convinced them today," I said.

"You convinced me," said Mildred. "I'm sure you convinced them."

"You know what I like about you?" I asked.

"What?"

"Everything."

And I do. She's my most fanatically loyal fan. As proof, let me leap one year ahead in this story of *Gilligan's Island* to November 1964. The show had been on the air for three months at that time. Mildred and I were at home on a Thursday evening when the phone rang. Mildred answered.

A lady at the other end said, "Good evening. This is the Arbitron Rating Service calling."

"Arbitron Rating Service?"

"Yes. We're a television rating service. We select homes at random to get samples of how many people are watching which shows."

"I see," said Mildred.

"Can you please tell me if your television set is on?"

"Oh, yes," replied Mildred.

"Can you please tell me what show you're watching?"

Without hesitation, Mildred answered, "*Gilligan's Island.*"

"But this is Thursday," the lady pointed out. "*Gilligan's Island* doesn't come on until Saturday."

"I wait!" answered Mildred.

That's what I call loyalty!

I'll bet that lady from Arbitron is still sitting there staring at her phone, trying to figure out Mildred's answer.

The Longest Journey Starts with the Dreaded Blank Page

"How did you ever get the idea for *Gilligan's Island?*"

I've been asked that question more often than Mary has been asked, "How does your garden grow?" Sometimes it's asked as a matter of simple curiosity. Sometimes it's admiration. Sometimes it sounds like an accusation that places me somewhere between Marquis and de Sade.

Some people think my idea for *Gilligan's Island* came from *Robinson Crusoe*. Or from *Swiss Family Robinson*. With all due respect to Daniel Defoe and Robert Louis Stevenson, I don't think so. However, without those antecedents, I'm sure I never could have sold *Gilligan's Island*.

Television is a copycat medium. Network executives today, even more than in 1963, want evidence that a similar project has been previously successful in some form, any form. They don't care if it derives from a best-selling novel, or a hit movie, or a Broadway play, or a comic strip, or even a previously successful TV series.

Please, nothing original. If it's derivative from a success from wherever, it gives the network executives what I call "an excuse for failure."

Television has an almost biblical reverence for begatting. Plays like *The Odd Couple* which begat the theatrical film *The Odd Couple*, begat the series *The Odd Couple*, which begat *The New Odd Couple*.

Anna and the King of Siam went from Broadway to film to series; so did *Barefoot in the Park*, *Annie Get Your Gun*, and *Stalag 17*, among others.

Peyton Place went from novel to film to TV. So did *Lassie*, *Topper*, *Spencer's Mountain*, and *The Thin Man*.

Some skipped films and went straight from book to series, like *The Hardy Boys*, *Perry Mason*, *Ellery Queen*, *Nero Wolfe*, *Nancy Drew*, and *Little House on the Prairie*.

Comic strips like *Superman*, *Batman*, *The Green Hornet*, *Buck Rogers*, *Dennis the Menace*, *Peanuts*, *The Incredible Hulk*, and *Spiderman*, all became TV series. Some then became films.

As for television shows begatting television shows, the list is almost endless. *All in the Family* begat *Maude*, *The Jeffersons*, *Good Times* and

11

Gloria. From *The Mary Tyler Moore Show* came *Rhoda, Phyllis, Lou Grant.*
From *Happy Days* came *Laverne & Shirley* and *Joanie Loves Chachi.* From *The
Andy Griffith Show* came *Gomer Pyle* and *Mayberry R.F.D.*

This is by no means an exhaustive study, merely examples which come to
mind.

Suppose there had never been a book called *M*A*S*H,* and suppose
there had never been a film *M*A*S*H.* Further suppose that a writer, even a
writer with the credentials of Larry Gelbart, arrived at C.B.S. in 1972 with an
idea to do a TV series about a mobile army surgical hospital in the Korean
War—a war that ended in 1952. Also suppose the writer wanted it to be a comedy series, with wounded soldiers landing in helicopters and being rushed to
the operating room.

What do you suppose are the chances for that series ever getting on the
air? A million to one? I think that's conservative. A billion to one? That's
closer, but still far from the mark.

But what about *Gilligan's Island?* Where did that idea come from?
Perhaps from my public speaking class at New York University, where I
received my Bachelor's degree.

Professor Borden was the instructor, and very often he would give us an
exercise in making an impromptu speech. He would provide a topic; each student would then get up as called upon and speak on that topic for one minute,
without any preparation.

One day the topic was, "If you were alone on a desert island what one
thing would you like to have?"

Two things were specifically excluded by Professor Borden. One, any
means of escape. And two, a woman. It was an all-male class. In fact, maybe
the exclusions were in the reverse order; one, a woman, and two, any means
of escape.

The first young man called upon said, without hesitation, "If I were alone
on a desert island, the one thing I would like to have most is a radio. In that
way I could learn what was going on in the outside world; all the news of the
day, the sports news, the financial news, and everything else."

After a few more generalizations about what he could learn from a radio,
he sat down.

Professor Borden called on another student, and he, too, chose a radio as
the one item he would most like to have on a desert island. He tried desperately
not to duplicate the same wording. He talked about news events, and as I
recall, threw in weather reports, and even obituaries, to sound somewhat
different.

As a matter of fact, Professor Borden's topic for that particular speech was
really quite limiting. A radio was such a logical choice that in quick succession
the third and fourth speakers all selected the radio as their number one choice.
Knowing they were duplicating previous speakers, they all squirmed as they
spoke, searching for a better way to say the same things.

Finally, the fifth speaker arose. "If I were limited to one thing on a desert island," said this young man, "I would like the *New York Times* delivered to my island every morning. In that way, I, too, could learn all the news of the day every day, and believe me, there's one thing you can do with the *New York Times* that you just can't do with a radio."

What followed was the biggest laugh I ever heard in my life, and I've worked with most of our greatest comics. Professor Borden gave him an "A" for that speech.

Was I that speaker? I'd love to take the credit. But it wasn't I. That young man was one of the few in the class who went on to become a doctor. A proctologist, I believe.

That speech is one of my favorite memories of college. Perhaps that's what inspired *Gilligan's Island*. After all, the Castaways' only connection with the outside world was the radio.

Truthfully, I don't honestly know where the concept for *Gilligan's Island* came from. I doubt if the writer of any work of fiction, plagiarists aside, can tell you where a specific idea comes from. Thought processes are simply too complex to trace.

I can't deny the possible influence of *Robinson Crusoe*. It was one of my two favorite books when I was a youngster. (The other was *Beau Geste* by Percival Wren. If I ever do a situation comedy series about the foreign legion, I confess in advance a probable debt to Mr. Wren.)

After leaving *The Red Skelton Show* and C.B.S., I worked on many ideas for TV series. Mostly comedy, because that's how networks perceive me — as a comedy person. It's useless for me to explain I could do a dramatic hospital show, for example, because of my background (graduate of pre-medical school, plus a master's degree in biological sciences and psychology). But over the years I've discovered we are not what we are, but what people perceive us to be. And television executives perceive me to be a writer and producer of comedy shows.

I spent weeks going from one concept to another, looking for a fresh idea; not another domestic sit-com, not a bumbling private eye, or a western spoof, or kids in a high school. I wanted something unique, a concept with which I could say something important even though it would be in comedy terms.

One day the idea of a group of diverse characters being forced to live together began to take shape. They would be a "family," but of a very different sort. But what brings them together? And why are they forced to stay together?

Maybe a desert island, I thought, there's little likelihood they would be found. And if their boat were wrecked, they couldn't escape.

A great many comic possibilities came to mind immediately, based on two major themes: the problems of modern man dealing with primitive life on an uninhabited island, and the conflicts among people as they are forced to adjust to each other.

The world, in a very real sense, is an island, where Americans and

Russians, Arabs and Jews, Turks and Armenians, Irish and English, Afrikaners and Blacks, all must somehow learn to live together if they are to remain alive at all. Rich nations, poor nations, religious nations, godless nations, big nations, small nations, modern nations, backward nations, all exist on this same island we call Earth.

The more I thought about this idea, the better I liked it. But how long would a series like this last? The same group of people? On the same little desert island? Would enough viewers tune in?

In television in those years, a program needed twenty million viewers each week to remain on the air. Can you imagine any other business where you would be a failure if you only pleased fifteen or sixteen million people a week? Television is a hard taskmaster. But that's the game I was in. If you want to play a game, you have to play by the rules.

Would there be enough stories? That question would take considerable exploration.

I began to make notes on various problems that would occur for a group of people stranded on a deserted island. Some of the stories were strictly problems with nature. Would the food supply last? Would a hurricane wipe out their crude huts? Would their water supply end? Would they have trouble with various wild animals? Or quicksand? Or poisonous insects? There certainly seemed to be a wide variety of catastrophes available to the Castaways.

What about stories concerning interrelationships? That, of course, would depend on the Castaways. Before attempting to develop stories, I'd have to settle on the cast of characters who were shipwrecked together. That jigsaw puzzle took me several weeks to put together.

First of all, how many castaways should there be on the as-yet-unnamed island?

In a half-hour format, it's very difficult to deal with a large cast. When you subtract commercials, opening, closing, and station breaks, there's about 23 minutes of actual air time.

So should there be six castaways? Seven? Eight? Nine? Certainly no more than nine. Less would be even better, to devote more time to story and character relationships. Maybe eight then. Or seven. Would an even number be better, or an odd number? More women, or more men? Or the same number of each?

As I started to work out the characters, the two people who immediately became fixed were the Skipper and his assistant. On a little charter boat, the Skipper wouldn't have more than one assistant. Almost from the first moment of conception, the luckless, hopeless Skipper's mate became the star of the show. And the importance of the relationship between the Skipper and his incompetent assistant was just as obvious right from the start.

The picture in my mind of the Skipper and Gilligan never varied from the instant I thought of them together. The Skipper was a large man, really

How many Castaways on the island, and what kinds of characters? It took weeks to decide on these seven. From left, the Professor (Russell Johnson), the Skipper (Alan Hale,) Mary Ann (Dawn Wells), Gilligan (Bob Denver), Ginger (Tina Louise), Thurston Howell III (Jim Backus), Mrs. Howell (Natalie Schafer).

big, and Gilligan was small and thin. Maybe I was influenced by the image of Laurel and Hardy, or Abbott and Costello.

Their passengers had to be carefully delineated to form the social microcosm I was attempting. After all, this limited cast would have to represent prototypes of many different personalities in our society. I also knew they would have to be extreme forms, more caricatures than characters. Caricatures may be one-dimensional or "cardboard," but they are very effective in television in making that role memorable.

Archie wasn't a *little* bigoted in *All in the Family*. He was *totally* bigoted in every conceivable way. That's what made him unforgettable. Lucy wasn't a *little* scatter-brained in *I Love Lucy*. She was *completely* scatter-brained, and equally unforgettable.

Jack Benny wasn't a *little* stingy. Mr. T. wasn't a *little* destructive. Fonzie wasn't a *little* "cool." Gary Coleman wasn't a *little bit* smart ass. *The Fall Guy* wasn't a *little* reckless.

And Dolly Parton is also unforgettable. For *two* reasons.

The five passengers aboard the S.S. *Minnow,* I determined, would be equally exaggerated. They would also have to represent extremes in social, intellectual and financial terms, as well as in background, personality, and even in size.

It's impossible to reconstruct all the thoughts that led me to my final decisions. But after weeks of juggling combinations of Castaways, the final result was five passengers: Mr. and Mrs. Thurston Howell III, married and super-wealthy; Ginger, single and super-beautiful; the Professor, single and super-intellectual; and Mary Ann, single and super-virginal.

In a further effort to make the characters prototypes rather than completely flesh and blood, I decided to call them only by first names or nicknames—excepting Mr. and Mrs. Thurston Howell III, of course, because that would have been out of keeping with their characters.

I don't know what prompted me to do the following. I got a roll of three-foot-wide white butcher paper and tacked it on the walls of the room where I worked. The paper encircled the entire room, except for windows and door. Then I spent about a week with a felt-tip pen writing sample storylines for the series on that butcher paper. Somehow I figured if I could fill those walls with storylines, there would be enough plots for episodes to keep the series on the air.

When I finally finished circling the room with my felt-tip pen, I had 31 stories written on that paper. I don't know if any other writer ever used that particular technique in developing sample stories for a series presentation, but it worked for me.

At this point, the show had no name. I knew I wanted the word "island" in the title, and I wanted the island to be named after the Skipper's hapless mate. Believe it or not, it took me three weeks to settle on the name "Gilligan." This may seem a terrible waste of time to some, but it was important to me.

There are many names that would make the series sound like a dramatic show: "Johnson's Island," "Thompson's Island," "Wilson's Island," etc. I also didn't want a ridiculous name, like "Winkelpleck's Island," "Hogfighter's Island," "Hokusfigger's Island."

So I just kept looking through telephone book after telephone book until I hit the name "Gilligan." I felt "Gilligan" was amusing enought to indicate a comedy series and acceptable enough to avoid burlesque.

Now that I had the names of the characters, I wrote short descriptions of

The characters had to be exaggerated to be effective. Ginger, as played by Tina Louise, was so sexy she could fog a robot's eyeglasses.

each of them: where they came from, occupations, interests, and why they were aboard this small charter boat near Hawaii. I also described the characters physically in order to help with the casting, if and when that ever took place. These descriptions became the "bible."

Incidentally, there's one serious problem all writers face. They are people. They eat and sleep. They catch colds. They have to take out the trash, change light bulbs, go shopping, and pay bills. Just like everyone else.

In addition to being people, some writers are also husbands, wives, or parents. Like me. During those months I was developing *Gilligan's Island,* I went to P.T.A. meetings, Little League games, school plays, music recitals, and I helped all four of our youngsters with homework and school projects.

Aside from these normal distractions and "the thousand natural shocks that flesh is heir to," other things happened while I was working on the presentation for *Gilligan's Island*.

One day some men were sawing down a huge eucalyptus tree in our backyard, not far from the room in which I was typing. The racket from that chain saw was godawful. I sat at my typewriter, unable to think. Not only that, the noise of the chain saw ripping through the wood set up such violent vibrations I had to clutch my typewriter to keep it from shimmying off the table.

When the men finally finished work, they rang the bell and asked if I wanted them to saw the eucalyptus in sections for firewood. I remembered eucalyptus was great for fires. It snapped and crackled and had a wonderful aroma. It would salvage something for me from that wasted day. I thanked the men for the idea, and they cut up the eucalyptus and piled it in the backyard.

The next day was Saturday, and I was determined to get something accomplished that weekend. That's one of the great advantages of being a writer. No matter how difficult the work is, you can do it seven days a week.

When I looked out the window later that day, I saw some dark clouds. Maybe it's going to rain, I said to myself. All that wonderful eucalyptus firewood is going to get soaked. I really should stack it in the garage.

I went outside where the hunks of eucalyptus were piled, picked one up and started toward the garage. My knees buckled. I couldn't believe a three-foot section of eucalyptus weighed that much.

I had bought a lot of firewood over the years, but I never had any trouble lifting it. It never occurred to me that the firewood I bought had been cured for many months, maybe years. This eucalyptus wood was fresh, full of water and sap.

I staggered to the garage and put the piece of eucalyptus down. How did I get so weak? I wondered. Maybe I needed vitamins. Or more exercise. Or both.

I struggled to the garage with the second piece of eucalyptus. Then I went back to the pile of wood and bent down to pick up piece number three.

That's how I remained! Bent over, with my hands down by my ankles! I couldn't move. I was in such agony I couldn't even breathe. I was frozen.

Using whatever air I had left in my lungs, I called to Mildred.

"Honey!"

Mildred came to the back door and saw me out in the yard bent over like a horseshoe. She called to me, "What are you looking for?"

"Nothing," I said, as loudly as I could. "I can't move."

"What do you mean, you can't move?" called Mildred.

"I can't move. I'm in such pain, I can't even breathe."

Mildred was properly sympathetic. "It's not as bad as childbirth," she pointed out.

I was in no position to argue the merits of that comparison. I could only call weakly, "Help!"

By this time, Mildred realized I was really in trouble. She walked over to me, amazed by my strange position.

"You really can't move?" she asked.

"I told you. I can't even breathe."

Mildred was really alarmed now. "I'll call the doctor." She started toward the house, but couldn't resist stopping and calling over her shoulder, "Don't go away."

Even if I had thought of a good answer to that wisecrack, I wouldn't have had the strength to say it. At least that's what I told myself.

Meanwhile, Mildred rushed into the house and called our doctor. He wasn't in his office, but his nurse told Mildred I needed an orthopaedic specialist. She gave Mildred the phone number of an orthopaedist.

Mildred phoned his office and described my condition to his nurse.

The nurse said, "The doctor's very busy, but I'll give you the earliest appointment I can."

"Good," Mildred said. "My husband's in terrible pain. He's out in the backyard bent over like a hairpin, and he can't even breathe."

"How about a week from Friday?" suggested the nurse.

"A week from Friday!" repeated Mildred, not believing she had heard correctly.

"That's the earliest appointment."

"What if it rains?" inquired Mildred. "You want me to stand out there and hold an umbrella over him?"

"I'm sorry. That's the earliest appointment."

"What about meals? And suppose he has an urge to use the bathroom?"

"Sorry."

"When you go home tonight, lift some firewood," said Mildred, slamming down the phone.

Then Mildred suddenly remembered some friends of ours who were very close friends of a well-known orthopaedist in Beverly Hills, Dr. Harvard Ellman.

They arranged an immediate appointment for me.

When Mildred came outside, I was still in the same position, bent over with my hands down by my ankles, taking very shallow breaths.

Mildred had to drive our car across the grass in the backyard to get to me. She jockeyed the car beside me, opened the back door, and tilted me in. I was still doubled over, lying on the back seat facing my feet.

The trip to the doctor was agonizing, but an injection quickly relieved the spasm in my lower back. An x-ray, however, proved I had done some longer-term damage to one of my discs.

For several weeks I remained in great pain, but continued the develop-

Gilligan, disguised as a tree, reacts as he's attacked by a woodpecker.

ment of *Gilligan's Island*. That's another advantage of being a writer. Even though you're in great pain, you can still work seven days a week.

In spite of the back problem I've just detailed, and numerous other annoying distractions, at the end of three months I was ready to present my project to the entertainment world.

One Ten-Cent Phone Call

"Are you outta your fuckin' mind?" asked George Rosenberg.

George Rosenberg wasn't seriously doubting my sanity. It's just the way he talked.

George Rosenberg, or Rosey, as everyone in Hollywood called him, was a very colorful character whose language was sprinkled liberally with four-letter words. Or to put it more precisely, his four-letter words were sometimes sprinkled with language.

It has always been a tradition in Hollywood to develop a distinctive image. And Rosey had one. Rosey talked with a deliberate "dese-dem-dose" kind of speech. Yet he went to the finest men's stores and his clothes were impeccable. He dressed like the Prince of Wales and spoke like Damon Runyan.

Even in the army, Rosey's uniforms were custom tailored. And he wore silk khaki shirts. That's where I met Rosey, in the army.

We were both in Armed Forces Radio Service. I had risen to the rank of corporal writing scripts for army shows, and Rosey was a sergeant in charge of casting. He, along with two sergeant/agents, Lester Linsk and Baron Polan, knew all the stars in the entertainment world. They themselves had been important agents before entering the army. As a result of their contacts with the famous and super-famous, they could, and did, schedule every important star of films, radio, and stage for appearances on army shows.

After the war, Rosey returned to his previous occupation as an agent, and I became one of his many clients. From 1946 through 1962, Rosey had helped guide my career. He had represented me in television on *I Married Joan, The Red Skelton Show,* and *My Favorite Martian.*

In addition to being my agent, Rosey had been a close friend. He was, in fact, the godfather of my son Ross. So we had more than a simple agent/client relationship.

In spite of all that, Rosey had read my presentation of *Gilligan's Island* and he asked me, "Are you outta your fuckin' mind?"

I tried to explain what I hoped to do with the show; how I wanted to combine broad comedy with a meaningful concept about people of various types learning to live together. I talked about the social microcosm aspect, but I stayed away from words like "metaphor" and "parable."

21

"Who the hell is gonna tune in week after week to watch those same god-damn people on that same goddamn island?"

"I think a lot of people will. That's why I spent three or four months work-ing out the presentation and all these storylines."

I indicated the white butcher paper that had formerly encircled my room. I had rolled it up into a long tube about three or four inches in diameter and put a rubber band around it.

"I have thirty-one feet of story ideas rolled up on this paper," I said.

Guess what Rosey advised me to do with that roll of paper?

"It's the craziest idea I ever heard of," continued Rosey, after giving me the advice you guessed. "Nobody's ever done a show with the same goddamn people on the same goddamn location every week."

"Nobody's ever done anything that nobody's ever done before," I answered.

"Don't give me that goddamn writers talk," said Rosey. "If you don't like *my* opinion, let's tell this idea to Bob."

Rosey was referring to Bob Coryell, his partner in the Rosenberg-Coryell Agency.

I knew Bob, but not as well as I knew Rosey. Bob was more concerned with their dramatic actors and writers, while Rosey serviced the comedy people. Sometimes they overlapped because of personal relationships with particular clients, but that's how it usually worked.

Rosey spoke to Bob on the intercom, and a moment later, Bob entered from his office.

"Hi, Sherwood."

"Hi, Bob."

"Sherwood, why don't you tell Bob this crazy idea of yours and see what he thinks of it?"

"Guess what Rosey thinks, Bob?"

Bob laughed. He knew Rosey better than anybody else.

"We disagree about a lot of things," said Bob. "Go ahead, Sherwood."

I outlined the idea of *Gilligan's Island* to Bob Coryell, while Rosey sat as quietly as he could under the curcumstances. He avoided interjecting his own opinions until I was finished. Then he couldn't resist.

"I told you it was crazy," he said.

"Well," Bob observed, "I don't think it's crazy, but it seems severely limited. I don't see how you can do enough stories with the same people in the same locale."

"See!" said Rosey, obviously feeling vindicated by Bob's remarks.

"I must say, however," Bob pointed out, "I don't know that much about comedy. Maybe those limitations are not as important in comedy as they are in drama."

"I don't think it makes any difference," I said, "whether it's drama or com-edy. *Gilligan's Island* could be a dramatic series, for that matter, and I think

His thinking is usually upside down, and sometimes Gilligan himself is upside down.

it could be successful. That's why I believe it makes such a wonderful comedy series. Because the foundation is dramatic."

The intercom buzzed, and Bob's secretary said he had an important call waiting. Bob was happy to leave the room, I'm sure. He exited.

By this time, Rosey probably thought he had been too harsh. He tried, in his own way, to smooth things over.

"Look," Rosey said, "I've represented everything of yours so far, why don't I take a crack at this, too? Whether I'm nuts about it or not."

"No thanks, Rosey. If you don't like it, I don't want you to handle it."

There was no point in asking Rosey to represent an idea which he felt had no chance for success. Literally thousands of ideas are submitted to the networks every year. Invariably they are submitted with great enthusiasm and the strong conviction that they'll prove to be hit shows. It was no place for an agent who had no faith in his product.

"Life is tough enough for you guys, Rosey. I know how hard it is to sell a show. So why don't we just exclude this particular idea from our arrangement? You're still my agent, and you can represent other things. But I would rather have someone else walking in with this one."

"Fine," agreed Rosey.

We shook hands. Rosey was delighted he didn't have to represent something he didn't like, and equally delighted we had retained our friendship.

I was disappointed in Rosey's reaction to *Gilligan's Island*. But even as I left his office, I already knew who I was going to call when I got home.

*

"Perry?"

"Hi, Sherwood. Good to hear from you."

I was on the phone with Perry Leff, an agent I had known for a long time. Perry had joined forces with Freddie Fields and David Begelman a few years earlier to form C.M.A., Creative Management Associates.

All three men were well-known agents, and from the moment they formed C.M.A., they had a long, distinguished list of clients, mainly performers, including Paul Newman, Judy Garland, Henry Fonda, Peter Sellers, and Phil Silvers, among others.

Perry knew I was a client of Rosenberg-Coryell, and he respected that. But many times Perry had said that if for any reason I decided to change agencies, he wanted to represent me. The opportunity had come.

I explained to Perry on the phone that I had a concept for a television series in which I had great confidence, but Rosey was not anxious to represent it. Would he like to talk to me about this one property?

"Sure," said Perry, "come on up and tell me about it."

The very next day I went to see Perry Leff at C.M.A. I brought a copy of the presentation, and my white butcher paper scroll with the rubber band around it.

I told Perry the idea of *Gilligan's Island*. Interestingly enough, Perry's views, in many respects, were the same as Rosey's.

"The same seven people on the same island?"

There were very few goddamns and fuckin's in Perry's speech. Perry was a Harvard law school graduate, and it showed in many ways.

Perry was very articulate and handsome enough to be an actor. In fact, he *was* an actor. Very often his behavior in meetings was a performance, complete with planned outbursts and even indignant exits. He used to tell me about this in advance so I wouldn't be upset by his actions.

While Perry's initial reaction to *Gilligan's Island* was similar to Rosey's, his attitude was completely different. Whereas Rosey told me it was crazy to try to write and produce this show, Perry put it in the form of a question.

"Do you think it's possible to write and produce a show that's so limited in cast and locale?"

"That's why I'm here, Perry."

"I guess that's right."

"I have here," I indicated the roll of butcher paper, "Thirty-one feet of plot outlines for stories. You want me to unroll it so you can see?"

"No. If you say it's possible, that's good enough for me. Leave the presentation with me and let me make a phone call. I've got an idea."

"Good. You want these storylines, too?" I offered Perry the tightly rolled scroll of paper.

"No," said Perry. "I don't want it in my office. Somebody might think I'm in the wallpapering business."

Two days later I heard from Perry Leff. He had made exactly one phone call about *Gilligan's Island:* to Dick Dorso at United Artists.

United Artists, as a result of a previous deal with Phil Silvers, had a joint arrangement with Phil Silvers' company, Gladasya Productions, and C.B.S., which was airing *The New Phil Silvers Show.* This arrangement called for development of a TV series for Phil's company in which Phil need not necessarily appear.

If Dick Dorso, representing United Artists, liked the idea, and Hunt Stromberg, Jr., and/or Jim Aubrey at C.B.S. agreed, Perry Leff was confident Phil Silvers would approve, and the S.S. *Minnow* would start its long journey toward *Gilligan's Island.*

It seemed very complicated to me, that tripartite agreement with all those approvals, but Perry was convinced it would all fall into place.

In less than a week, it did.

On May 13th, 1963, I signed a deal memo with United Artists, the first of dozens of documents involving the financial relationships among United Artists, Gladasya Productions, C.B.S. and myself, and the S.S. *Minnow* raised anchor for that fateful trip.

If Rosey had made one ten-cent phone call—that's all it cost in those days—who knows?

In the Beginning Was the Word

"How would you and Rocky like to write the pilot of *Gilligan's Island* with me?"

I was speaking to my younger brother, Elroy. He and his family had moved out to California from New York recently. He had been writing audience participation shows there, but he wanted to write variety and/or situation comedy. Almost all those shows had moved to the West Coast by 1960.

However, when Elroy arrived in Hollywood, to write comedy shows, he was suffering from a double dose of that dreaded Hollywood disease, S.N., suspected nepotism.

I had had that problem myself when I first started writing because my older brother, Al, was already an important writer. My own talents were suspect for a long time, particularly when my first job was on the Bob Hope radio show, where my brother Al was head writer.

Elroy had two older brothers to contend with in 1963. Our reputations were a hindrance to him rather than a help in his quest for acceptance as a comedy writer.

Elroy had teamed up with Austin Kalish, known to one and all as "Rocky." The two of them had gotten assignments on some situation comedy shows, and they had written a few half-hour scripts together. If Elroy and Rocky and I could work together on the pilot script of *Gilligan's Island,* I felt it would be a relationship that might prove symbiotic, synergistic and serendipitous.

I've always wanted to use those three words together, and I know I could never do it in a network meeting.

In truth, all three words applied. Working on a pilot script for a new series would be beneficial to the budding careers of Elroy and Rocky. At the same time these two talented young comedy writers would be equally beneficial to me. Symbiotic.

Our past writing experience came basically from three different fields of comedy: Elroy, mainly audience participation; Rocky, mainly situation comedy; and I myself, mainly variety entertainment. Therefore, the whole very easily could be greater than the sum of its parts. Synergistic.

In addition, our personalities were so diverse, as we worked together, I hoped for some accidental benefits along the way. Serendipity is only something you can hope for; planned serendipity is a contradiction in terms.

I had sold the show on the basis of my presentation and the character "bible." In fact, the outline of the pilot script was incorporated in the presentation. In architectural terms, the steel supports, the cement, the beams were in place to form the walls and the floors. It was now up to Elroy, Rocky and me to add the painting, the carpets, and the furniture.

In addition to writing the script with Elroy and Rocky, I was also the producer of *Gilligan's Island*. I knew there would be many meetings for me with C.B.S. and United Artists.

There would be creative differences among us. There are always creative differences.

I also knew I would have to defend and/or change whatever we were writing to take into account suggestions from United Artists and C.B.S. executives.

I returned to Elroy and Rocky after those meetings with some victories, some defeats, and a lot of Maalox.

A wiser man than I said, "Scripts are not written. They're rewritten."

That's an understatement.

Scripts go through more changes than a three-month-old infant.

Most people have never been in writing sessions. It's impossible to describe the debates and discussions which affect every word that finds its way to paper.

Three writers can argue for an hour about the length of a line of dialogue. If it's short, it's punchier. If it's long, it's more conversational. If it's *too* short, it sounds jerky. If it's *too* long, it's boring.

Is it too obvious? Or is it too subtle? Too contrived? Too simple? Too this? Too that?

Is it in character? Dialogue had to make the Castaways come to life, with words each character should properly say. The same is true of written descriptions or actions in the script. Each Castaway should be called upon to do things consistent with that particular character.

We debated every line on every page: content, context, and continuity. We argued over descriptions and actions.

Writing comedy is nothing to laugh at.

That's particularly true when you're writing a pilot script, the script that will serve as a model of many scripts to come. It's careful, precise, painstaking, meticulous work.

When we were finished, I paid my mandatory visit to C.B.S. and United Artists, where I received suggestions for all kinds of changes. Very often their changes were in direct conflict with each other. Whether I agreed with any or all of these changes or not, each had to be given consideration. These two companies were planning to spend hundreds of thousands of dollars on this project, and were entitled to express their opinions.

The Professor is supposed to be smart, but look what he's trying to get rescued from.

Many meetings were held at C.B.S with Hunt Stromberg, Jr., and with Peter Robinson, his associate in program development. I also had to fly East to confer with Dick Dorso and his associates at United Artists.

One time I flew to New York to attend just one "creative" meeting with Dick Dorso. Usually I stayed one or two days for several meetings at United Artists or C.B.S.

I automatically checked into the Plaza Hotel, my usual lodging in New

York. After that one meeting, I went back to the Plaza and checked out to fly back to Los Angeles. I had been in New York for only three hours.

The desk clerk asked me if there was anything wrong with the room. I explained I hadn't even been in it. I had checked in from force of habit. The clerk asked me to wait a moment while he talked to the manager.

The manager refused to charge me full price for the day. Half price is what they asked for, and half price is what I paid.

Perhaps that incident will give you some insight into the state of my mind after a few dozen of those meetings.

I was desperately trying to protect my concept and my characters, without alienating my partners at United Artists and C.B.S. The idea is to give as little ground as possible. It's a TV creator/writer's version of the territorial imperative.

This is a process through which every new series goes before you see it on television. Hundreds of scripts are forced through dozens of rewrites every year. Meetings on both coasts involve hordes of network executives.

Millions of dollars in development are spent annually in this mad scramble to shovel new shows into the giant furnace of television. And the viewers at home press their little buttons and it's "burn, baby, burn."

With all the care, and all the meetings, and all the creative thought from writers, producers, and executives, approximately one out of every six new shows even comes back for a second season. And of these, about one out of five become "hits," in the sense they'll last enough years to go into syndication and pay back all deficit financing.

Is this any way to run a billion-dollar-a-year industry? Is there a better way? I don't know. I know this is the way it's done in television.

In order to accommodate the network's suggestions, and the production company's suggestions, and the stars' suggestions, writers and producers are often faced with so many compromises that they hardly recognize their own project by the time it gets on the air.

"A camel," it is said, "is a horse put together by a committee." Back in 1963, if you fought hard enough, you could limit the size of the hump on your horse. But if you allowed them, they humped you to death.

Today the networks are so powerful, your horse turns into a camel at your first network meeting. Then, slowly, inexorably, it changes into a giraffe, a rhinoceros, a dragon and finally a creature that would have stumped Darwin himself.

If I had submitted to the pressures of various executives, every single character in *Gilligan's Island,* without exception, would have been changed. In addition, *Gilligan's Island* would have become *Gilligan's Travels,* with Gilligan and the Skipper taking different groups on various charter trips each week.

There would have been no "social microcosm," no comedy/drama of people being forced to live together, and certainly no allegory, no matter how subliminal, about the importance of finding a means to coexist in the world in which we live.

But that was 1963, and it was still possible to "fight City Hall," to retain your concept, to survive the demands for changes.

It was still possible, but it wasn't easy.

6

The Songbird from Passaic

"Hi, Sherwood."

"Hi, Perry."

During the writing of the pilot script, Perry Leff had explained more about the C.B.S./United Artists/Gladasya Productions arrangement.

Right after the popular *Bilko* show, Phil Silvers was a very "hot" TV property. In order for C.B.S. to air the new TV series, *The New Phil Silvers Show,* in which Phil played foreman in a factory, C.B.S. had to agree to another part of the deal. That part was a commitment by C.B.S. to provide development money for another series for Phil Silvers' company, Gladasya Productions, in which Phil Silvers would not have to appear.

United Artists, anxious to participate in the development of pilots with C.B.S., the Dick Dorso/Jim Aubrey axis, gladly advanced the development cost of the pilot script of *Gilligan's Island.* They also agreed to take over the financial and contractual obligations of making the pilot film, providing most of the money for the filming, with C.B.S. covering the balance.

As Perry Leff had predicted, Dick Dorso for United Artists, Jim Aubrey for C.B.S., and Phil Silvers for Gladasya Productions had all agreed upon *Gilligan's Island* as the project that would fulfill the C.B.S. commitment to Phil Silvers.

As time would later prove, *Gilligan's Island* became far more important financially to Phil than *The New Phil Silvers Show;* even more important financially than the *Bilko* show, which had made him such a major TV star.

In any event, the Tinkers-to-Evers-to-Chance combination of Dorso-to-Aubrey-to-Silvers provided the funds for the final script I had written with my brother Elroy and Rocky Kalish.

Perry Leff's predictions in this, and on other important occasions, were right on target.

Perry was a man who had the courage of my convictions. That's right, the courage of *my* convictions. If that sounds like an insult, it's not meant to be. When you're a writer or producer, it's terribly important for your agent to feel as strongly as you do about a project.

Originally, Perry had had some doubts about the concept. But once I convinced him I believed in it, he believed in it, too. He never questioned it again.

Perry fought just as hard as I did to preserve the show as I originally conceived it. In fact, without Perry Leff I could not have gotten *Gilligan's Island* on the air.

"Well, tomorrow's the big day," Perry reminded me.

"Yeah, I know."

Perry was referring to *the* meeting. It was a final meeting in August at C.B.S. Television City to determine which projects now in final draft would go from script to pilot film. It was the culmination of months of work, dozens of meetings, and an infinite number of rewrites.

Like the previous crucial meeting with Mr. Paley and Dr. Stanton to determine which ideas would go from development to script, this was a twenty-minute, no more/no less, meeting. In a sense, the previous full-scale meeting had been a mid-term. This was the final exam.

This time there was a final script, containing C.B.S. East Coast input, United Artists East Coast input, C.B.S. West Coast input, and United Artists West Coast input. I was grateful they had no North Coast and South Coast. I'm sure they would have inputted, too.

It was Monday evening about 7:00 p.m. when Perry phoned. My meeting with all the C.B.S. and United Artists executives was the very next day, Tuesday, 10:00 a.m.

"This is it," said Perry, "It's now or never."

"Did you call me up to make me nervous?" I inquired. "I can manage nicely by myself, thank you."

"No, no. I called you up to warn you."

"Warn me?"

"About Jim."

Perry meant Jim Aubrey. Obviously, Jim was going to be at the meeting. His opinion would not only weigh heavily in the decision. It would *be* the decision.

"Jim's going to take another shot at you about the problems of exposition in your format. He still wants to do it his way, with the little charter boat taking a different trip each week. *Gilligan's Travels.*"

"I've told him a dozen times there won't be any exposition. *Gilligan's Island*'s main title will have a theme song to cover the whole back story."

"I know you keep saying that, but Jim's not buying it. He's going to raise that same issue. And it may knock you right out of the box."

"I'll tell him about Sir Lancelot."

"Sir who?"

"There's a popular new singing star named Sir Lancelot. He does calypso songs, and he's very popular right now. He's available, and he'll do the opening theme."

"It's too late for that now."

I didn't understand what Perry was driving at.

"Too late for what?" I asked.

"Too late for anything," said Perry. "You can't *talk* about a solution to this problem any more. You better *have* a solution."

"Are you crazy or something?" I asked as I finally grasped the nature of this phone call. "It's 7:15 p.m. You want me to have a calypso song about *Gilligan's Island* sung by Sir Lancelot, with a recording which I can play tomorrow morning at 10:00 at the meeting? Is that what you're telling me?"

"I'm not telling you anything," replied Perry. "Except that Jim is going to raise the same objection and you can't say it's not a problem. I'm simply saying you have to solve it."

"Thanks a lot, Perry. You have indeed handed me a sedative for a good night's sleep. Couldn't you have made this phone call last week?"

"It wasn't urgent last week," replied Perry. "Tomorrow's the meeting. Now it's urgent."

Perry was wrong about that. It wasn't urgent. It was beyond urgent. It was impossible. It was probably beyond impossible.

Any thought of trying to contact Sir Lancelot that night was out of the question. Even if I could talk to him, I had no song. Even if I had a song, I couldn't make a recording by 10:00 the next morning.

I had several friends who were songwriters, but who could I call at 8:00 p.m. to write a song by morning? I would have to explain the whole idea of the show and get someone to incorporate in the lyrics all the exposition I wanted in the song. No, that was hopeless.

I had never written a song in my life. But I had taken violin lessons for several years when I was a kid, and I have a good ear for music. I can pick out most tunes on a piano after I've heard them once or twice.

In addition, I knew exactly what I wanted the lyrics to say. I wanted them to describe the little boat, tell about the shipwreck on the island, and indicate that they were to remain there.

I also knew I wanted the song to be a happy, rollicking calypso tune. But what did I know about calypso? I was raised in Passaic, New Jersey, three thousand miles north of Harry Belafonte.

Fortunately, a few weeks earlier I had bought a few albums of calypso music because I knew eventually that's how I wanted to treat the opening theme. I bought some by Belafonte, and some by Sir Lancelot. Belafonte was too important to approach for a theme song. But I was sure we could make a deal with Sir Lancelot.

Ignoring the fact that I was trying to do something that couldn't possibly be done, I began to write the lyrics for *Gilligan's Island*.

I sat down at the piano, scribbling lyrics while I tapped out some Schwartz calypso.

Lyric writing is considerably different from script writing. Many thoughts have to be said in very few words. In a song where you're trying to tell a real story, that problem becomes acute.

My battle with a calypso melody was even more bloody. For two hours I tried to get the words to fit the music, and then the music to fit the words. I gained new respect for Rodgers and Hammerstein, Lerner and Loewe, and Andrew, Lloyd, and Webber.

Fortunately, I felt it didn't have to be a *good* song. It only had to be a song which would show Jim Aubrey his fears about exposition were groundless. The song was not meant to be number one on the Hit Parade or win a gold record. It just had to prove a point.

I planned to get these lyrics mimeographed—this was B.X., Before Xerox—and pass them around to the executives at the table, if and when Mr. Aubrey raised his expected objection.

The meeting was 10:00 the next morning. It was almost midnight now.

I phoned my secretary, Mary Strohm, apologized for the late call and explained the urgency. I asked her to meet me at C.B.S. at 8:00 the next morning. I would need twenty or twenty-five copies of the lyrics to take to the meeting at 10:00. Mary had been my secretary for several years, was very efficient, and understood the critical nature of the situation. She promised to be there promptly at eight.

Meanwhile, I spent the rest of Monday night, and most of early Tuesday morning, polishing the lyrics and improving the calypso melody. Finally, they seemed to match, at least to my ear. I fell into a troubled sleep until 7:00 a.m. I had the sort of dream you're even afraid to tell your psychiatrist.

At 8:00 I met Mary at C.B.S. I gave her the lyrics and she typed them onto one of those blue waxy master sheets for mimeographing. She went off to the mimeo room and returned some minutes later with twenty-five copies of the lyrics of the theme song. I put them in a folder which I mentally labeled "to be used only in case of emergency."

I spent the next thirty minutes rehearsing my remarks for the 10:00 presentation.

At 10:00, when I opened the door to the conference room, I was, in many ways, better prepared for this meeting than I had been for the previous full-scale C.B.S. executive conference.

I was a little surprised that Mr. Paley and Dr. Stanton weren't present at this meeting. But just about every other C.B.S. top executive was there: Jim Aubrey, Michael Dann, Oscar Katz, Frank Shakespeare, Jack Schneider, Hunt Stromberg, Bob Lewine, plus a half dozen other vice presidents of one thing or another.

There's a joke about General Custer's last words at the battle of Little Big Horn. He's supposed to have said, "Did you ever see so many Indians?" That's how I felt about C.B.S. executives when I walked into that room. But at least I was not alone. I was flanked by Perry Leff and Dick Dorso.

Dick Dorso, Executive Vice President of Programming for United Artists Television, was the top creative officer in that company's TV ventures. He had midwifed several major hits in the past few years. This year Dick's career was at its peak, with a dozen pilots in development, some already approved for filming. Most of his company's projects were with C.B.S., and his close association with Jim Aubrey was widely known in the industry.

Dick Dorso was shorter than Jim Aubrey, but just as lean. However, Dick seemed tougher physically, as though his leanness were due to exercise; Jim seemed thinner by nature, without Dick's Marine-boot-camp look.

Later, I heard that Dorso's special athletic achievement was tennis and Aubrey's was women. I guess they give you different sorts of lean looks.

Aside from his athletic ability and his achievements as programming chief at United Artists, Dick was even better known for a sartorial idiosyncracy. He never put his arms in the sleeves of his coat, whether it was a suit, sport jacket, or top coat. Dick's coats were always draped across his shoulders. We had been in many meetings and I had never seen his arms in his sleeves. I sometimes wondered idly how he managed to keep his jackets on as he moved and twisted and turned. I would have suspected Velcro on his shirt collar, but it had not yet been invented.

In or out of his sleeves, Dick Dorso was an important man in TV, and if even half of his pilot commitments became successful series, he would become a legend in the industry. A rich legend.

Dick sat directly to my left, and Perry Leff to my right as I began my twenty-minute presentation.

Without Mr. Paley and Dr. Stanton, Jim Aubrey was now the senior C.B.S. executive in the room. His opinions and decisions would be absolute. Nobody in that room would question his judgment in any matter big or small. Jim knew that as well as they did, and he accepted it in his usual fashion. He slouched his long, slim body back in his chair, casual and detached, and waited for me to begin. I think everybody in that room knew it was just a battle between Jim and me.

The classic western confrontation.

Except Jim was the only one with a gun.

I began.

Everybody was familiar with the concept of *Gilligan's Island* and the characters from previous meetings. So I quickly recapped concept and characters and spoke about the script, which had now been completed. I was careful to stress the broad comedy. Literacy was out. Humor was in.

"The show opens on the island," I said, "and the Skipper is the first one ashore. He yells 'Gilligan, Gilligan.' Gilligan hears the Skipper's voice. In a panic Gilligan yells 'Oh my gosh!' Man overboard! He dives headlong over the side of the *Minnow*. We hear a body thud off screen, and when the camera cuts to Gilligan, he's half buried in the sand."

There was general laughter from the group in the room as they envisioned the scene. Even Jim chuckled.

But before I could continue describing the pilot film, Jim interrupted. "We all know it's funny, Sherwood," he said. "That's never been the problem. I like the Skipper, I like Gilligan, and I like the little boat. The problem is the

A mystery *on* Gilligan's Island: *the Skipper and Gilligan concerned about grapes and watermelon, and paying no attention to the peach between them.*

exposition. How the hell is the audience going to know what they're doing on that same damn island every week?"

Jim knew how to get right to the point.

"I know we've been around and around about that, Jim," I replied, "But there's a theme song that will take care of the problem. In sixty entertaining seconds the lyrics will tell it all."

"You keep saying that. But I still think it's a problem."

As usual, when Jim spoke, the other executives in the room were seized by an acute attack of silence. I don't think they even breathed as the scenario played itself out.

"Jim," I replied, "I know how strongly you feel about this. So instead of discussing the problem any more, I've solved it."

"Oh? Solved it?"

"Instead of talking about a song, I've written one. These lyrics tell the audience everything they need to know."

As I said this I opened the folder with the mimeographed sheets, and I started to hand them out. Before I had a chance to distribute more than one or two, Jim interrupted.

"Just a minute. You say that's a song?"

"Yes. These are the lyrics."

I tried to continue distributing the pages, but again Jim interrupted.

"Sherwood, songs weren't meant to be passed around. Songs were meant to be sung."

Once the implication of Jim's remark registered, all the blood flowed out of my brain, out of my arms, out of my legs. I expected to see it in a pool around my feet.

When I was finally able to speak, after two or three eons, I tried to make a small joke. "Jim, I'd be happy to oblige, but I forgot my piano."

My remark was followed by the kind of quiet you hear in a graveyard at midnight. And the temperature of the room suddenly dropped two hundred degrees.

"I'd really like to hear the song," said Jim with a smile. Now I truly understood his nickname. I could hear the flute music beginning, and I could see the basket starting to open. Was Jim's neck starting to expand, or was that just my imagination?

I made one more attempt to escape the deadly Fangs. "It's a calypso song, Jim. 'I'm hoping to get Sir Lancelot to sing it. Sir Schwartz is terrible."

More silence. The chill in the room got worse. I felt like a side of beef in a meat locker. Beef that was soon to become hamburger.

"Sherwood," said Jim quietly and gently, "Are you going to sing, or are you not going to sing?"

Dick Dorso, on my left, kicked me in the shin. "Sing!" he hissed.

We have all had moments of decision that influence our lives, an instant that shapes our destiny in one way or another. Sometimes it happens on a freeway when a car is coming at you on the wrong side of the road. Do you veer left or right? If you guess wrong, you've wasted a lot of money on long-term magazine subscriptions.

In cases like that, they say your entire life passes before you. My life didn't pass before me. Too bad. I would have welcomed watching a few moments of my early days in New Jersey, my high school graduation, even my attack of scarlet fever. Anything.

If I didn't sing, Jim's objection would remain unanswered. He would not okay the pilot film, and there would be no series. All the months of meetings, all the writing and rewriting, all the dreams of *Gilligan's Island* would be over; the S.S. *Minnow* would truly be wrecked.

But *me sing?* The only time I had ever sung publicly was at my Bar Mitzvah. And that was in Hebrew, a language I didn't even understand. And my whole audience was made up of friends and relatives. It was rigged.

When this group heard me sing, they might lynch me. And a jury would probably consider it justifiable manslaughter.

Clearly, not singing would kill the project. Just as clearly, singing might kill me. Dick Dorso was willing to take that chance with my life.

So was I, actually. I got up to sing "The Ballad of Gilligan's Isle."

It would be wonderful to report that I sang brilliantly; that everyone loved the song and there was great applause when I finished. But that's not exactly what happened.

There was an additional problem: the film. In addition to singing, I had to describe what was on the screen to match the lyrics I was singing.

I'll never forget those few minutes as I sang to those executives in the Court of St. James.

Since the lyrics were in rhyming couplets, I decided to describe the scene, sing one couplet, describe the next scene, sing another couplet, and so on. This meant, of course, that after each description I would somehow have to get back into the melody, on key, and sing the next two lines.

There are people who graduate summa cum laude from Julliard who can't do that. Maybe Frank Sinatra can do it. Maybe Barbra Streisand can do it. But neither one of them was available, and I was.

It's often been said there are no atheists in foxholes. Well, there aren't many at network meetings either. So calling on help from high, I began.

"We start the main titles with a helicopter shot of a busy marina at a Caribbean island."

Then, in my best calypso style, I sang:

SCHWARTZ CALYPSO
Off Florida coast many hundred miles
Is tropical sea full of tropic isles

Between lyrics, I described the action:
"WE ZOOM IN TO A CLOSER SHOT OF tourists around some small charter boats."

SCHWARTZ CALYPSO
This is the place where tourists flock
Renting boats at the busy dock

More description:
"Then WE ZOOM IN CLOSER ON the S.S. *Minnow*. The Skipper stands near the sign welcoming tourists to his boat. The five passengers who will be co-stars in the series climb aboard the *Minnow*."

I desperately tried to pick up the melody:

SCHWARTZ CALYPSO
The S.S. *Minnow* sailed the ocean blue
With able Captain and able crew

"The able crew," I explained, "is a reference to the Skipper's assistant, Gilligan, who is getting himself completely entangled in the rope used to secure the boat. The Skipper glares at him, then shrugs off his frustration. Within the first five seconds of the film the Skipper/Gilligan relationship is established."

I waited a moment for some reaction. Would there be a sign they understood what those five seconds of the theme song had accomplished? A quick glance, all I had time for, indicated no sign. Thus heartened, I continued:

"The little boat starts out of the harbor toward the open sea."

SCHWARTZ CALYPSO
Tourists come, tourists go
Tourists go on S.S. *Minnow*

"Suddenly there's a terrible storm. Lightning and thunder. Huge waves start to toss the little boat."

SCHWARTZ CALYPSO
The winds they howl, the waves they shout
Angry sea toss the boat about

"We see the Skipper desperately trying to hold onto the wheel, while Gilligan is sliding around the deck. The passengers are below. Gilligan comes sliding into the Skipper and knocks him away from the wheel. The wheel begins to spin like crazy."

SCHWARTZ CALYPSO
The wheel is loose, without control
S.S. *Minnow* do the rock and roll

Again I took a quick look around the room for some sign of approbation from the executives. I felt a little like Lizzie Borden looking for a friendly face at a P.T.A. meeting. However, I'm not a quitter:

"Gilligan and the Skipper try to stop the wheel from spinning as the boat is lashed by the storm."

SCHWARTZ CALYPSO
Tourists come, tourists go
Tourists tossing to and fro

"On one last violent tilt of the boat THE CAMERA SPINS as though the boat is turning like a top, and then we DISSOLVE THROUGH TO Gilligan's Island, a small, deserted tropical isle."

SCHWARTZ CALYPSO
Now the sea is calm and the weather grand
Where is the *Minnow*. . .?

"Now WE CUT TO the shore of the island. We can see beautiful palm and a lovely tropical jungle in the background, but in the foreground is the S.S. *Minnow* lying on its side."

SCHWARTZ CALYPSO
. . .up on the sand.

"The CAMERA STARTS TO ZOOM TOWARD A CLOSER SHOT of the S.S. *Minnow.*"

SCHWARTZ CALYPSO
What happens now will make you smile
The story of the Castaways on Gilligan's Isle

I stopped singing. This was obviously the end of the song, but there wasn't a sound in the room. Not a single comment.

To make sure they understood, I said, "That's the end of the song."

There was still no comment. I sat down and waited. From the first, this whole business of the musical opening had been a bone of contention between Mr. Aubrey and me. There wasn't a person in the room who would even clear his throat lest it sound like an opinion. Not till Jim spoke first.

Even Dick Dorso and Perry Leff, my staunch allies, knew there was nothing they could do or say at this point. And so there was a silence. I could see pages drop off the calendar like they do in the movies: Tuesday, Wednesday, Thursday, Friday.

Finally, Mr. Aubrey spoke. "Sherwood," he said quietly, "I think you can fix up those middle lyrics a bit."

In effect, that was the end of the meeting.

As good or bad as my calypso singing was, the lyrics were somehow able to illustrate what I had been trying to tell Jim for months.

I must say this about my relationship with James T. Aubrey, Jr.: He has always heard me out. I'd had other disagreements with Jim before that day, and I've had them since. He never made it easy. But when I could show him the logic of my position, he was willing to let me try it my way.

He may have been "the smiling cobra" to many others in the industry, and I carry some scars from his fangs, but with me he never used venom.

Once Mr. Aubrey's opinion was voiced, there were loud murmurs of approval from the assorted vice presidents. Everybody loved the way I had handled this sticky problem of exposition.

In a matter of moments, by unanimous decree—that is to say, Mr. Aubrey's opinion—*Gilligan's Island* took the next big step up the ladder: approval from C.B.S. to go from script to film.

I've always considered it ironic that although I had spent many years writing and producing, and had had considerable experience and success in both fields, those years and those successes didn't count when the chips were down. In that critical meeting, my ability to write a song and carry a tune, something for which I had no training or experience, turned the tide.

In the past twenty years I have created and sold many other series on television. Yet I'm convinced that without the enormous success of *Gilligan's Island*, which gave me my initial track record as a creator/writer/producer, none of the other series would have happened. And it was all because I took a chance and sang.

There was another writer, William Shakespeare, who had something so say on this subject. It was in his play *Julius Caesar*:

There is a tide in the affairs of men,
Which, taken at the flood, leads on to fortune;
Omitted, all the voyage of their life
Is bound in shallows and in miseries.
We must take the current when it serves,
Or lose our ventures. (IV, iii)

In that meeting, I took Shakespeare's advice. And old Bill turned out to be right.

Recently, Mike Dann told me that in his years at the network he had been at two or three hundred presentations, comedy and drama, and mine was the only presentation in which anybody ever sang a song.

He also told me he never thought I would get up and sing, in spite of Jim's challenge. He also told me that when I left the room there were many comments about my performance.

He also told me I don't have a very good voice.

Sometimes Smoke Gets in Your Eyes

"I told you that you'd convince them," Mildred said.

She wasn't referring to my most recent meeting at C.B.S. where Jim had deliberately, and some said sadistically, forced me to calypso myself in public. She was referring to the earlier meeting attended by William Paley and Frank Stanton. She knew I was still disturbed by the fact I had used the phrase "social microcosm," which seemed to bother Mr. Paley.

Mildred also knew I was even more disturbed by the fact that Dr. Stanton hadn't asked a single question nor made a single comment during my entire presentation of *Gilligan's Island*. He had sat quietly, slowly puffing his pipe as I answered questions from the other men, mostly from Mr. Paley. I was unable to tell if he had been deeply attentive or simply disinterested.

In spite of the obvious assurance I now had from Jim Aubrey that *Gilligan's Island* was going to move from script to film, I was still uneasy about Mr. Paley and Dr. Stanton. Regardless of Jim's power, the Chairman of the Board of C.B.S. and the President of C.B.S. could still overrule him.

Remarkably, it was Dr. Frank Stanton himself who put my fears to rest. Any doubts about whether Dr. Stanton was paying attention to my presentation on *Gilligan's Island* vanished when I received from him a copy of three lectures that had been given at the Colby College Sesquicentennial Convocation in 1962. One of the lectures was by Dr. Frank Stanton.

That's what Mildred was referring to when she said she knew I had convinced them. We were both astounded by the remarkable coincidence of the topic of my television series, and the topic of Dr. Stanton's lecture at Colby College the previous year.

After receiving those lectures, I wrote to Dr. Stanton. Here's a copy of my letter to him, reprinted in its entirety.

Dr. Frank Stanton
Columbia Broadcasting System
485 Madison Avenue
New York, New York

Dear Dr. Stanton:

A few weeks ago, at our meeting at Television City, when I was describing the format and the future plans of GILLIGAN'S ISLAND, I was unaware of the topic of your lecture at the Colby College Sesquicentennial Convocation in 1962. Since that time, as you know, I received a copy of the three lectures delivered at Colby College. The topic of the Convocation, "The Heritage of Mind in a Civilization of Machines," as you must imagine, delighted me.

While Dr. Gerard Piel's essay dealt with an appraisal of this question from the viewpoint of pure science, and Dr. Oscar Handlin's speech treated the industrial and technological aspects, it was your lecture, oriented to the humanistic, psychological, and sociological phases of the theme, which drove home the coincidence most clearly: the interesting parallel between the subject of the Convocation and the television series I am preparing for C.B.S.

Obviously, we are attacking this subject from totally different directions. Your lecture, delivered in an intellectual university atmosphere, treated the subject with eloquent earnestness. It is certainly a far cry from the broad comedy and slapstick fun which form the backbone of GILLIGAN'S ISLAND. But we are, I'm sure you will agree, posing the same questions and making the same observations, each in our own way.

When you ask, "Can man use his resources and capacities wisely — not only for his own advancement but for his own survival"; and when you state, "Man's curiosity about himself and his behavior has always gone hand in hand with his probing curiosity about his environment"; you are examining the very reefs upon which Gilligan's Island was formed.

Let me quickly emphasize now — lest the tenor of this letter gives you misgivings about the humor-hand at the helm of the future of GILLIGAN'S ISLAND — I have spent some eleven years aiding Bob Hope and Red Skelton clown their way up in the ratings. There is, I believe, no regulation which makes pratfalls and philosophy mutually self-exclusive.

Thank you for having the Convocation lectures sent to me.

Yours sincerely,

Sherwood Schwartz

Where, When, How and with Whom

"I'm in pre-production on my first feature film," said John. "I can't re-arrange the dates."

I was talking to John Rich about directing the pilot film of *Gilligan's Island*. United Artists and C.B.S. both agreed that he was a wonderful choice.

John was an old friend and co-worker. He had directed dozens of my scripts on the *I Married Joan* series, which had been his first introduction to directing a film show rather than live, and had been my first film TV series as well. John had gone on from there to win several Emmy Awards for *The Dick Van Dyke Show*, and he was now considered one of the top television directors, particularly in comedy.

It was unfortunate that John was unavailable to direct the pilot, but C.B.S. and United Artists, as well as I felt John Rich was so valuable that United Artists made a deal with him to go into effect if *Gilligan's Island* went to series. John would become my co-producer on the series, direct eight episodes, and supervise the directing on the others. In addition, Hal Cooper, a colleague of John's, would become the associate producer. I would be the producer, script editor, and writer of as many episodes as I felt appropriate.

United Artists had no studios of their own. They rented space on major lots to film their features or television shows. Gladasya Productions, Phil Silvers' company, was doing his new show, *The New Phil Silvers Show,* on the Fox lot. It was natural, therefore, for me to set up the *Gilligan's Island* production unit at Fox also. In fact, *The New Phil Silvers Show* was just going on hiatus, and many of the people associated with that show became available to work with me on *Gilligan's Island.*

One of the first people I met at Fox was Rod Amateau, the director/producer of the *New Phil Silvers* series. He had also been the director/producer of *Dobie Gillis,* and other hit TV series for United Artists. With John Rich unavailable to direct the pilot, Rod Amateau immediately came to mind.

Based on his credits, Rod, with whom I had never worked before, seemed like an excellent choice. In fact, since this was my first film series as a producer, and Rod had more producing experience, Rod became the executive producer of *Gilligan's Island* as well as the director.

The Skipper, disguised by vines to avoid the headhunters, learns the vines are poison ivy.

In those years, Rod made an immediate impression. His head was shaved clean. This was before Yul Brynner and *Kojak* made it popular. And long before Mr. T tried to duplicate the feat, but missed a ridge in the middle.

Because he was producing and directing *The New Phil Silvers Show* on the Fox lot, Rod Amateau already had offices there. We set up space for *Gilligan's Island* in the bungalow area of the lot. Series of cottages were clumped together in twos, threes, and fours to satisfy needs of different production companies. They were small white cottages, painted and repainted so often I think it was the paint that kept them from falling apart. I'm sure they were there from the days of silent movies. Maybe from the days of daguerreotypes.

Actually, *Gilligan's Island* didn't need much in the way of office space.

We were thinking only in terms of a pilot film at that moment, not series, and we knew we'd be doing the pilot on location somewhere rather than on a stage. We needed offices only to conduct meetings with the production designer, art director, wardrobe people, props, special effects, and, of course, casting.

We were now beginning the first phase of production, which is called pre-production.

The production phase, which most people not in the industry think of as "producing the film," is the actual filming on sound stages, or on location.

The third phase, post-production, is everything that occurs after the shooting of the film. During post-production, the music, sound effects, "loop" lines, opticals, are all added in a final step called "dubbing." It's during this dubbing process that all the elements come together to form the finished product.

Pre-production, which we were starting then in three cottages at Fox, was only the beginning. However, in many ways, it's the most crucial phase of production. The results of the meetings in those small buildings would determine where, when, how and with whom the pilot film would be shot. It's a very complicated time for the producer because many things have to be considered at once.

In one of the cottages, casting began. Potential Skippers, Mr. and Mrs. Thurston Howell the IIIs, Gingers, Professors, and Mary Anns were coming and going as Rod and I went through the selection process inherent in the casting of every new show.

In another cottage, there were meetings with location scouts to determine where the film was to be shot. In a third cottage, budget meetings were being held with production executives to limit costs, without hurting the look of the show.

Many other production meetings were also taking place, some of which were to have a profound and permanent effect on the series. For example, in one of those meetings, wardrobe man Ray Summers suggested the highly identifiable red rugby shirt for Gilligan, and the bright blue short-sleeved shirt for the Skipper. It was a perfect idea to make them a visually memorable twosome. Gilligan's and the Skipper's wardrobes, which were to remain throughout the series, seem natural now, but someone had to think of those unforgettable outfits. It was Ray Summers who did it.

Equal consideration had to be given to the wardrobe of the other five characters. Only two of them, Mr. and Mrs. Thurston Howell III, were intended to have changes of costume — and extensive changes, at that.

Parenthetically, I should say here that the second most frequently asked question about *Gilligan's Island* is, "Where did the Howells get all those clothes on that desert island?"

The answer to that question is philosophic, like some other things in *Gilligan's Island*. The endless wardrobe was symbolic comment. It was my way of saying rich people manage somehow to have the best of everything, no matter what the circumstances.

(By the way, the *most* frequently asked question is, "Did Gilligan and the Skipper ever get hurt when the coconuts hit them on the head?" The answer to that question is, "No, because we used rubber coconuts.")

But the question being asked by United Artists and C.B.S. in September 1963 was, "Can't we film this pilot at a close location?"

United Artists, which was undertaking the major share of the financing, was concerned about the budget. Cost control at distant locations is difficult. United Artists wanted to film *Gilligan's Island* somewhere on the California coast, the closer to Los Angeles the better.

C.B.S. also wanted the show filmed nearby. While they were interested in budget, they were even more interested in creative control. The further away a project is filmed, the more difficult it is for a network to keep that production under constant supervision.

As for me, I had never shot anything on distant location in my life. All my shows had been done on sound stages, with scenes on local locations. I would have been perfectly happy to film *Gilligan's Island* someplace nearby, like in my own backyard.

However, in order to make the pilot film of *Gilligan's Island* convincing, it had to be filmed in some area that looked like the South Seas, with palm trees and tropical vegetation, and with absolutely no signs of civilization—no roads, no houses, no telephone poles, no telegraph wires, not even a McDonald's or a Baskin-Robbins.

One might think that there would be plenty of palm trees and lush foliage along the Southern California coast. But our location managers examined the beaches from the Mexican border to Santa Barbara. There were roads in plain view everywhere, or telegraph poles, or cars, or transmitters, or oil rigs dotting the landscape. No place had that totally deserted feeling.

It would have cost enormous sums of money to "dress" the areas, to truck in our own palm trees and tropical vegetation to hide all those signs of civilization and make it look like a deserted tropic isle. In addition, none of the beaches had the real look of the South Seas, with their wide stretches of white sand and bright blue ocean.

With great reluctance, United Artists and C.B.S. finally decided to shoot the pilot film in Hawaii. But where in Hawaii? The Honolulu area, which had the best facilities for filming, presented too many visible signs of life by 1963. Most of the coastline of Oahu was already dotted with signs of civilization. Huge hotels had been built; highways were everywhere, as were telephone wires, buildings, and people. Even miles away from the heavily populated Waikiki Beach and Diamond Head area, we couldn't find an ideal deserted beach that suited our needs.

Our search finally took us to the island of Kauai, and to Moloaa Bay. Moloaa Bay had everything we needed; the beautiful white sand beach, the bright blue Hawaiian waters. Coconut palms, royal palms, and many other varieties crowded the hillside leading to the beach, and tropical vegetation was everywhere. The landscape was rich with beautiful South Seas flowers: antherium, orchids, zymbium, and birds of paradise. There was only one dirt road, and it little more than a trail, that led down to the beach. The trail could be hidden easily from the camera, with some properly placed tropical bushes and small palms.

We had finally found our "Gilligan's Island."

Gilligan, the Skipper Too, the Millionaire and His Wife, the Movie Star, the Professor and Mary Ann

"Who's going to be in it?"

That's what the viewer wants to know.

It's the people on the tube to whom the viewers relate. It's not the writer, or the director, or the producer, or any of the dozens of people who are responsible for the look, the sound, or the feel of the show.

The director of photography, casting director, set designer, film editor, wardrobe, makeup, hair dressers, lighting personnel, location manager, cameraman, set decorators, props, carpenters, painters, and even grips are essential ingredients, as are the composer, the musicians, and the engineers in the dubbing rooms, but the average viewer takes all those background people for granted.

The viewer connection to the show, particularly in a series, is the actor. Do I like him? Do I love her? Is he attractive? Is she cute? Is he funny? Is she beautiful? Is he evil? Is she mean?

How does that actor make me feel? Good? Sad? Happy? Depressed? Great? Nauseous?

An actor's effect on a viewer is what makes the viewer tune in the following week. Or not tune in. Therein lies the rating, and as a consequence, the fate of the show.

Of course, without the right concept, the right words and the right action, the most talented actor will fail. However, the viewer doesn't know all that. As important as the writer, the director, the producer, and all the other elements are, the success of a series depends on a love affair between the audience and the performers.

Can you imagine *All in the Family* without Carroll O'Connor as Archie Bunker? Can you imagine *I Love Lucy* without Lucille Ball? Or *The Cosby Show* without Bill Cosby?

Hit series are invariably accompanied by a superpersonality—one whose special ability transcends mere "acting." The actor and the role become one.

Later on, this identification with a character proves difficult for performers to overcome. They become furious that they have been "typed." But in the beginning, there's a great unity of purpose. The writer, the producer, the casting director, the production company, the network, *everybody* wants every performer to become a superstar in his or her role.

In a series called *Gilligan's Island,* it's obvious the number one casting problem is Gilligan. Who's going to play the title role?

Physically, Gilligan as described in the presentation and the "bible," required someone young and smallish, someone guileless and gullible, someone honest and sincere, but irrevocably, hopelessly incompetent. Obviously, James Mason, John Wayne, and Sir Laurence Olivier were all wrong.

I had never met Bob Denver. I knew Bob only from his role as Maynard G. Crebs on *Dobie Gillis.* It never occurred to me to connect the bearded beatnik and his hip talk with my image of Gilligan. Like many producers, casting directors, and executives, I fell temporary victim to the evils of typecasting. Bob Denver was not my first choice for Gilligan.

However, there was another young comedy actor whom I knew quite well, Jerry Van Dyke.

Jerry had arrived in Hollywood with high hopes and low finances. More than anything, he wanted to be Jerry Van Dyke rather than Dick Van Dyke's brother.

Actually, Dick and Jerry are quite different. Dick has an urbane, sophisticated look and manner. You somehow don't expect to see him in a sweatshirt. You not only expect to see Jerry Van Dyke in a sweatshirt, you expect to see a hole in it.

Jerry seemed just right as Gilligan. I phoned him, and Jerry and I had lunch together. I described the project and the character, and gave him the script to read. Jerry told me he would think it over and discuss it with his agent.

But Jerry Van Dyke's agent was Rosey—George Rosenberg. Would he advise the promising young comedy actor to take the lead role in a series he himself didn't want to represent? Of course not! Instead, he recommended a different role in another pilot film, which never became a series.

To this day, every time I meet Jerry, he never fails to bemoan the fates that denied him the starring role on *Gilligan's Island*.

Hollywood is filled with stories like that. Actors turn down parts in motion pictures or television series which later make enormous stars of the actor who eventually takes the role. That's one of the fascinations of show business. Very often it's the third or fourth, and sometimes the eighth or ninth actor who gets the role that wins an Oscar or Emmy. Those that could have had it are kicking themselves around the block. If it's any consolation, however, both winners and losers are probably telling their stories to psychiatrists.

Thanks to the recommendation of some of my friends at the William Morris Agency, I met Bob Denver. Even though I didn't know Bob personally, I had heard a great many things about him from mutual friends in television. In addition, I knew of his incredible popularity on the *Dobie Gillis* show.

From time to time, a co-star, a "second banana," actually becomes more important on a series that the actual star of the show. This happened with the Fonz on *Happy Days,* with Mr. Spock on *Star Trek,* and with Bob Denver on *Dobie Gillis.* Audience research and fan mail clearly indicated there were thousands of Bob Denver fans.

It took only one meeting with Bob Denver to convince me he was indeed the Gilligan that was in the script and in my mind. Rod Amateau reinforced my own conviction that Bob Denver was perfect for the part.

Bob himself is very quiet by nature, extremely bright, and very well read. In fact, he had been a teacher before becoming an actor. But it's amazing how truly gifted performers can give a flawless characterization in a role that's so counter to their own personality.

Bob saw the potential in *Gilligan's Island,* loved Gilligan's relationship with the Skipper, and was fascinated by the concept involving the interrelationships of this odd assortment of characters.

United Artists and C.B.S. quickly approved the selection of Bob Denver as Gilligan, and I went on to the next natural casting element, the Skipper.

Instinctively I knew the Skipper would be the hardest character to cast. Very often, when you believe somthing is going to be the most difficult, it turns out to be the easiest. Not in this case. The Skipper was without doubt the toughest casting job in *Gilligan's Island.*

The Skipper had to combine the gruff, forceful strength of a lion with the gentleness and warmth of a pussy cat. You had to love the Skipper even while he was bawling out the sympathetic, well-meaning Gilligan for some blunder. No matter how stupid the mistake, and no matter how vicious the scolding, it was imperative that the audience still love the Skipper.

On *Gilligan's Island* there were to be no villains among the seven Castaways. The villainy came from the forces of nature — storms, lightning, quicksand, tidal waves, volcanoes — or from wild animals, poisonous shrubs, savages from other islands. The Castaways themselves were all designed to be likable characters — though with very different sets of natures.

The Skipper, being the ultimate authority figure on the island as he was on the boat, was the most difficult to make lovable, particularly in his relationship with Gilligan. It required an actor who brought to the role so much innate warmth and humanity that you would love him no matter what. The actor who played the role would have to combine the worst features of Attila the Hun with the benevolence of Edmund Gwenn in *Miracle on 34th Street.*

I wrote a special test scene between the Skipper and Gilligan. It wasn't in the script. It was a scene that made the Skipper as angry, unforgiving and unsympathetic as possible. This uncompromisingly merciless scene was

The fumbling, bumbling Gilligan, magnificently portrayed by that highly intelligent, versatile actor, Bob Denver.

designed to make you hate the Skipper, no matter which actor played the part.

Maybe it was unfair to make the test so severe, but I felt the Skipper-Gilligan relationship rested on the ability of the actor to make you like the Skipper in spite of everything he said or did. And the whole show, in a large sense, rested on the Skipper-Gilligan relationship.

Bob Denver was very generous with his time and talent in playing this test scene against dozens of prospective Skippers. Rod Amateau was equally generous, devoting many hours, days, weeks, directing those video tapes. They both realized the importance of chemistry between the Skipper and Gilligan.

Time after time we videotaped that scene with one character actor after another. Many of them were well-known names who went on to become stars of other TV series. Like Carroll O'Connor, for example, who, I'm sure, is delighted the role of the Skipper escaped him.

We tried all the recommendations from the casting departments, from C.B.S. executives, United Artists executives, plus my own ideas. Bob himself made several suggestions. Nothing worked. Every Skipper flunked the sympathy test. As they chewed out Gilligan for his inept behavior, you hated their guts. There seemed to be no Hardy for our Laurel.

The pilot film was to be shot in November in Hawaii. Weeks were slipping by as we continued to test performers for the Skipper role. Unhappy with the results on the West Coast, C.B.S., through its New York facilities, made video tapes of various New York actors, primarily stage, playing the scene against an East Coast version of Bob Denver.

Five of those actors seemed promising enough to bring to Hollywood to test against Bob Denver himself. Much to our disappointment, we had the same results.

Was I too harsh in that test scene? Was it simply impossible for anybody to play the Skipper? I was tempted to change the scene and let the Skipper be a little easier on Gilligan. But I kept reminding myself how important it was to insist on the magic of that relationship: a Skipper whose love for Gilligan would shine clearly through any verbal abuse.

We were encountering difficulties with other casting as well. However, they were the usual difficulties a producer encounters in casting. Some performers were unavailable. Others didn't work out in readings, or in tests. In the case of the two young ladies, Ginger and Mary Ann, there were matching differences between the two women to consider: age, height, hair color, attitude. The parts of Mr. and Mrs. Thurston Howell III, and the Professor, presented their own difficulties, but I was always convinced we could find the right performers.

Not so with the Skipper. That role kept gnawing at me, particularly as November approached with hurricane speed. All of us went through our lists of candidates again and again. We turned the pages of the Academy Players Directory more and more slowly, hoping to find an actor whom we had overlooked. It was very discouraging. Time was running out. It was either settle, or pass up the opportunity to do the pilot film that year.

*

"I don't know what to do."

"Have another drink" suggested Mildred cheerfully.

I didn't even smile. Mildred knew the situation was serious.

"We're supposed to start shooting in the middle of November, around the fourteenth."

"That's your birthday," she reminded me.

"Right," I said grimly.

We were having dinner at a restaurant on Santa Monica Boulevard, near Westwood Boulevard, in West Los Angeles. We had never dined there before, but some of Mildred's friends had recommended it.

I was sipping a vodka martini on the rocks, and Mildred was sipping her vodka gimlet, also on the rocks, as we contemplated my "Gilligan's Island" project, which, at that moment, also seemed to be on the rocks.

Very often Mildred had come up with good ideas for casting, but this time she was as stumped as we all were.

"Any point in going through the casting book again?"

"We've been through it a dozen times."

"Nobody's even close?"

"Close isn't good enough. The Skipper-Gilligan relationship is the most important one in the show. If that's not perfect . . ."

"There must be *someone*."

I gave her a look. We had all been saying that to each other for a month now.

"Maybe you should wait till next season," said Mildred. "That'll give you another year to find the right Skipper."

"It doesn't work that way. If I don't get this project off the ground now, it will be dead. Next year it will be an old project competing with new projects. You have to strike while the iron's hot, 'cause it cools off mighty fast."

"There's still three weeks." Mildred was trying to be comforting. "Anything can happen in three weeks."

"Sure. I could get hit by lightning. That would solve my problems. Maybe I should have another drink."

I looked around for the waiter, and as I did, something caught my eye across the restaurant. There was a table of four men dressed in civil war cavalry uniforms. In Hollywood, near the studios, you sometimes see unusual sights like that. This restaurant was located just behind what used to be the backlot of Twentieth Century–Fox Studios.

Then suddenly my eyes were riveted on one of those four men.

It was Alan Hale!

"That's the one!" I exclaimed to Mildred.

"That's the one what?" asked Mildred.

"He's sitting right over there!" I pointed. It's impolite, but it's effective. "That's Alan Hale, isn't it?"

"That's the Skipper! He's perfect! For some reason he's not in the book. And for some reason nobody's mentioned him."

"He really looks right" said Mildred, still staring at Alan Hale. "I wonder why his name never came up."

"Any number of reasons. He might not be available because of this movie. He might not want to do a series. He might be in a pilot already and C.B.S. would never settle for second position. There are lots of reasons. Maybe nobody thought of him. Maybe his agent never heard of the project. Maybe anything, but that's the guy."

The more I looked at Alan Hale, a big, blonde, huggable teddy bear, the more convinced I was he'd be perfect as the Skipper.

Unfortunately, I didn't know Mr. Hale personally, and I never approach a performer except through an agent. Most producers follow that procedure. It avoids placing you in a business/legal relationship with performers and puts that in the hands of agents and business affairs people, where it belongs.

"I just hope he's available three weeks from now. I'll call his agent first thing in the morning. Let's have some dinner. I'm hungry."

"I thought you wanted another drink," said Mildred.

"Not any more."

*

"Hi, Bob. I'd like to talk to you about Alan Hale."

I was on the phone with Bob Lounsberry of the Bill Shiffrin Agency.

"Is he available for a series?" I asked.

"Yes," said Bob, "depending on the dates, the material, and naturally, the money."

It was a logical agent response.

"The date is the important thing," I replied. "United Artists and C.B.S. can talk to you about the money, and I'm sure the role is perfect for Alan. But availability is critical because this pilot film shoots in three weeks."

"Well, that shouldn't be a problem," said Bob. "Bud's in a movie right now, but he'll be available in two weeks."

"Bud" was Alan Hale. That's when I first learned that everybody who knew Alan Hale well called him Bud.

"Wonderful. When can I get together with Alan?"

"As soon as he gets back from Utah," answered Bob.

I was flabbergasted.

"Utah! He's here in town. I just saw him at dinner last night."

"That was last night. He left at five this morning for St. George, Utah. That's where they're doing the location on that civil war movie."

"Somehow I've got to get him back here to do a test scene with Bob Denver," I said to Bob.

"That's going to be tough. As you know, they shoot six days a week on location. And their location is down in a gorge. They have to reach it on horses and the equipment has to go down on mules."

"I've got to get him back here somehow, even if it's on a Sunday."

"Look," said Bob, "I haven't even seen this property, and neither has

Bud. And I'll have to make some kind of deal with United Artists or C.B.S. before I bring him back from Utah."

"I'm not worried about the deal, I'm just worried about the test with Bob Denver."

"There's plenty of film on Bud. I can get it over to anybody at C.B.S. or United Artists."

"It's not the film. It's the relationship. Besides, C.B.S. has an absolutely ironclad rule. Nobody in a starring role can be signed without a screen test for that particular role."

Networks had run into problems with performers in judging them by film clips that were a year old, or even six months. In the interim, actors and actresses had lost weight, gained weight, or their appearance had changed considerably for some other reason. Therefore, the rule: current screen test. The other networks had the same rule.

I told Bob I would send him a couple of copies of the script and asked him to get one to Alan Hale. I also asked Bob to find out how to lift Alan out of that gorge in Utah on the coming Sunday, or the following Sunday. Those were the only two possible days left to test him before the shooting date of our pilot film.

I phoned Hunt Stromberg at C.B.S., and told him about the problem.

Hunt agreed that Alan Hale was certainly worth testing. However, C.B.S. video tape facilities were down on Sundays. Hunt would have to try to hold them open in the event Alan Hale could return from location.

I wasn't exactly sure whether Bob Denver would be available on both Sundays. He had been super-cooperative thus far.

A quick phone call to Bob Denver gave me his assurance that he would make himself available. Then Hunt Stromberg phoned back with good news about the C.B.S. facilities. He would hold them open on either Sunday.

The remaining problem, and it was a big one, was getting Alan Hale to Hollywood for the test. Assuming Alan and his agent both liked the project and the script, and a deal was negotiated, how could Alan come up out of the gorge, get to Hollywood, and return to his film company, all in one Sunday?

I don't know who first said, "Where there's a will, there's a way," but I know it goes back a long way. Maybe it was Eve when she offered Adam the apple.

Alan read the script and loved it. He knew the only way he could get the part was to get to Hollywood on Sunday, and he took direct action. He asked a buddy of his, Skip Homier, another actor in the film, to ride with him out of the gorge up to the highway, and stay there with Alan's horse until he returned from Hollywood.

That buddy must have been an awfully good buddy, because he had to wait by the side of the highway with Alan's horse for over six hours.

Casting the Skipper was incredibly difficult, but the lengthy search was worth it. As the Skipper and his "little buddy" Gilligan, Alan Hale and Bob Denver are one of the most memorable comedy duos in television history.

During those six hours, Alan hitchhiked a ride on a truck from St. George, Utah, to Las Vegas, Nevada. Then he flew from Las Vegas to Los Angeles and took a cab to the studio.

Bob Denver and Rod Amateau and I were waiting at C.B.S., and the facilities were available. After a few rehearsals, Bob and Alan did the scene that had proven disastrous for every other potential Skipper.

Anybody who has ever seen an episode of *Gilligan's Island* knows the magic between Bob Denver and Alan Hale. It was evident immediately. No matter how Alan ranted and berated Gilligan, you knew he loved him every second. There was never any doubt about the test. Everyone who saw it knew that Alan Hale was the Skipper and the Skipper was Alan Hale. They were meant for each other.

But Alan couldn't even wait around for results. He flew back to Las Vegas, hitchhiked to St. George, met his friend and his horse, and both men and both horses rejoined the film company down in the gorge.

It was a very exciting day for Alan Hale, and it was an equally exciting day for me. Finally, *Gilligan's Island*'s two main equations were completed: Bob Denver = Gilligan, and Alan Hale = the Skipper.

Gilligan and the Skipper provided the broad slapstick comedy. It was urgent to supplement this with wit and satire, comedy of an entirely different sort. Mr. and Mrs. Thurston Howell III were on the island to provide that balance.

I had written the role of Thurston Howell III with my good friend Jim Backus in mind. However, there were two problems in casting Jim Backus, both of them crucial.

One difficulty was availability. Jim had done a pilot film many months earlier and was still contractually obligated to keep himself available.

The second problem was money. Jim was a very important actor and had co-starred in a few series of his own. The money in the budget for that role was far less than Jim was accustomed to receiving.

Meanwhile, we had found two good character actors who could play the part of Thurston Howell III. Both were good, but neither could give the part the sort of perfection that Jim alone could bring to that role. Neither one had the Thurston Howell III voice I heard in my head, or the face I pictured on the screen. But since I had to assume Jim was simply unavailable, we began negotiating with the two alternatives.

During these negotiations with the other actors, Jim Backus suddenly became available. It was exactly six days before leaving for Hawaii to do the pilot film. On that date, the option on Jim for the other series ran out, and Jim's agent, Tom Korman, phoned me. Was the role still available?

The answer was yes. But it was a qualified yes. The other problem with Jim now reared its monetary head. What about the budget?

I knew two things. One was that United Artists, who was supplying the deficit financing, wouldn't agree to double the weekly salary for that role. That's what it would cost if we could get Jim.

On the other hand, I knew that Hunt Stromberg at C.B.S. was very fond of Jim and would love to see him in *Gilligan's Island*. During casting, I had told Hunt that Jim was my prototype for the role for Thurston Howell III. I knew Hunt agreed.

I phoned Hunt at C.B.S. and told him Jim Backus had suddenly become available. Would C.B.S. come up with the extra money? Money above and beyond the call of budget?

Jim Backus and Natalie Schafer were a formidable comedy team as Mr. and Mrs. Thurston Howell III, the only people who ever took a three-hour tour with 300 outfits.

With no hesitation, Hunt spoke for C.B.S. "Jim is perfect. You've got the extra money."

It was one of the many times Hunt Stromberg, Jr., helped me with *Gilligan's Island*. Later, there were times when he drove me up a wall. But there's no question that without Hunt, the show never would have gotten on the air.

I phoned Tom Korman, Jim's agent, and told him to get in touch with United Artists and C.B.S. Business Affairs. Then I phoned Jim.

That's where my long personal relationship with Jim Backus became very important.

When I didn't think we could get Jim for the role, the part of Thurston

Howell III in the pilot script wasn't emphasized. It became a major role only after I found out Jim was available.

I phoned Jim and told him about the pilot film, and the role of Thurston Howell III. He was excited about the idea.

"Get me a copy of the script right away," Jim said.

There was no way I would show that script to Jim Backus. He wouldn't take the part. He was a man used to important starring roles. I don't think Thurston Howell III had more than ten or eleven lines in the original *Gilligan's Island* script. Or, as Jim himself puts it, "My original part was shorter than the wine list on an airplane."

I said, very honestly, "Jim, if you see the script, you won't do the show."

"Do you expect me to sign a contract to star in a series without reading the script?" asked Jim.

"Yes," I answered.

"Well," he said, "since you put it that way, okay."

The addition of Jim Backus to *Gilligan's Island* was of immeasurable importance to the series. His satiric wit as the madcap billionaire was exactly what the series needed to balance the Gilligan-and-Skipper slapstick. The large percentage of adult viewers that *Gilligan's Island* attracted, a percentage it still enjoys in syndication, is largely attributable to the zany, sophisticated dialogue between Jim Backus and Natalie Schafer, Mr. and Mrs. Thurston Howell III.

By emphasizing the importance of Jim Backus to *Gilligan's Island,* I'm in no way diminishing the contribution of Natalie Schafer. Where would Thurston Howell III be without his Lovey?

Here too I'm indebted to Hunt Stromberg. Natalie Schafer was his casting suggestion.

I remembered Ms. Schafer from dramatic films, and from the stage. But Hunt's father, Hunt Stromberg, Sr., was an important film producer who had used Natalie in some of his movies. Hunt remembered she had played high comedy, and played it very well.

One meeting with Natalie Schafer was all it took. I was convinced Mrs. Thurston Howell III was in the room with me.

However, playing opposite Jim Backus is no easy task. Jim's characterization of Thurston Howell III was so strong and colorful, it required equal vigor and flamboyance on the part of his wife.

Mr. Howell somehow felt writing a check that was large enough could stop a hurricane. By the same token, Mrs. Howell expected somebody to come ashore every Thursday to dust the island and polish the coconuts. It took two extremely talented performers to play these characters who lived in their own little world, preoccupied with finances, culture and social amenities on this remote deserted isle.

Mr. and Mrs. Thurston Howell III's concept of the real world was entirely

Dawn Wells and Tina Louise took over the roles of Mary Ann and Ginger after the pilot was sold. They were as carefully "matched" for complementary heights, hair colorings, etc., as their characters were matched for complementary personalities.

different from the other Castaways'. Nevertheless, they were never intentionally nasty to the others. They simply didn't understand how the other half lives.

This was a common theme in many stories in *Gilligan's Island*. Each of the Castaways was forced to look at life through the eyes of others, and to examine his own life, as well.

That was my purpose in creating this social microcosm. That was the basic theme I was trying to examine: the understanding each of us must try to have for the other person's problems.

It's difficult to discuss the casting of Ginger, the Professor, and Mary Ann,

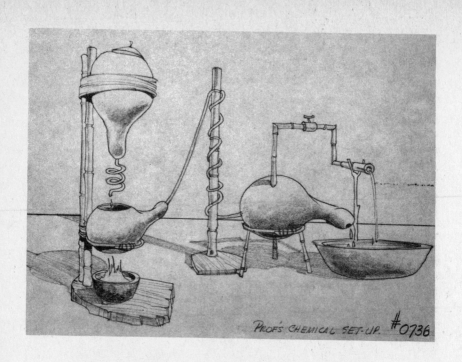

PROF'S CHEMICAL SET-UP #0736

because those three cast members were changed after the pilot was sold and *Gilligan's Island* became a series. I mention their names here—Kit Smythe, John Gabriel, and Nancy McCarthy—with warmth and gratitude, because they were obviously good enough in their roles to help me sell the series. They also helped the pilot get terrific scores in audience testing. For these accomplishments they forever have my thanks.

A word about recasting roles: A new performer brings a new approach to a part. Therefore, the writing of that role has to be reexamined. In addition, the relationship of that new performer to all the other performers has to be reexamined.

The part of Ginger is an excellent example. The original actress in the pilot film played the part of Ginger as a slick Hollywood actress, with a sarcastic kind of wit. That's the way the part was written.

After meeting Tina Louise, who was the new Ginger in the series, it became apparent that the concept of Ginger had to be rewritten to make better use of Tina's natural abilities. Tina wasn't really comfortable as the wisecracking, brassy, Hollywood Ginger. But she was marvelous as a wide-eyed, innocently sexy Hollywood starlet.

Tina's Ginger was soft, feline, narcissistic. Tina almost floated in and out of scenes. This approach emphasized Tina's fantastic figure and added a sexual dimension to life on the island. Tina Louise had her own vast crowd of loyal *Gilligan's Island* viewers every week.

Actually, we were fortunate to sign Tina Louise for that role. I had remembered her from *God's Little Acre*. She had a face and figure that were hard to forget. But she was in a Broadway musical at that moment, *Fade Out, Fade In*, with Carol Burnett. In order for her to play Ginger, we had to buy out her contract for the balance of her guarantee to the play.

It was well worth it to bring Tina's very special presence to *Gilligan's Island*. Ethel Winant, head of C.B.S. casting, was able to engineer the contractual arrangements necessary to clear the Broadway hurdle.

As Tina's Ginger became wide-eyed and innocent, Mary Ann stopped being wide-eyed and innocent, and became more realistic and down-to-earth. She was still virginal, but not from innocence. From determination.

Dawn Wells was an ideal choice for the new Mary Ann, particularly after Tina Louise was cast as Ginger. Her energetic, pretty, girl-next-door look made a wonderful contrast with the tall, glamorous, sexy Tina Louise.

By the way, if you think pretty girl-next-door types are out of fashion, guess who always got the most fan mail in the cast of *Gilligan's Island?* You guessed it: Dawn Wells.

Opposite, top: *Production sketch for one of the Professor's inventions.* Bottom: *The Professor working with a piece of "scientific equipment" much like the one conceived in the sketch. It was up to Russ Johnson to give the Professor believability; it was up to the production department to give him props. Following this chapter are more production sketches for the Professor's island inventions.*

How about the role of the Professor? Was this character important? Vital? Essential? Much more than that. Inestimable! The Professor was the glue that held the more colorful characters in place in the *Gilligan* mosaic. And Russell Johnson played him perfectly: intellectual, serious, sincere. He supplied the logic on the island, and he supplied it so well that he convinced the other Castaways, and the viewers as well, that whatever he said was scientifically sound.

And more often than not, what he said and did actually had a scientific basis, thanks to my years in pre-med, plus the research the writers did. All the Professor's experiments seemed absolutely legitimate. Russ Johnson knew that, believed that, and instilled that believability in the show. No matter how weird or bizarre the Professor's scheme might seem, Russ made it sound perfectly plausible.

For instance, in one episode, the Professor, basing his calculations on the wind currents, decided the Castaways could escape the island in a balloon. He sealed off the ends of the sleeves of their raincoats and filled them with hot air, making a weird-looking, but practical, balloon.

Far-fetched? Bizarre? Unbelievable? That's what a critic in one of the trade papers said about that particular episode back in 1965.

Nevertheless, in September 1983, a family of four in Czechoslovakia made a balloon by sealing the ends of the sleeves of six raincoats and filling them with hot air. Thanks to wind currents, they escaped Russian persecution by sailing across the border to a safe democracy. They even used the same number of raincoats we used.

Maybe they watch *Gilligan's Island* in Czechoslovakia. If they do, the Professor must have convinced them it would work, even if he couldn't convince some of *Gilligan's Island*'s critics.

We needed Russ Johnson to give that air of calm believability to the role of the Professor, just as we needed Bob Denver as the perpetually bumbling Gilligan, Alan Hale as the forceful yet compassionate Skipper, Jim Backus and Natalie Schafer as the completely eccentric yet lovable billionaires, Tina Louise as the voluptuous, somehow innocent Ginger, and Dawn Wells as the sweet young thing you'd like to bring home to your mother. That is, if you trusted your father.

I'd like to thank the lady most responsible for assembling those Castaways: Ethel Winant.

I don't know any ensemble shows in television that have been cast any better.

On the following pages are several of the island inventions created by the Professor, with the help of the C.B.S. art and prop departments. Some of them are labeled with the title and number of the episode for which they were specifically built; others, like the Howell's lavatory basin, the wheelbarrow, the "stove," the phonograph, and the fan, were used in many episodes.

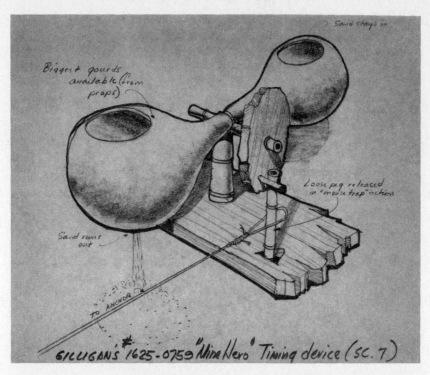

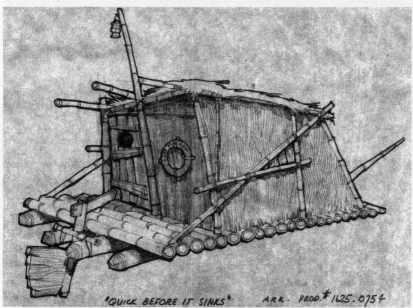

Top: *Timing device for "Mine Hero." Bottom: Ark for "Quick Before It Sinks."*

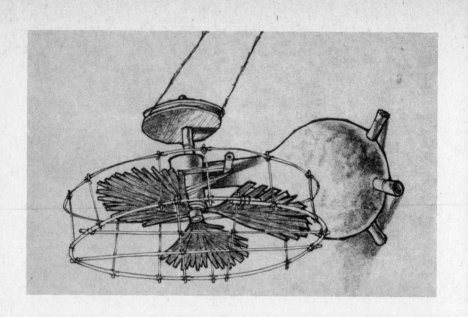

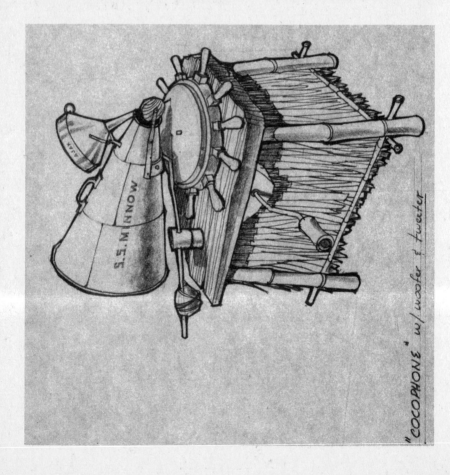

"COCOPHONE" w/woofer & tweeter

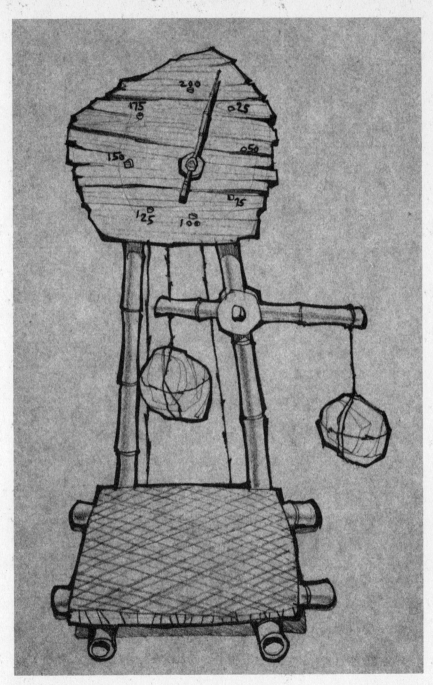

Above: *Scale for "Physical Fatness" episode.* Opposite, left: *"Cocophone" with woofer and tweeter.* Opposite, right: *fan (powered by bicycle).*

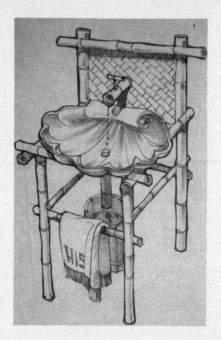
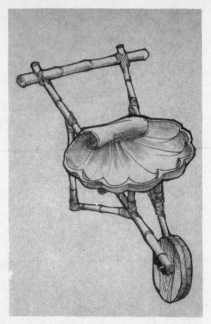

Top, left: *Howell's lavatory basin.* Top, right: *wheelbarrow.* Bottom: *"Rock & Sattler" cooking range (with plate warmer and condiment shelf).*

10

The Hills Are Alive with the Sound of Crickets

"What the hell are we doing in this relic?" Rod Amateau wanted to know.

It was November 15, 1963, and about a dozen of us were headed for Honolulu, on our way to Kauai and our location at Moloaa Bay. We were flying in old propellor-driven aircraft, and Rod was angry.

Our group consisted of Mildred and me; Rod Amateau; Lottie Cagle, his secretary/assistant; Bill Porter, our production manager; Miles Middough, the assistant director; Charles Van Enger, our director of photography; Ray Montgomery, our dialogue director; and Mr. and Mrs. Bob Denver and their three children.

To this day Rod Amateau is still furious with our production manager because he arranged our transportation in that old propellor-driven Constellation. By 1963, jets were already in use, but a production manager's job is to save money, and jets were more expensive.

Some of the people in the crew had already left for the Hawaii location the previous week. They were the people involved in the physical production who would be preparing the Moloaa Bay site to become our deserted tropical isle: Jack Senter, art director; Charles Stevens, the construction foreman; Richard Ragland, carpenter; Frank McCarrey, transportation; Jack Gertsman, unit manager; Earl Spicer, gaffer; Walter Fitchman, key grip; Fed Lutz, landscape; Joe Krutak, painter; followed by Carl Cabibbi, best boy; "Jock" Christie, second grip; Norman Rockett, set decorator; and Joe Thompson, prop man.

The following Monday, November 18, the other members of the cast, Alan Hale, Jim Backus, Natalie Schafer, Kit Smythe, John Gabriel, and Nancy McCarthy, arrived in Kauai, along with the rest of the crew.

Our Friday group spent the first night at Coco Palms near the southern end of the island. Preparations were being made for us at Hanalei Plantation at the north end of the island near Moloaa Bay, where we would be filming.

Hanalei Plantation consisted of a large main building with a series of small private cottages leading down a steep hill to Hanalei Bay. That's the bay where *South Pacific* was shot some years earlier. In fact, it was the production designer on *South Pacific* who designed Hanalei Plantation and its cottages.

The main building at Hanalei Plantation was to house the crew, while the cast and executive personnel were given individual cottages along a private road down to the bay. In some ways, the cottages, although better accommodations, were less desirable. The road leading up to the main building was so steep the management had to send special jeeps down to collect us because walking was extremely difficult. In addition, all the hotel facilities, restaurant, gift shop, lobby, etc., were in the main building.

There was another problem: frogs. Every night frogs would gather by the hundreds, maybe the thousands, outside the door to our cottage.

By morning it was almost impossible to open the doors because of the weight of the frogs. At times it was scary. Mildred was terrified of the slimy green creatures. I told her one of them might be a prince. If she kissed all of them, she'd be sure to find the right one.

Mildred picked up a pillow. I pretended to duck. This time she threw it.

Work had already been started by the personnel at Moloaa Bay who had preceded us to the filming site. That location was just a few miles from Hanalei Plantation. As soon as our group arrived, we joined the others in making preparations for the first day of shooting. That date was to be Tuesday, November 19.

My personal major concern was the script. There were two main problems.

First, it's one thing to write scenes in the comfort of your office in Hollywood, imagining the scenes, the location of the palm trees, the width of the beach, etc. It's quite another thing when you get to location and nothing is quite where you imagined it would be. This required on-site rewrites for adjustments in dialogue, and description, to fit the movement in the scenes.

The second script problem was my guarantee to Jim Backus. He had agreed to become one of the stars of *Gilligan's Island* with the promise that his role would be improved and enlarged. This was not only my obligation to Jim, but it was my obligation to the series as well. As a character, Thurston Howell III had a great deal to offer. I had to rewrite the script and build up that role properly, incorporating Mr. Howell in more of the plot, and improving his scenes with the other Castaways.

I made a quick visit to Moloaa Bay with Rod Amateau, Bill Porter, Norman Rockett, Jack Gertsman, Miles Middough, and Charles Van Enger, to see what changes would be required in the script based on the specifics of location. Happily, they didn't seem too extensive. I made a small sketch of the area for myself as a guide. Then I left the rest of the group to the many physical production problems—construction, cameras, special effects, etc.—and I returned to my cottage to wrestle with the script.

As usual, the pressure of time dominated everything. Shooting was to start the following day, and the changes I was making affected all the actors. My new final draft would have to be mimeographed so they could have the pages in the morning.

Fortunately, there were mimeographing facilities at Hanalei Plantation. Unfortunately for me, they were up in the main building. That's where Lottie Cagle, the secretary I shared with Rod Amateau, had her room. As a result, everything I wrote in my cottage would have to be run up to her in the main building.

"Lottie," I said, "we're going to have to finish this entire new draft tonight. The only feasible procedure is to get the rewrite to you eight or ten pages at a time. You can type it final and put it into the mimeo while I start rewriting the next section."

"Fine," said Lottie. "I'll be up in my room waiting for your rewrites."

That was our arrangement.

I returned to my cottage down by the water, and I sat down at my portable typewriter, with the rough sketch I had made of the location. Mildred left me to my work. She strolled through Hanalei Plantation, while I strolled through the script.

Nothing is very easy when you rewrite a final draft. Every change you make may affect three or four other scenes, and every line of dialogue affects the speeches of all the other actors. These were scenes and lines that had already undergone innumerable rewrites based on innumerable suggestions. If I had to violate certain executive suggestions in this final rewrite, so be it. There was no time to consult with United Artists, or C.B.S. They would get copies in the morning like everybody else. These were emergency conditions.

It was evening when I finished the first eight pages of my rewrite, and I decided to get that section to Lottie so she could start retyping them for mimeo.

Meanwhile, Mildred had returned from her tour of the Plantation.

"Why don't you phone Lottie and make sure she's there?" advised Mildred. "It's a rough climb from our cottage up to the main building."

That was a very practical suggestion, so I phoned Lottie. The phone rang and rang, but there was no answer.

"Maybe she went out for a bite to eat," Mildred speculated.

"She promised she would be in her room waiting for the rewrite. She knows how pressed we are for time."

"Maybe she's in the bathroom."

Mildred's theories were always very practical.

"I'll try her gain," I said, dialing her number.

This time I confirmed her room number with the switchboard operator in the main building. Yes, it was the right number. No, there was no answer.

Gilligan, always on the lookout for some new hope of rescue which he could render hopeless.

The best thing for me to do was continue my rewrite for another few pages and then phone her again. If she had gone out for a bite to eat, she'd be back shortly. And it certainly can't take more than a two-page rewrite for anyone to go to the bathroom.

Half an hour later I phoned Lottie again. No answer.

This time I decided to find out what, if anything, was wrong. I pushed open the front door to leave our cottage, scattering frogs in all directions. Then I started up the hill toward the main building. It was quite a climb at that severe angle and I was really out of breath by the time I finally reached the top.

When I entered the lobby, I asked the desk clerk if he had seen Miss Cagle. He hadn't.

I went up to her room, and started to slip the pages under her door. Whenever she got back she could start retyping them for mimeo.

Much to my surprise, Lottie opened the door.

"Where have you been?" I asked. "I've been calling for almost an hour."

"I was waiting for your rewrite. I haven't left the room," said Lottie.

There was no point in discussing whether or not she left the room. There was work to be done.

"Let's not get into that now. Here are the pages."

I explained some of the more complicated arrows and scribbles to indicate how I wanted the scenes typed, and I started to exit.

Lottie felt I hadn't believed her, so she reiterated: "Honestly, I haven't left the room. I was waiting for the rewrite."

"Okay. Maybe something's wrong with the switchboard."

I left Lottie to her work, and returned to my cottage.

Going down the hill was much easier than climbing up. When I got to the cottage a new group of frogs was piled up at the door — or maybe they were the old group regrouped. I hated to be rude, but I used the door to push them away, went inside, and continued my work.

About an hour later, I finished two more sequences, and I phoned Lottie to see if she had finished retyping the first pages. I was amazed when there was no answer.

"I don't understand this," I said to Mildred.

"Maybe she finished those pages and went out for a cup of coffee," Mildred suggested.

Writers don't think of those logical things.

After a few minutes, I rang the room. No answer. I checked with the switchboard operator again. There was no mistake. Lottie wasn't answering.

I was really puzzled because Lottie was a very responsible secretary, and I knew she realized the importance of this rewrite.

I decided to run, or at least walk, these additional pages up the hill.

Frogs flew everywhere as I pushed open the door. I climbed the steep incline to the main building.

This time I knocked at Lottie's door. Lottie opened it.

"Do you have more pages?" she asked. "I finished the other ones awhile ago."

"Did you leave the room after you finished them?" I asked.

"No," she answered, "I've been right here waiting for your rewrite."

"I can't figure it out because I've been calling. Anyway, here are more pages."

Once again, Lottie felt called upon to defend herself. "I swear, the phone hasn't rung. I didn't even go out for a cup of coffee. I didn't even go to the bathroom."

There must be some mysterious brainwave communication among women.

"Okay. I'll call you as soon as I finish with the rest of it."

I left Lottie's room and went down to my cottage.

There were the frogs again. They were jumping over each other in their anxiety to pile up against the door. In spite of my problems, I noted with some satisfaction that I still retained my sense of humor. That was the first time in my life I ever saw frogs playing leap frog.

Still shaking my head in bewilderment over Lottie and the strange game of hide-and-go-seek we were playing, I continued on the script.

Writers have to ignore the world around them under script pressure. Especially comedy writers. I remember writing an entire act of an *Ozzie and Harriet* script while Mildred was in labor with one of our sons.

So, doing my best to ignore my strange problem with Lottie and her phone, I finished rewriting the script. Once again, I phoned Lottie. By this time I was sure there would be no answer.

There was no answer.

There was no point in trying to figure it out.

Frogs flew from our front door like planes leaving an aircraft carrier as I flung it open.

I struggled up the hill and knocked at Lottie's door. Sure enough, she answered.

"I know," I said, "the phone hasn't rung and you've been waiting for these pages."

"Right," said Lottie. "I've been sitting right here waiting for the phone to ring."

I decided to ignore the whole question of the phone calls, as Lottie continued.

"And if that mystery wasn't enough, there's a cricket that's been driving me crazy."

"A cricket? We have problems with frogs down at my cottage, but none with crickets."

"There's a cricket in this room that I've been trying to locate. Every ten or fifteen minutes it chirps so loud it's been driving me out of my mind."

"I've never heard a cricket while I've been here."

"It comes and goes."

"Well, never mind the cricket. Here's the rest of the script."

"They must have lots of trouble with crickets here," said Lottie. "I found a can of insecticide spray in the closet. I sprayed everywhere. Especially near the phone. That's where that chirping seems to come from. In fact, I sprayed the phone."

Suddenly a big electric bulb turned on above my head, like in comic strips.

Hanalei Plantation was one of the first places to install the new Swedish phones that didn't ring like American phones did at the time. Instead of the traditional ring, they chirped.

My problem with the phone calls, and Lottie's problem with the cricket, were one and the same. Every time I phoned, she tried to kill the cricket. Lottie had been spraying my phone calls.

When I explained this to Lottie, she was absolutely mortified. She was so embarrassed, she made me promise not to tell anyone else about the incident. I thought it was simply a very funny misunderstanding, but Lottie was afraid she would be humiliated if the others found out.

It's more than twenty years later now, and I don't think Lottie will be embarrassed by this story. I'm sure she'll realize it's an amusing anecdote now in an otherwise grim evening of rewriting.

Lottie's efficiency was unimpaired by the events of the night. The next morning the cast and crew all had copies of the revised script she had retyped and mimeographed.

In spite of that elusive cricket.

11
Everybody Remembers That Day

"Did you hear about the storm last night?" asked Rod Amateau.

"No," I answered. "I was busy all night with the rewrite." (I wanted to say "crickets," but I had made a promise to Lottie.)

We were down on the beach at Moloaa Bay, where hectic activity was in progress as a result of that storm. The unexpectedly heavy waves had loosened the pilings our crew had sunk into the sand the previous day, about forty feet from shore. These pilings were to anchor the thick metal cable to be used in an important routine in which Gilligan was to be pulled around the ocean by a hugh fish. A heavy winch was needed for this special effects sequence. The pilings had to be resunk deeper and more securely to prevent their loosening again.

Divers were out in the water now resetting the pilings. It was enormously difficult work because the Pacific was still very turbulent below the surface. Fortunately, this work could go on out of camera range while filming began on the beach.

Rod was starting with simpler scenes first: scenes around the wrecked S.S. *Minnow*, confined to a relatively small area. While the first day's work was deliberately scheduled to be relatively easy, nothing is easy the first day. And nothing is easy when it requires moving heavy equipment around on sand.

Meanwhile, the ever-changing script required ever more changes. They say a woman's work is never done. Neither is a writer's. Pity the woman writer. She's never done either way.

A special little hut was constructed for me on a nearby section of beach. It housed me, my typewriter, and what was euphemistically referred to as "the script." I was dressed in swim trunks, a hat made of palm fronds, and a nose coated white with zinc oxide. The rays of the tropical sun had already painted my nose bright red.

I spent most of that first day running back and forth between the camera and my little hut making changes. Bob Denver has a prize photo he himself took of me at work in that little hut, rewriting as we filmed.

Those four days of filming on the island of Kauai were filled with crisis after crisis, but there were also amusing incidents along the way.

One occurred on Monday, November 18, the day before we started

On the Gilligan's Island *set, with Gilligan, the Skipper and Gilligan's dialogue coach.*

filming. There were no small charter boats on Kauai that fit our needs as the S.S. *Minnow*. Our scouts found an old one in Honolulu Harbor. It was the right size for a two-man crew and a limited number of passengers. It had a flying bridge, which we needed for filming. (That's where Gilligan and the Skipper would be wrestling with the steering wheel trying to ride out the storm.) We had to tow the small craft to Kauai and demolish it to make it look like it had been wrecked during a storm.

In order to make the boat really wrecked-looking, we pulled it up on the beach and workmen with huge sledge hammers began to smash gaping holes in the sides. I was watching this procedure, to make sure the holes were big enough and in the appropriate places in the boat.

An old Japanese gentleman happened to be walking along the beach at that time. He had no idea who we were or what we were doing. He stood quietly and observed what was going on. He watched carefully for quite a while as the workmen pounded huge holes in the sides of the boat. Finally, the Japanese gentleman turned to me and said very seriously, "They keep doing that, boat no float."

He said that with such calm logic and reason I almost choked trying to suppress my laughter. I'm sure he would have taken it as ridicule. I assured him that was our intention exactly, to make sure the boat couldn't float.

The Japanese gentleman considered this for a moment, shrugged, and moved away, mystified by the peculiar behavior of this strange group of people.

Amusing incidents, unfortunately, were at a minimum compared to the complications that plagued our filming. Many people are amazed that movie films cost as much as they do. I'm amazed that any film ever gets finished, considering the problems, both expected and unexpected, that become permanent guests at every production.

There's no point in detailing the problems involved in the actual filming. One expects the unexpected, and one is never disappointed. No matter how careful the crew is, cameras roll off dolly tracks, and grains of sand find their way into delicate pieces of equipment. The sun moves faster or slower than one anticipates, and the same holds true for the tides. Clouds constantly change the exposure during shots, airplane noises interfere with dialogue tracks, winds blow over gobos and prop palm trees, and sunburns plague the cast. Murphy's law, which is true on sound stages, is even more true on location shooting: "Whatever can go wrong, will go wrong." Not once, but two or three times.

As the writer of *Gilligan's Island,* a lot of these problems were not in my province. However, since I was also the producer, they were very much my concern. Fortunately, Rod Amateau, the director, had a great deal of experience in filming under difficult conditions, and he was somehow able to handle the problems as they occurred. Since he was also the executive producer, he was even more responsible than I for keeping the filming on schedule, and the problems under control. He dealt admirably with a never-ending series of major and minor catastrophes.

The biggest shock of all came on Friday, November 22.

On November 23, we were scheduled to film in Honolulu Harbor. Even though that was our last day of location filming, the scene at Honolulu Harbor was to be the very first sequence in the *Gilligan's Island* pilot, where the S.S. *Minnow* leaves on its fateful excursion.

That Friday, November 22, was the last day of filming at Moloaa Bay. It was late in the morning, when somebody came running down to our company on the beach, claiming he had just heard a disc jockey on the radio say that President Kennedy had been shot. Nobody believed him. It was too preposterous. Just another one of those crazy rumors, we all thought. When you're thousands of miles from the mainland, news reports don't seem very realistic somehow.

But during the next hour, we began to listen to a small radio someone had on the beach. There were further reports, very garbled, about this tragedy. Gradually the realization dawned that this was not simply a rumor. President Kennedy had indeed been shot.

Filming continued, but with great difficulty, as reports trickled in on the President's condition. As concerned as we all were about our President, this was our last day of filming on Kauai, and we had to finish somehow. It was incredibly difficult to continue work as it became clear with every passing hour that the President's condition was critical. We gathered around the radio between rehearsals and takes, listening to one news bulletin after another.

Finally we learned that Lyndon Johnson was being sworn in as President. President Kennedy was dead.

I think everyone knows exactly where he was when he first heard about the assassination of President Kennedy. That's were we were, and that's how we heard the first of a trio of assassinations that were to shock the United States and the world.

I still don't know how we were able to complete the filming that day on Kauai. Not that there was anything we could do about this tragic event. It simply gives you an extra measure of helplessness when you're 5,000 miles away.

Saturday, November 23, we were supposed to complete location filming at Honolulu Harbor. Friday night we left Kauai and checked into our hotels in Oahu.

When we arrived at Honolulu, we learned that Honolulu Harbor, along with other United States naval and military installations, was to be closed Saturday and Sunday, as a period of mourning for President Kennedy. We would be unable to film there.

As the producer of *Gilligan's Island,* I had a very practical problem to consider. Filming in Honolulu Harbor was our last day of location shooting. The whole cast and crew were scheduled to leave Saturday night or Sunday morning and fly back to Los Angeles.

We were told by the authorities that Honolulu Harbor would reopen Monday and that our original permission to film there on Saturday could be transferred to Monday. Later, the official day of mourning was declared to be Monday, and our filming was changed to Tuesday, November 26. This necessitated carrying the cast and crew for two additional days. That's a considerable sum of money, and our budget was already overextended.

The United Artists representative, when I informed him of this problem, answered by simply turning his pockets inside out. He suggested I call C.B.S. for this additional sum.

I had dipped the bucket into that well several times, and C.B.S. had always been cooperative. I hated to make another call for more money, but there was really no alternative. I phoned Hunt Stromberg in Los Angeles, and explained the circumstances. And again Hunt came to the rescue of *Gilligan's Island*.

Fortunately, Hunt himself, and Bob Lewine and his wife, had visited Kauai during the filming, and they were delighted by what they saw. They thought we were making an outstanding pilot film, and that helped when I phoned Hunt for the additional money. C.B.S. agreed to pay the extra costs, and the cast and crew remained in hotels in Honolulu that weekend.

It was there, in the lobbies of our hotels in Honolulu, that we watched on live television while the next episode in a violent drama unfolded. We could scarcely believe our eyes as we watched Jack Ruby pump those bullets into Lee Harvey Oswald. Again, the distance from the United States made everything seem more unbelievable, more bizarre.

On Tuesday, November 26, we finally filmed the sequence in Honolulu Harbor were the S.S. *Minnow* starts on the fateful trip that will strand the Castaways on "Gilligan's Island."

In *my* script, this sequence was to be shot as 60-second background to introduce the crew and passengers for the main title theme song.

Much to my amazement, however, additional scenes had been added to the script without my knowledge or consent. These new scenes consisted of pages of script showing each passenger's preparation for departure.

I've tried to track down the writers of this material. I have followed several leads from people who supposedly knew the writers, but in every case, I was met with denial. The only thing I know for certain is that these pages of additional scenes were written under the supervision of Hunt Stromberg, and sent by C.B.S. pouch to Rod Amateau. Rod was advised by United Artists to "shoot it and keep 'them' happy."

Whether these additional pages were inspired by Hunt Stromberg himself, or the instructions came from Jim Aubrey, or some other C.B.S. executive, I'm sure I'll never know. It's the mysterious generic "they" or "them" who are always responsible for things that suddenly materialize.

What those additional pages accomplished were four minutes of what Rod Amateau calls "fixin' to get ready" scenes. They simply delayed the start of the picture by four interminable minutes. In addition, their intrusion at the beginning of the film precluded the use of my theme song as back story for the series.

These added scenes also prevented me from starting the pilot with a wonderful sight gag: Gilligan, not aware that the boat has been beached during the storm, jumps overboard thinking to rescue the Skipper from the ocean, and dives into the sand instead. I wanted that sight gag to start the film with immediate broad comedy. Instead, it was now preceded by four minutes of dull footage that could only make an audience tune out.

Somewhat similar problems existed with the ending. At that point, to appease Jim Aubrey, the pilot was still called *Gilligan's Travels*. Also for Jim, I had had to add a "tag" sequence to the pilot to indicate a future episode in which the charter boat is repaired and Gilligan and the Skipper embark on another adventure with different passengers. It involved two gangsters, pretending to leave on a charter trip. As soon as they climbed aboard, they pulled out guns and commandeered the boat, holding Gilligan and the Skipper as hostages. This "tag" sequence ran about a minute.

There was a great difference between the opening scenes which were added and the tag which was added.

In the first place, I was fully aware of the tag and participated in writing and producing, even though I was determined never to use it. I had agreed to do it to appease Jim. That wasn't true of those opening scenes.

In the second place, the pilot film would be completely over before the "tag." The tag would not interfere in any way with the preceding film. On the other hand, the "fixin' to leave" opening footage would destroy audience interest before the story even started.

By this time, I guess Jim Aubrey knew I would continue to be obstinate about my original concept of *Gilligan's Island:* keeping the Castaways on the same island and devoting the series to their adventures and the development of the new little isolated community.

Jim was so sure I was wrong and he was right that he immediately set in motion another series, conforming, to his approach to *Gilligan's Island.* It was called *The Baileys of Balboa.* My Alan Hale "Skipper" role was played by Paul Ford. My Bob Denver "Gilligan" was played by Sterling Holloway. Jim Backus' "Thurston Howell III" was played by John Dehner. The humble little charter boat, the S.S. *Minnow,* was played by the humble little charter, the *Island Princess.* This series was produced by Keefe Brasselle's company, Richelieu Productions. (Keefe was a close friend and associate of Jim Aubrey.) On *The Baileys of Balboa,* the little charter boat took different people on different trips each week. Just like Jim wanted.

There are many reasons for success in television: the right night, the right time period, the right lead-in, the right casting, etc. But whatever the reasons, *The Baileys of Balboa* lasted one season. *Gilligan's Island* is still going strong.

Maybe the right concept had something to do with it.

12

Left at the Post

"Sherwood, this is Larry Heath, our film editor," said Rod, as he introduced us.

Larry had worked with Rod Amateau many times before and was an excellent film editor. Larry was to become very important in the history of *Gilligan's Island* later on.

However, during the next few weeks, Larry's editing room became a battlefield where Rod and I, who had gotten along with a minimum of friction, suddenly parted company.

Rod was apparently satisfied to follow orders when they came from above. When United Artists, in the person of Dick Dorso, and/or C.B.S., in the persons of Jim Aubrey and Hunt Stromberg, asked for certain scenes to be excluded, or included, shortened, lengthened, undercranked, overcranked, drop-framed, or double-printed, Rod was anxious to accommodate their wishes. Very often, however, those wishes and my wishes were not exactly the same.

Larry Heath first cut the film to please the director, Rod. Then he would recut it to please the producer, me. Then he would have to recut it to please the executive producer, Rod. Rod and I would argue about our differences.

Then Rod would call Dick Dorso in New York and explain the dispute. Dick, whose proudest boast was that he knew exactly what Jim Aubrey wanted, invariably sided with Rod, for a very simple reason: because Rod cut it the way Dick thought Jim wanted it cut in the first place. It all boiled down to editing the film by second-guessing Jim Aubrey's opinion.

It became a ritual. We would disagree. We would call New York. Dick would agree with Rod.

Post-production is truly one of the most fascinating parts of producing. Ordinarily, I love it. I love the hours in the editing room. I love the music and effects run. I love the scoring. And dubbing is a very special art. I love all of it. The technical people continue to amaze me with their skills. I find all of those post-production elements creatively challenging.

But the post-production on the *Gilligan's Island* pilot, because of the continuing friction in editing, left me frustrated and thwarted. They wouldn't allow my theme song, or any theme song, to explain the back story. There were whole minutes I wanted to remove, entire sections I wanted to recut, and I was handcuffed.

It was my concept, my show, my script, and in many ways, my film, but I couldn't edit it the way I wanted.

Aside from everything else, there was the pressure of time. It was now late December and the network was anxious to see the pilot.

The Bible says that there's a time to sow and a time to reap; a time to be silent and a time to speak. Now it was time for me to be silent. Because it was simply impossible for me to win an argument. I sent the pilot film of *Gilligan's Island* to C.B.S., edited the way "they" wanted it.

Later it would be time to speak. And I had laid the groundwork for that moment.

13

You Can't Win 'Em All

"I can't believe it, Sherwood! I can't believe it! It's never happened before!"

"What's never happened before?"

I was talking to Dick Dorso. Or rather, he was talking to me.

I had just passed through the lobby of Mount Olympus, otherwise known as C.B.S. Television City, on my way to a meeting with Hunt Stromberg.

I wasn't even sure if we would have that meeting. All meetings were subject to cancellation without notice in December. That was the month, back in 1963, when network executives from the East flew West to get a preview look at the pilot films for the following season.

Pilot films were generally not finalized at that point. Editing was incomplete, without stock shots, and the pilots were seldom dubbed with final sound and music. They were usually submitted to the networks for appraisal at this stage, but only because by that time the networks would be driving the production companies crazy for a look at the pilots. The networks wanted to start planning their schedules for the following September. This was especially true for C.B.S. because they were the first to announce next season's schedule, a ritual that occurred in mid–February.

Like birds flying south for the winter, the network executives from the East would fly to Hollywood in December for a look at their crop of pilot films. Then the production executives on the West Coast would fly to New York in February to convince the East Coast network executives to buy their series. Every year, like swallows flying south and north, Eastern execu-birds would fly West, and then the Western execu-birds would fly East.

The trade papers were always filled, at that time of year, with inside information involving potential schedules. Certain pilot films were "hot" and others were "cold," according to *Variety* and the *Hollywood Reporter*.

Advertising agencies began jockeying for the new series that showed the most promise and would benefit their sponsors. In those years, sponsors and ad agencies were still very powerful in making decisions on programming because most TV shows were sponsored by one or two companies.

When the East Coast network chiefs gathered in Hollywood, only the heads of production companies were allowed to screen the pilot films with the networks in the executive viewing rooms. Producers, writers, actors, directors, were all specifically excluded from these screenings. Perhaps this was to shield the delicate ears of the creative people from the kinds of remarks network executives were likely to make as the pilots unreeled on the screen.

I've been in countless screenings with network executives and with production executives, but never in those super-top-level screenings. Not in the December West Coast selling season, nor in the January East Coast selling season.

Anyway, I was on my way to my meeting with Hunt, armed with some last-minute notes I had written; ideas to promote *Gilligan's Island* if it got on the air. I started down the first-floor hallway toward the elevators, when the door to the executive viewing room opened and disgorged a matched set of well-tailored executives. Leading the group was James T. Aubrey, followed by at least ten or eleven of his underlings, including Hunt Stromberg. Accompanying them was Dick Dorso, the only non–C.B.S. person I saw. Dick was annointed for network screenings because he was the executive in charge of programming for United Artists. Apparently, Dick had been showing some of his pilots to the network.

Dick saw me coming down the hall, and broke away from the group and ran toward me. In my entire life I have never seen a man in a wilder state of exultation. On a scale of euphoria from one to ten, he was somewhere around 182, the boiling point. Any higher and they put you away.

Dick grabbed me by the arm and exclaimed, "I can't believe it, Sherwood! I can't believe it! It's never happened before!"

"What's never happened before?"

Dick didn't even hear me. He was so excited he just babbled on.

"Every single one! I can't believe it! What a day this is!"

Somehow Dick managed to put an arm around my shoulder without losing his jacket.

"Sherwood, I broke every record. I just screened all my pilots for Jim today. All of them. And I'm sure this has never happened before."

I couldn't believe what Dick Dorso was saying. Surely he hadn't sold all five pilots to C.B.S. Yet . . .

"You mean you sold everything?"

"That's right! *Calhoun, Kibbee Hates Fitch, Mark Dolphin, John Stryker—.*"

Suddenly Dick broke off as he realized to whom he was speaking.

"Sherwood." He used my name again as he became aware. "I'm sorry, I'm really sorry. I was so excited I didn't realize. It wasn't *all* of them. It was *almost* all. I'm afraid *Gilligan's Island* didn't make it."

Dick tried to figure some way to apologize. "Jim just didn't go for *Gilligan*. He loved all the other ones, but somehow—I'm sorry."

"Well," I said wryly, "You can't win 'em all."

Mr. Dorso was rather anxious to do two things at that moment. One was

In spite of that "come hither" look, nobody came to rescue Ginger for years and years.

to leave me as soon as possible after that blunder. The other was to chase after the C.B.S. flock, which Shepherd Jim was leading toward the elevator to their handsomely appointed fold on the third floor.

"Look," Dick said, "I know Jim better than anybody. I know what he liked in the film, and I know what he didn't like, so I still might be able to save it."

"Thanks," I said.

"I mean it, I'll give all my notes to Rod."

With that, Dick hastened toward the elevator.

All my work—the writing, the rewriting, the casting, the filming, the editing, the dubbing—all down the drain. Somehow it seemed much worse because all of Dick's other shows had made it. Only *Gilligan's Island* was unsold.

How was I to know that on the September 1964 C.B.S. schedule, Dick Dorso and his company, United Artists, would have exactly one new series on the air and that series would be *Gilligan's Island?*

You have very few choices at a time like that. If you're six years old, you cry. If you're past twenty-one, you go out and get drunk. But if you're about forty, and you have a wonderful wife, and four great kids, and you have plenty of ideas for other shows, you try to remember the optimists' creed. My glass was still half full.

Besides, there was something I knew that Dick Dorso didn't know.

Dick was aware I had continually disagreed with him and Rod Amateau about the editing of the film. As I said before, after each disagreement, Rod phoned Dick in New York. Dick always supported Rod and Rod always supported Dick. Because they "knew" what Jim liked.

Intellectually, I could understand that, because Dick Dorso and Rod Amateau had shared several major hits in television. Also, realistically, Rod outranked me. Even though it was my show, my creation, I was only the producer. Rod was the executive producer. It was natural for Dick to side with Rod. This was my first pilot film, and they knew more about pilot films than I did.

Emotionally, however, it was hard to accept. Just because someone has more experience doesn't mean he's right. It doesn't mean he's wrong. But he's not automatically right either. It was useless to point this out to Dick right now. Or to Rod, for that matter. They had made the final cut of *Gilligan's Island* over my objections, and that film had now been rejected by Mr. Network, Jim Aubrey.

It had been my duty, as the producer, to send that cut of the film — Rod and Dick's cut — to C.B.S. I fulfilled that duty. However, there was another duty I had. To myself, to my show, and to C.B.S.

I had disagreed with so much of the editing, I hadn't felt it was fair to me, to *Gilligan's Island,* or to C.B.S. to let them assume I was satisfied with this version of the pilot. So along with the film, I had sent a letter to C.B.S. In that letter I stated there was, in my opinion, a good pilot film in this footage, but not the way it had been edited. I disavowed this version of the pilot, divorcing myself from this cut of *Gilligan's Island.*

It was a very dangerous thing for me to do. What if C.B.S. loved it the way it was? What if they tested it for audience reaction and the audience loved it that way, too? My disclaimer would effectively remove me from my own show.

What made me sure I was right? What made me sure two men with much more extensive experience were wrong?

I wasn't sure. In a matter of judgment, the only thing a creative person has is his opinion. I was exercising mine.

I was also depending upon my close relationship with C.B.S. I had rescued *The Red Skelton Show* when it had been on its way to oblivion. I had also solved the problems they were having with *My Favorite Martian*.

I suspected the pilot film would be rejected. And if it were, then perhaps—just perhaps—C.B.S. would take another look at *Gilligan's Island* if I recut it and I presented it again, my way.

I must point out that I never received a reply to my letter, neither by return mail, nor by memo, nor even by a phone call.

Yet I'm sure someone somewhere at C.B.S. read my letter because of what eventually happened.

Left at the Post Again ... and Again

"Jesus, if we cut out all this stuff, there'll be nothing left."

I agreed. "The whole pilot will run about sixteen or seventeen minutes," I said.

Rod Amateau and I were at Fox discussing the notes he had received from Dick Dorso.

Frankly, I didn't even think Dorso meant what he said about "notes" and "saving the film" after the Jim Aubrey screening at C.B.S. I thought he was only trying to make me feel a little better after the rejection. But Dick had been in the room with Jim when they screened the pilot; and, true to his word, he had made some notes, including what scenes Jim had liked.

"If we string those scenes together, it'll be like film clips," I said to Rod. "I'm not even sure the plot will make any sense. Jim Aubrey might not even like the scenes he liked before, cut together like this."

Rod's attitude was simpler than mine. "If Dick Dorso wants it cut this way, let's cut it this way." He repeated the same thing I had heard time and time again: "Nobody knows Jim Aubrey better than Dick Dorso."

It was pointless for me to argue about this. Rod would call Dorso in New York, and Dorso would tell me the only possible alternative left was cutting the film to suit Jim Aubrey.

The editing of the first version of the pilot had been frustrating and aggravating because of all the disagreements I had had with Rod. However, cutting it the way Dorso suggested, Rod and I had few disagreements. We simply butchered the first *Gilligan's Island* pilot. We chopped it to pieces to fit a Dick Dorso version based on his interpretation of Jim Aubrey's reactions. When we finished we sent this truncated pilot to Dick Dorso in New York.

Several days later we heard the news. It was not unexpected. Dick called from New York to say, "Jim saw this new version. He simply doesn't go for the show. Sorry."

At this point, Rod threw up his hands. He had done his job. He had followed instructions. He was finished. We didn't exchange fond goodbyes, for lots of reasons.

But then a new knight rode in on his white horse.

"Never mind Dick Dorso," said Hunt Stromberg. "Nobody knows Jim

Aubrey better than I do." It seemed that everybody knew Jim Aubrey better than everybody else.

From previous experiences with both Hunt and Jim, I was aware they really were very close in many ways. Hunt was Jim Aubrey's West Coast alter ego.

Hunt's suggestions included not only recutting the film, but doing some retakes, inserts, and a few short added scenes.

I was somewhat surprised that Hunt would go through this additional expense on a pilot film that had already been rejected in two other forms. But there's an old saying, "Where there's life, there's hope." I've always believed it. In fact, Jim Backus always called me "Pollyanna Schwartz."

Besides, what did I have to lose? If West Coast C.B.S. thought those changes would make it acceptable to East Coast C.B.S., my feelings were obvious. Let's try it!

I wrote a letter to Dick Dorso on January 15, 1964, outlining Hunt's suggestions and enclosing my own script changes for the retakes, inserts, and added scenes. *Gilligan's Island,* for Jim Aubrey's reasons, was still called *Gilligan's Travels* at that time.

Dorso's response was immediate and natural. "Do it," he said.

We did it. It took only a day to do the required shooting for the additional footage. Then Larry Heath and I cut this new material into the pilot film, and added back the scenes Hunt had suggested.

There were now three versions of *Gilligan's Island*—the Stromberg Version, the Dick Dorso Version and the original Rod Amateau Version.

None of these versions had my theme song, or any theme song, for that matter, to explain the show. All of them contained pieces of the deadly dull opening scenes in the marina.

Larry Heath's editing room was so filled with different versions of different scenes for the different variations of the pilot, there was enough film there to make *Gilligan's Island* an 84-part mini-series.

The Stromberg Version was now shipped to New York to be shown to Jim and/or audience tested.

In a few days the results came back: another rejection. In baseball, three strikes and you're out.

Luckily, we weren't playing baseball.

Setting *Gilligan's Island* Free

"Hi, Dick,"

That was me on the phone to Dick Dorso in New York.

"Hi, Sherwood. What can I do for you?" Dick was still in an expansive, exuberant mood. Why not? He still thought he had just turned five TV pilots into four series, a truly remarkable achievement.

"I'd like to have the film and the negative of *Gilligan's Island*," I said.

"What for? You want to make ukulele picks?"

Dick chuckled as he said this. It's one of the oldest jokes in show business. Dick knew it, and he knew that I knew it. It's just one of those things you say about film that's absolutely worthless.

"Not exactly," I replied. "I want to recut the film."

"What for? Jim turned it down. Three times. And so did C.B.S. research. It's been rejected."

I knew I needed United Artist's permission to work on the film because they owned it. I didn't want any arguments or any recriminations about its past history. I simply needed his authorization to get my hands on the film.

"I think I can improve it."

"What's the point? Why recut something that's been rejected by everyone?"

"That pilot film didn't even have the theme song in it."

"You're really stubborn, aren't you?"

"I'm not stubborn," I insisted. "I'm determined."

"What's the difference?" Dick wanted to know.

"It all depends on whether I turn out to be right or wrong."

Dick chuckled again and replied, "Okay. If you want the film, I'll authorize the release. But there isn't anything left in the budget."

"I'm not asking for any money," I answered. "I'll get it recut somehow."

"And you might as well forget about a theme song. There's no music budget," Dick reminded me.

"I know. I'm just asking you to release the print and the negative. Okay?"

"Okay."

"Thanks."

My next talk was going to be more difficult: I had to tell Mildred what I was planning to do. Any woman who has watched her husband go through the battles of making a pilot film isn't anxious for her Sir Lancelot to try to slay the fire-breathing network dragon again. My Lady Guinevere reacted as I expected.

"Aren't you just beating your head against a stone wall?" she wanted to know.

"Just think how good it'll feel when I stop."

Mildred didn't even smile at that ancient punchline.

"Has anyone ever sold a pilot film that's already been rejected by everybody?" she asked.

"I'll look it up in the *Guinness Book of World Records*," I answered. "Besides, remember the letter I wrote, disavowing the pilot film, the way it had been edited?"

"You don't even know if anybody read that letter. Nobody's ever mentioned it to you."

"That doesn't mean nobody read it. Besides, I'm convinced there's a wonderful pilot buried in that film."

Mildred is a sculptor. A very good one, too. In fact, our house is the only one in Southern California guaranteed not to blow away in a hurricane, thanks to several tons of her marble. I decided to use her work as a point of reference.

"Didn't you once say 'inside every piece of stone there's a sculpture waiting to be set free'?"

"No. It was a different sculptor who said that. Michelangelo, I think. But I get your point."

"That's all I'm trying to do, set *Gilligan's Island* free from the rest of that film."

"Are you talking about recutting the whole picture?" Mildred wanted to know.

I had a feeling she was going to ask another one of her practical questions. The kind I hate. She did.

"How can you finish it in time? Doesn't C.B.S. announce its schedule in a week or two?"

"I didn't say it was going to be easy."

"Is it possible?"

"I don't know," I answered honestly. When Mildred didn't respond, I added, "Aren't you going to try to talk me out of this?"

"No," said Mildred. "I know you're not stubborn, Honey, but I know you're determined."

She'd heard me use that phrase many times.

The next person I phoned was Larry Heath, the film editor who had worked on the pilot.

Larry and I had gotten along very well. He's an excellent editor, but like all editors, he was forced to change the film according to final authority. In the case of television, final authority is the executive producer. While I was editing the film with Larry, and Larry was making changes in accordance with my instructions, new instructions would come from Rod Amateau. Thanks to my changes, Rod's changes, Dick's changes, and Hunt's changes, the film had been cut, recut, and recut again until it was mostly splicing tape.

I told Larry I was planning to recut the pilot yet again and add the theme song. I also told him I didn't think there was anything left in the budget for more editing, but I'd make sure he got paid anyway.

The next morning I was in Larry's editing room at Twentieth Century–Fox, with Larry and his assistant, Mike Brown. We were looking at the pilot film that had been turned down by C.B.S.

"There's no way we can start cutting this film again," said Larry. "It's been cut and recut so many times, it'll tear as soon as we start work on it."

"You mean, back to square one?"

"Right. We're going to have to start with dailies, if you're talking about major recutting."

Dailies! It was January 20! It would take a couple of days to get reprints of all the dailies. Then they had to be numbered before we could even start cutting them.

The C.B.S. schedule would be coming out in less than three weeks. We would have to cut Saturdays, Sundays, and even if we did, could we—?

As difficult as I imagined the work would be, I never fully realized what the next weeks had in store. We worked Saturdays and Sundays. We had lunch in that editing room, and took naps there at night when it was too late to go home. I'll forever be in Larry's debt.

It's amazing what you can do, if you don't know that you can't do it. Starting with the dailies on January 22, we recut virtually the entire pilot film.

In the editing process, we eliminated some six or seven minutes. Much of the footage was removed from the deadly slow opening which C.B.S. and United Artists had secretly authorized writers to write — the "fixin' to get ready" sequence at the marina. Four deadly minutes that lasted forever, or longer.

With Larry Heath, I could start the film the way I wanted to: after the *Minnow* was wrecked on the island. Virtually the first thing the viewer would see was Gilligan diving into what he thinks is water and landing in the sand.

For those readers, and I guess that means most readers, not familiar with film editing, recutting and reediting film may sound like simple addition or subtraction. Nothing could be further from the truth. Editing is a highly creative process. Performances are often made or destroyed in an editing room. So are plots. So are moods. So are pilot films.

I've already mentioned the removal of several needless minutes at the beginning of the pilot. That was simple elimination. But let me give an example of another type of editing. There was a sequence in which Gilligan hooks a huge fish and battles it toward the shore. The fish pulls him out to sea and he pulls it back to shore, wrestling in the water with it.

It was a very funny sequence, and it lasted about thirty or forty seconds on screen. It was so funny, it should have been longer. I ordered several reprints of each shot in the sequence, and I built the battle between Gilligan and that fish until it was almost a minute and a half, three times the original length. Each time Gilligan dragged the fish toward the shore, the fish dragged him back out again, and when he finally started grappling near shore with the fish the added film made it a wrestling match worthy of an Olympic gold medal. This additional footage was accomplished by having the film lab change sizes on some of the shots, reverse action on others, and "flop" several more (i.e. print them backwards, facing the other direction).

Thus a good comedy scene was turned into a hilarious sequence that became the most important sustained comic scene in the entire show. The results of the eventual audience testing of the pilot film clearly indicated the importance of that Gilligan/fish battle. It tested higher than any other part of the show and sustained itself for the full minute and a half. It was so successful that it would be used in all advance promotion to advertise *Gilligan's Island* that fall.

That's how much creative editing can mean. It's not simple addition or subtraction.

Larry and I were able to effect many other changes of this kind during those sleepless, lunchless days in the editing room. For instance, in addition to cutting, changing, and recreating scenes in the pilot film itself, we had to cut the background shots for the main title to appear on the TV screen behind the theme song.

The theme song! At long last, the theme song!

This time I wanted professional help with the music. This was no time for an encore from the Songbird from Passaic.

I called George Wyle, a wonderful musician and composer who had written a number of successful songs. (Many of you would become familiar with George later on as the conductor on *The Flip Wilson Show* where he was also a performer, as he was on the *Andy Williams* specials.) George, witty and clever with lyrics as well as music, had been a close friend for a number of years.

I told George my problem. I needed a terrific song, to be recorded with orchestra and vocal, and there was absolutely no money in the budget to pay for anything.

George responded characteristically. "What are friends for?" he asked.

Professional musicians, thanks to a very strong union, would have to be paid. Somehow we would have to record the song without union musicians. George thought it was possible.

Suppose we had a group, like three or four fellows with guitars. If they sang the theme, we wouldn't have to pay them, providing the performance was for private use, like screenings for the executives. When their vocal and music became public, then they would be paid for that performance. In fact, each time their performance would be repeated, they would get residuals. George was sure he could find some new group anxious to perform under these conditions.

Meanwhile, we needed different music from Calypso. We had filmed the pilot in Hawaii, and calypso, of course, is indigenous to the Caribbean area.

I screened the pilot for George so that he would know the main title shots I intended to coordinate with the theme to help tell the back story. George was full of enthusiasm and talent, helpful in every creative way. My phone call to him had been an inspiration.

We discussed the possibility of Hawaiian music. Neither of us was enthused about that. The slow hula one associated with Hawaii didn't seem right. Neither did the furious beat of Hawaiian war chant tom toms. Both seemed wrong for a rollicking comedy show called *Gilligan's Island*.

"How about a sea chanty?" asked George.

I didn't know much about sea chanties, but in a few minutes at my piano, George showed me what he meant. The rhythm was just right. It had the feeling of the ocean, rather than that of a specific place like Hawaii or Jamaica, and there was rousing good spirit to the musical form.

We spent several hours together that day. George was working on a melody line. I worked on changing the lyrics from my calypso song to fit the new music.

The lyrics had to conform with the sequential order of the main title, which introduced the characters and told the back story of the voyage and the wreck. Also, the characters had to be introduced in a certain order because of contractual obligations. Changes followed changes as I conformed the lyrics, with a great deal of help from George. Fortunately, I knew enough about music to adjust George's melody to fit the back story and the contract demands. In truth, the credits at the end of each episode reflect the way we eventually worked things out: "Lyrics and music by George Wyle and Sherwood Schwartz."

I continued to work with Larry Heath at Twentieth Century–Fox, where the editing was difficult, but going smoothly. There was no Rod Amateau, no Dick Dorso, no Jim Aubrey, no C.B.S., no United Artists, to suggest changes. They weren't even aware of what I was doing.

I had even neglected to tell Perry Leff, my agent. I wasn't trying to keep it a secret. I was so completely consumed in my work that it never occurred to me to tell anyone.

It took several days before the music and lyrics for the opening theme were finalized. They had to run exactly sixty seconds, because that's the maximum allowed for the main title in a half-hour series.

Janos Prohaska, a stuntman who played many different creatures on Gilligan's Island, *chats with Tina Louise.*

The film footage, of course, had to be cut to tell the same story as the lyrics. This required only minor readjustment because the main title, without song, had been edited in much the same way.

"I've got some good news, and some bad news, and some terrible news," said George on the phone.

"Start with the good news," I suggested.

"I found a really nice group, three fellows who call themselves 'The Wellingtons.' They all play guitars and they have a very nice sound."

"Great. What's the bad news?"

"The bad news is that recording studios cost a lot of money. I haven't been able to make any kind of deal, and I've pulled every string I have."

"I'll get the money somehow. What's the terrible news?"

"You wanted the recording by Monday, for Tuesday's dubbing. There isn't a single decent studio in town available on Saturday. Even if you have the money."

"And Sunday?"

"They're all closed."

"That's not simply terrible news, George. That's catastrophic, calamitous and cataclysmic."

"Sounds like the name of my law firm," said George.

"Get a new law firm," I suggested, and hung up.

I had made arrangements for a dubbing session on Tuesday so I could get an answer print by Thursday and send the new version of the *Gilligan's Island* pilot to C.B.S. New York on Friday. That way, the executives could see it the following week and audience-test it before they announced their fall schedule.

Somehow I had to have the theme song ready for the Tuesday dubbing. That meant I had to get the recording made over the weekend. And every place was booked or was closed.

Not every place.

I turned to another close friend of mine in this time of need: Mel Shavelson, a man I had known since 1939, when we both worked on Bob Hope's radio show. In fact, Mel was our "official" photographer when Mildred and I were married.

Mel is an avid ham operator, electronics genius and possessor of more technical equipment than C.B.S. itself. The antenna on his house is so high, planes have to avoid it on their way to L.A.X.

"Mel, I'm desperate."

"Sherwood, everyone in television is desperate."

"I need a favor."

"Everyone in television needs a favor."

"Mel, I need your equipment this weekend."

"So does Lucille."

Then Mel saw I was serious. The jokes stopped, and the help started.

Mel and Lucy weren't going to be home Saturday, but they'd be there Sunday. Mel promised to help me any way he could.

I phoned George Wyle and told him about Mel. We worked out the following plan.

Early Sunday, about 10 a.m., George would come over to my house with the Wellingtons, the group he had found. We would rehearse the song for an hour or so. Then we would go over to Mel's house — only about five blocks from mine — and record it.

As scheduled, George and his singing group arrived at my home Sunday morning. They were, as George had assured me, nice, bright, young men, and sang in an upbeat, casual style. It took awhile, with George at the piano, to find the right chords for their guitars and to give the various voices the proper levels. In addition, we found it more effective if a few of the lyrics were sung solo by one of the group. It took about two hours to get the sound we wanted, and to make the Wellingtons comfortable with the song. Then we all drove over to the Shavelsons—and walked into an astonishing scene.

The Shavelson's house was bustling with enormous preparations for a big luncheon affair for some charity. The living room, where I was hoping to record the song, was set up with ten or twelve round tables surrounded by folding chairs. There were waiters scurrying about with table cloths, silverware, and place settings. A boiler room would have been quieter.

"I forgot all about this when I spoke to you," said Mel cheerfully.

"Don't worry about a thing," his wife Lucy assured me. "When you're ready to record, I'll whistle. The waiters will stop moving. I've already talked to them. I'll show you."

She whistled and sure enough, the waiters stopped moving and the room became quiet. Lucy's a good producer herself.

Mel was in the next room in his private electronic haven—the one filled with enough equipment to keep six satellites in orbit at once. As George and I and the Wellingtons were preparing for the recording session, Mel ran back and forth from the electronics room to the microphones in the living room where the Wellingtons were tuning their guitars.

The next hour was like a scene from a Marx Brothers movie. While George and I were trying to get a recording of "The Ballad of Gilligan's Isle" in the living room, Mel kept adjusting the microphones and dashing back to the control room. On cue, Lucy kept whistling for the waiters to stop the clatter of dishes during actual takes. Sometimes they did and sometimes they didn't.

Seen in retrospect, I'll bet it would really make a hilarious scene. But as with many scenes that are funny in retrospect, we were all quite serious. George, the Wellingtons, and I, Mel and Lucy, and even the waiters, were pulling for one good take.

We got it. And it happened just as guests were starting to arrive for the affair.

With profuse thanks to Mel and Lucy, and our apologies for all the inconvenience we had caused, we left, a recording of "The Ballad of Gilligan's Isle" in hand.

Usually theme songs for main titles are produced on scoring stages with a large orchestra, a multitude of microphones placed at precise points for all the various instruments. Engineers balance the instruments individually and with each other. This is done with infinite patience so that the ultimate musical sound is a perfect equilibrium of strings, brass and percussion.

In a control room there's an engineering panel that looks something like the Mission Control Center in Houston, only a lot more complicated. The engineers can increase or decrease the highs and lows in any combination with any of the instruments. The tender loving care that goes into a scoring session for a theme song is incredible.

With this as background, consider the theme music I brought to Twentieth Century–Fox on Monday morning. It was the tape I made at Mel Shavelson's house with the three Wellingtons playing their guitars into two microphones while they sang the lyrics. If you listen ever so carefully, you might even hear the rattle of a dish as the waiters obeyed Lucille's instructions to cool it during that take.

However, the question that Larry Heath and I faced on Monday morning, as we prepared for the dubbing session the next day, was not quality but length. The music and the film had to be the same length, to the exact frame. In addition, the lyrics were supposed to introduce the various characters as they appeared on the screen, so the film and music had to be in exact alignment. We had been flying blind at the Shavelson house, with no film to guide us. Now Larry and I had to line things up on the moviola and see how close we came.

We came pretty damn close!

We couldn't tamper with the music. That couldn't be changed at this point. So we trimmed some of the cuts, added to others, and in a relatively short time the main title and "The Ballad of Gilligan's Isle" were finally united.

The long battle was over — the battle that had started months earlier with Jim Aubrey, and had included my *a cappella* calypso solo. I finally had the theme song I always wanted: one minute of entertainment that told the whole back story.

Larry turned this final piece of film over to post-production for negative cutting. The rest of the recut pilot had already been sent there. Now we had *Gilligan's Island* in negative cutting. The "answer print," the print not yet fully corrected for minor details, would be ready on Thursday.

Larry and I were both exhausted, not only from working day and night for four weeks straight. It was the kind of exhaustion that results from nervous tension — solving problems while working against an immovable deadline. And we weren't even sure what the deadline was!

We had given it our best shot, and we were both wrung out. Limp.

I remember shaking hands with Larry. "I don't know what's going to happen now," I said, "but the point is, we did it. You've gone far beyond the call of duty. And of money, too."

"So have you," replied Larry.

"That's different," I said. "It's my project, and I'm trying to prove something. You've been working when you knew there was no money in the budget for your services. Working night and day."

"Don't worry about it."

"No, no. I'll see that you're paid. And if it sells, there'll be a bonus for you."

"I told you. Don't worry about it."

"Instead of sending it straight to New York, maybe we should send it by way of Lourdes."

Larry was Catholic, and I thought that would please him. It did. He smiled.

"I'd pay the postage for that," said Larry.

This time it was my turn to say, "Don't worry about it."

"We've got a tough day tomorrow," Larry reminded me.

He was referring to dubbing. All the previous work in dubbing the original pilot film, the process of combining film, sound track, music, effects, and laugh track, was now worthless. There had been so many changes made in the reedited film from the first pilot, we would have to start from scratch. Larry and I would spend that entire next day, Tuesday, February 4, 1964, in the dubbing room.

"Didn't we do this once before?" asked one of the engineers.

"Yeah," I answered.

"And we're doing it again?" he wondered.

"We're going to keep doing it till we get it right. Right, Larry?"

Larry was dedicated and faithful, but he wasn't crazy. "I don't know about that," he countered, not sure I was just joking.

I laughed and we continued the dubbing session.

We had known in advance it would be a long difficult day. It was. But we were delighted with the results. Adding the theme song to the main title at the beginning, eliminating those dull minutes at the opening, trimming scenes, adding footage, cutting skip-frame opticals with which I disagreed—all these changes were very effective. At least, they were to me and to Larry. Dubbing engineers seldom voice an opinion. They've seen it all and they've heard it all. They do their own work efficiently and expertly, and don't get involved in creative judgments. They had no comments.

There was nothing further for Larry and me to do until Thursday, when we would see the answer print from the lab. We were told it would be ready at 5 p.m. Thursday.

That night I made a phone call.

"Hi, Perry."

"Hi, Sherwood. What's going on?"

"I just finished."

"You just fiinshed what?"

"The pilot film. I just finished dubbing the pilot film."

"What are you talking about? What pilot film?"

"Gilligan's Island."

"Sherwood, are you feeling okay?"

It was then I realized I had failed to tell Perry, of all people, that I was recutting the pilot. It suddenly hit me that Larry, Mildred, Mike Brown (Larry's assistant) and myself were the only ones who knew about this.

"Who authorized this?" asked Perry. "C.B.S.? United Artists?"

"Nobody. I asked Dick Dorso if I could have the film, now that C.B.S. has rejected it, and he said okay. If you want an exact quote, he asked me whether I was going to cut it up and make ukulele picks."

Perry's mind, like most agents' minds, went to money.

"How'd you do the cutting and dubbing and everything? Was there anything left in the budget?"

"I don't think so," I answered truthfully. "I just ordered things here at Fox, and I guess we still have the same charge number. I don't know."

"I never heard of anything like this," said Perry. "But I guess we're not talking about a lot of money anyway." Then he added, "What made you do it? I mean, after C.B.S. rejected it."

I explained to Perry about the letter I had sent along with that first cut of the pilot, disavowing that particular version. My past association with C.B.S., I believed, might cause the executives to take another look. Conceivably, it could lead to more audience testing.

"I've got to tell you, Sherwood. This is really crazy."

"Perry, they told Edison he was crazy. They told the Wright Brothers they were crazy. They told Samuel Morse he was crazy."

"There's one big difference," answered Perry. "They weren't, and you are! *Gilligan's Island* has already been rejected."

"I know."

"You're repainting a building after it's been condemned."

I knew that, too.

I couldn't blame Perry for being sarcastic. After all, I was presenting him with a *fait accompli*. I guess I should have discussed it with him, or at least made him aware of what I was doing.

"Perry, I'd like you to take a look at the answer print, Thursday, at 5 p.m., at Fox. The new pilot of *Gilligan's Island*."

"Okay, I'll be there. I don't really understand this, but I'll be there."

Thursday, at 5:00, in one of Fox's large viewing rooms, we watched the new version of the pilot of *Gilligan's Island*. "We" included Perry Leff, Larry Heath, Mildred, and me. There was no representation from United Artists, and none from C.B.S.

The film started, and Perry watched it with growing fascination and excitement.

By the time it was over, Perry could scarcely contain himself.

"It's a new fucking picture!" he exclaimed. "It's a new fucking picture!"

Mildred said, with a smile, "There's a lady present."

Perry said, "I know. And I want the lady to know *it's a new fucking picture!*"

Mildred laughed. I did, too. Perry seldom used four-letter words, with or without ladies present. He was obviously very, very excited about what he had just seen.

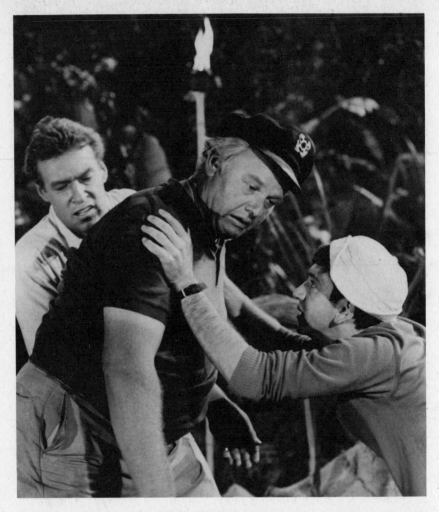

The Professor and Gilligan attend to the Skipper, who seems to be afflicted with some island sickness. The look on Skipper's face reminds me of how I felt when Perry Leff told me the C.B.S. schedule was coming out earlier than I'd planned.

Then, suddenly, Perry was all business. "What are you planning to do with this film?" he asked. A sense of urgency underlined his question.

"I'm airmailing it first thing in the morning to C.B.S. Their schedule is coming out soon. I want to make sure this pilot gets there by Monday."

"Too late! The C.B.S. schedule is coming out on Monday," Perry said. "Monday!"

The elevator dropped my stomach three floors.

All that work, a newly edited pilot, and the C.B.S. schedule would be released Monday, before they could view the film.

"This pilot film has to be in New York first thing tomorrow," said Perry. "So the C.B.S. brass can get a look at it tomorrow morning!"

"But how—"

I started to ask questions, but Perry didn't even hear. His mind was racing ahead.

"I'll charter a plane! Don't you see? This film has to be in New York Friday morning so the executives have all day to view it. If they like it as much as I do, they'll have Saturday and Sunday to do audience testing. That's the only way it can get on the C.B.S. Monday schedule."

Then Perry turned to Mildred. "Would you call the airport? I've never chartered a plane before."

Mildred picked up a phone as though she had been chartering planes all her life. She started making inquiries.

"We have to call Dick Dorso in New York," Perry said to me.

I wasn't too thrilled about talking to Dick Dorso. "What for? The last thing he told me was to make ukulele picks," I reminded Perry.

"Forget the ukulele picks," said Perry. "We have to let United Artists know what's going on. If C.B.S. looks at the film and likes it, they'll call United Artists. Dick Dorso won't know what they're talking about. You can't leave him in the dark, for your own sake."

Perry's argument was flawless. If Dick Dorso knew nothing about this recut version, that might cool interest on the part of C.B.S. That could be fatal.

"We've got to talk to Dick right now," said Perry.

Right there, from the Fox viewing room, Perry placed a call to New York. It was about nine o'clock in New York, so Perry phoned Dick Dorso at home. Dick and his wife were out to dinner, Perry learned from their housekeeper.

In the next few minutes, Perry earned every penny of his packaging fee for C.M.A.

Perry told the Dorso's housekeeper to keep phoning their favorite restaurants until she found them. He gave the housekeeper our phone number in the viewing room. He told her we would wait right there for a call from Mr. Dorso no matter how many restaurants she had to call.

We waited there. The engineers all left. Even Larry left. But Mildred and I waited there with Perry.

Mildred, meanwhile, had learned there was one new flight, a T.W.A. midnight flight, that arrived in New York the next morning around 8 a.m., New York time. There was apparently no need to charter a plane, if we got the film on that flight.

We had to hear from Dick Dorso. After about a half-hour, we did.

Perry was just as excited on the phone with Dick as he had been when he first saw the recut pilot film. "It's a new fucking picture, Dick! The song up front makes a tremendous difference, and the whole film moves faster. I don't even know why, but it's a new fucking picture!"

Perry offered me the phone, but I turned it down. At that point in history, I had no desire to get into a discussion with Dick Dorso.

"Okay, okay," Perry was saying on the phone. "I want you to see it first. You have to know what you're talking about if C.B.S. discusses it with you."

As anxious as I was for C.B.S. to get the film, I could understand the logic of letting Dick Dorso see it first.

"We're putting it on the T.W.A. flight tonight," Perry was telling Dick. "Good. Tell your messenger it's on the midnight flight. But promise me one thing. No matter what you think of it personally, I want your word that you'll take it over to C.B.S. Right. Sherwood and I both want your promise on that."

Evidently Perry got his assurance, because he hung up, and he said to me, "Let's get this show on the road."

"You mean, on the plane."

"Save your jokes for the scripts," observed Perry. "We've got to get moving."

"I'll call Transportation for a driver," I said as I reached for the phone. And encountered another problem. As sometimes happens at studios, there were no teamsters available.

People outside the industry may not know this, but ordinary mortals are not allowed to move film off the lot. Only members of the Teamsters Union are privileged to perform that sacred task.

It was now well past seven. Any drivers on the lot were assigned to a crew and therefore unavailable to us. Drivers off the lot might not be coming back for hours if they were on location.

There was only one thing for Perry and me to do: we had to smuggle the three reels of film off the lot to the airport.

Perry insisted on using his car and doing the driving so I wouldn't be blamed in any way. A producer could get into trouble with the Teamsters Union. But an agent has no real relationship with them anyway.

Hiding the metal cans under our jackets like criminals, Perry and I sneaked the reels of my own film into the trunk of Perry's car. Then Perry drove to the airport.

I knew Perry very well. He wouldn't let those cans of film out of his sight until he saw them on board that midnight flight. With his own eyes. So Mildred and I drove home.

There seemed to be no end of questions we could ask each other. Would the film get to United Artists the next morning as it was supposed to? Assuming it did, would Dick Dorso think the reediting made that much difference? Would he keep his word and show the film to C.B.S. no matter what he thought of it?

Would the C.B.S. execs like the show better now? Would they like it well enough to retest it with an audience over the weekend?

Would that audience like this new version? Would they like it well enough to turn those dials, raise those numbers, and move the lines on those graphs up there into the seventies?

Each of those questions had to be answered with a very emphatic "yes" to get *Gilligan's Island* on the air.

Mildred and I knew all the questions. We also knew what all the answers had to be. So we didn't ask. We didn't answer. We just drove.

The next morning I received a call from Dick Dorso in New York. He phoned to say he had received the film, screened it, and understood why Perry had been so excited about this new version of the pilot. Dick was extremely complimentary about what I had accomplished with the film and admitted my changes had "indeed made it seem like a new pilot."

In spite of our many differences about many things connected with *Gilligan's Island* over those past months, I must give credit where credit is due: That couldn't have been an easy phone call for Dick to make, after all our disagreements.

He assured me he would make certain to screen it for Jim Aubrey and other C.B.S. executives that day. If they liked it half as much as he did now, they would surely test it on the weekend.

In writing this book, I had a recent meeting with Perry Leff and found out an additional sidelight. Perry thought Dorso might not want to risk his relationship with Aubrey by asking him to view yet another version of the same pilot. So he set up an alternative plan if Dorso failed to keep his promise.

Perry phoned Mike Dann, second in command to Jim Aubrey in New York, with whom he had a very close relationship at that time. Between them they arranged an audience testing of the latest version of *Gilligan's Island* at the Preview House in Hollywood that weekend even if Dick Dorso didn't follow through.

I didn't know anything about that at the time. I was pinning everything on Dick Dorso's promise.

I wasn't disappointed. And neither was Dick Dorso.

16

A Meeting at Mount Olympus

"Congratulations. I still hate your fucking show, but the audience seems to love it, so we're putting it on," said James T. Aubrey, President of C.B.S. Television.

That was the gracious phone call from New York that told me *Gilligan's Island* was going into series.

I thanked Jim for his congratulations. I meant it. The conditions of acceptance were not important to me. The news was.

"Just remember this," added Jim, "you're not going to keep those people on that same damn island."

It's funny how there's always bad news along with good news.

I thought my battles with Jim over my concept of the show would end with his admission that the audience loved it, and that C.B.S. was buying the series. Evidently that was not the case. Our disagreement over this basic approach to the series still existed.

There was no point turning this congratulatory call into an open argument. Not while the C.B.S. schedule was still subject to change.

"Suppose I make this pilot with the Castaways on the island a two-parter," I said. "After all, I have a number of very good ideas and storylines to draw from."

"I guess that would be okay," replied Jim.

"And suppose that second part turns out well, what would be wrong with making it a three-parter?" I asked.

"All right," Jim grudgingly consented, "a three-parter."

"And suppose the third part—"

That was as far as I got.

"Listen, you son-of-a-bitch, you're not keeping those Castaways on the island."

Actually, Jim's "son-of-a-bitch" was said without anger or rancor; almost with a touch of amusement at my persistence.

"I'll make you a promise, Jim," I said. "The moment the audience begins to lose interest in the Castaways and their adventures on the island, I'll fix their boat, get them off, and do the series your way."

Jim hesitated.

106

"I'm very ratings-conscious, Jim," I reminded him. "I love shows I'm producing and writing to be up there in the top of the Nielsens. I like to feel my work is pleasing an enormous number of people. That's why I work. Not for fame or for money. Not that I object to those things either. But those are not my motivations."

Jim knew these things were true from my previous dealings with his network. After another pause, he said, "Okay. Do a multi-part series of episodes on the island"—this was before the phrase "mini-series"—"but that does not mean indefinitely. As soon as there's any slippage in the ratings, you promise to get them off the island."

"You've got a deal, Jim. You have my word on it."

On that note, our conversation ended.

I had sold the first pilot film I ever made. I must confess it was a triumphant moment in my life. Not only because the pilot had sold, but the way in which I had sold it.

Several tentative C.B.S. schedules had been printed in *The Hollywood Reporter* and *Variety* the previous week. *Gilligan's Island* had never appeared on any schedule. *Gilligan's Island* was never even mentioned in the trades as a possibility. That was the week during which my final frantic activity had finished the revised pilot film.

Perry's alert handling of the situation had resulted in the incredibly delicate weekend time table, starting with the T.W.A. Thursday night flight to get the film to New York in the proverbial nick of time. A messenger had picked up the newly edited and dubbed print of *Gilligan's Island* at Idlewild in New York (now called John F. Kennedy Airport) on Friday morning, and delivered it to United Artists. Dick Dorso viewed it, and true to his word, arranged a screening for the Eastern C.B.S. executives, including Jim Aubrey. Jim, apparently impressed by the reedited film whether he liked *Gilligan's Island* or not, agreed to retest the pilot on Saturday with the C.B.S. audience testing facility in New York.

The results of that Saturday testing were so extraordinary that the C.B.S. research department insisted on testing it again on Sunday. The Sunday test was just as extraordinary.

I've examined the results of both tests. In placing one graph over the other—the reactions of two different audiences on two different days—it was remarkable how the curves matched exactly. The highest points of audience interest on one graph were identical to the highest points on the other.

The fishing sequence, the scenes I had tripled in length by means of optical reprints, was the high point of the show. In fact, it sustained that high audience level through the whole sequence. It may have been the decisive factor in raising the average numerical evaluation so much that C.B.S. simply couldn't ignore *Gilligan's Island*.

Acceptance of *Gilligan's Island* by Jim Aubrey indicated Jim's perception of the nature of his position as programming chief at C.B.S. In 1962, when

C.B.S. had fourteen of the top fifteen shows, I'm sure Jim didn't love every single one of them. Obviously, they were programmed to achieve the greatest success possible for the C.B.S. network. That enabled C.B.S. to charge higher rates to the sponsors for network time than N.B.C. or A.B.C. It was clear Jim Aubrey believed such achievements to be his job, and he was doing that job better than anyone else ever had.

In fact, Jim's programming success was so phenomenal that N.B.C. and A.B.C., in those years, waited for the C.B.S. schedule to come out before they formulated their own. They would then program shows on various days at various hours to compete with shows already announced by C.B.S.

It was an incredible time in television history. Jim Aubrey, the programming chief on one network, was, in effect, directly responsible for the programming on all three networks.

*

The trouble with victory in television is that there's no time to celebrate. As soon as I learned that *Gilligan's Island* was to be a series, I had to prepare for immediate production.

The most likely facility for the show was the C.B.S. film lot in the valley, C.B.S. Studio Center. *Gunsmoke* and several other C.B.S. shows were filmed there. There was a backlot where a lagoon could be built, and it was close to Stage 2, one of the larger stages. *Gilligan's Island* would need a big stage to house a complex of huts where the Castaways would live. There also had to be plenty of space for tropical foliage: palm trees, South Sea island flowers, ferns, vines, etc.

We would need a surrounding "cyc," a backdrop of blue sky that would make this indoor set look like an outdoor tropical island. The foliage and palms would blend into the "cyc." The stage also had to provide an area for a dining, cooking, and congregating space in the foreground for the Castaways.

I was still basically a writer at that point in my career. But I had a greater knowledge of producing than most writers. That's because I had been a head writer for many years, and I had worked closely with producers. Also, I had been fortunate enough to work with Pinky Wolfson, Cecil Barker, and Jack Chertok. They were producers who welcomed me in casting sessions, editing rooms, scoring sessions, and dubbing sessions, so I was thoroughly familiar with many aspects of producing with which "pure" writers are seldom involved.

However, I needed production people to help the images in my head become a reality. I would have to put together a production designer, art director, and set decorator. But first things first. I needed a production team. A co-producer and/or a line producer and/or associate producer.

As I thought about likely candidates for these important positions, I received a phone call from Hunt Stromberg.

"You know John Rich, don't you?" asked Hunt.

"Sure. John and I go way back."

Sometimes Hunt's phone calls were wonderful. Other times his calls made me sorry Alexander Graham Bell had ever been born. Or even Don Ameche. But this call about John Rich was welcome indeed.

"How would you like John to be your co-producer on *Gilligan's Island?*" Hunt asked me.

Without hesitation, I replied "Great! If he's available. I wanted him to do the pilot."

"I think you two would make a great team," said Hunt.

"So do I," I agreed. In addition to being an excellent director, particularly in comedy, John had a great deal of experience in physical production, and in post-production as well.

"We can make that co-producer deal with John," said Hunt, "if we give him the first eight episodes to direct and work with the directors on all the rest. You can write as many scripts as you want, and be the script editor on the others."

I recognized that deal. It was the one John Rich had made with United Artists the year before, in case the pilot sold and *Gilligan's Island* became a series. If Hunt, for some reason, wanted to take credit for that arrangement, it was okay with me.

I could see the attractive nature of this combination from C.B.S.'s point of view. John Rich was the winner of the 1962 Emmy Award for comedy directing, and I was the winner of 1961 Emmy Award for comedy writing and was nominated again in 1962. That would be good for network sales promotion.

John Rich was a bargain in another way. Hal Cooper, a close friend and associate of John's, was anxious to become involved in a film series. He had been a director for years in live television; a fine director, in fact. But making the transition from live to film was a difficult one for directors. With the promise of some directing assignments in the offing, Hal Cooper agreed to join the staff of *Gilligan's Island* as the associate producer.

Guiding the S.S *Minnow* through the straits of United Artists, and the Bermuda Triangle of C.B.S., and finally to series, was all behind me now. I had a talented old friend as my co-producer and director, and a talented new friend as my associate producer. We could go about the business of pre-production in April, May and June. With any sort of luck, even bad, I felt we'd have five or six final scripts ready for filming in early July. That would give us a choice of two or three episodes to follow the pilot film in mid–September. The *Minnow* was in calm waters.

Yes sir, it was "smooth sailing from now on," I said to John Rich and Hal Cooper. It was a phrase we would repeat to each other sardonically time and again in the weeks ahead.

But on that optimistic note, John, Hal, and I started preliminary work at

Fox. This was mostly for casting purposes, to replace Ginger, the Professor, and Mary Ann.

After about a month or so in the same little off-off-white cottages where I had done pre-production and post-production on the pilot, our *Gilligan's Island* production unit moved to C.B.S. Studio Center for the series. C.B.S., presumably, could keep us under closer surveillance at their own facility.

C.B.S. Studio Center, now called C.B.S./MTM Studios, had formerly been Mack Sennett Studios, Mascot Studios, Republic Studios, and Four Star Studios. It was a relatively small studio complex compared to Universal, M.G.M., or Twentieth Century–Fox. There were only eight or nine stages, and the executive and production offices were contained in one or two story Spanish-style buildings. There were no high-rise office structures at C.B.S. Studio Center in those years.

The combination of low Spanish architecture and the limited area and few stages gave an intimate, informal feeling to Studio Center. It had a friendly feeling I have never experienced in any other studio.

Now there's an eight-story administration building, and stages have been added. There's a harried activity today not present in 1964. The "Mom and Pop" atmosphere has given way, as it has in most things, to progress.

*

In April, 1964, John, Hal, and I started work on the first year of *Gilligan's Island*.

There's an excitement about the beginning of the first year of a series that's like no other excitement I know. It's all new. There's no "last year" experience to look back to for guidance and no "next year" to look forward to, because you have to prove yourself in the market place in order to get there. The first year is now-or-never time—that's what makes it a great adventure.

Our first order of business was pre-production. Many people think of producing a film as though it begins with a cast in front of a camera, emoting, while the director watches every move, ready to call "action" or "cut." Actually, before a single camera turns on the stage, a weekly series should have five or six scripts ready for filming; directors for those scripts should be assigned; and major casting should also be complete. The better organized pre-production is, the smoother production becomes; with correspondingly fewer sixteen-hour shooting days and less damage to the budget.

What's true for scripts is equally true for the physical aspects of pre-production. Blueprints for construction have to be okayed, sets have to be built, crews have to be assembled. The better prepared the physical aspects, the simpler life becomes for everyone involved. But sometimes even simple instructions can be very hard to follow.

"Does that look bad enough, Mr. Schwartz?"

"No, no. Make it look worse, Bill."

"It really looks terrible."

"Believe me, Bill, it's still too good."

"Look at it from this angle. It's terrible."

"I'm sorry. You'll have to do it over."

"I can't make it look worse, Mr. Schwartz. People will laugh."

"Fine. This is a comedy show."

"Please. Let them laugh at the jokes. Not at my work."

"Nobody's going to laugh at your work, Bill. These Castaways were wrecked on a deserted island. None of them are carpenters. They don't have equipment. They don't know how to build anything. They can't make a hut that looks as good as that."

"But it looks awful. Those bamboo supports are more than two inches off line."

"The first time you built this hut they were one half inch off line and you thought it looked terrible. That's because you and your men are great carpenters."

"What do you want?" he asked, reluctantly.

"I don't know. Maybe I want it six inches off line. Maybe nine inches. I want it to look like seven people who don't know what they're doing have built this hut out of stuff they find on the island, bamboo poles and palm fronds. They have one hammer, one saw and a bunch of vines to hold it together. Make it look so terrible that tonight you won't be able to sleep."

"Okay. But that's not going to be easy."

"Nothing's easy, Bill."

Grumbling, Bill moved away to talk to his carpenters.

The trouble with real experts in any field is that they think people notice the slightest deviation from perfection. Studio technicians on Hollywood sound stages are the greatest in the world. The cameramen, soundmen, carpenters, painters, electricians, propmen, special effects men, all are master craftsmen. They do their work with incredible skill.

When you ask them to do things poorly, however, there's a problem. Their idea of "poorly" is the average person's idea of wonderful. The hut in question was the prototype for several that were to form the basis of the little *Gilligan's Island* community. It was important that these huts, and everything else on the island, look like the Castaways had done it themselves.

As Bill left me to talk to his carpenters about rebuilding the *Gilligan's Island* huts, I turned my attention to the "cyc"—the backdrop—and the foliage in the foreground. In order to make the indoor *Gilligan's Island* stage look like the outdoors, the background painting, with sky and hills and palm trees, had to blend in with the "real" jungle growth on the stage. This also called for some delicate foliage on the stage. Hidden wind machines would make the setting look "live" by making the palm fronds and vines sway.

As I looked around the stage that was about to become my home for the

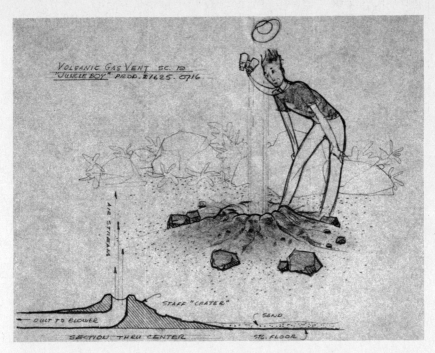

Throughout the entire run of Gilligan's Island, *the art and production crews proved ingenious in creating props and effects needed for the various episodes. Above is a production sketch showing how the "volcanic gas vent" for the "Jungle Boy" episode was accomplished. At left is a sketch for the raft used in "Castaway Pictures Presents."*

next three and a half years, I was called to the phone. Edna Ewing, my secretary, was phoning from my office in the Producers Building. Edna was British and still retained most of her delightful accent. She was a lovely lady, and in many ways, she was the prototypical proper Englishwoman: always a bit of dignity and never a bit of fluster. This time, however, there was more than a bit of fluster. About a ton, I would say.

"Mr. Schwartz," she started. Edna never called me Sherwood, even in an industry where everybody calls everybody by first names, whether they've ever met before or not. In twenty minutes, Pope John would be "Johnny" in the Polo Lounge at the Beverly Hills Hotel. Or maybe "Jack."

"Mr. Schwartz, you've had an urgent phone call from Television City. There's a crisis meeting." My British secretary was royally upset.

"Calm down, Edna," I replied. "Who phoned, and when do I have to be there?"

It was Mr. Stromberg's secretary," she answered. "She said it was a crisis and for you to be there as soon as possible. Shall I ring them back for particulars?"

"Don't bother. You won't get any particulars, because they don't want me to have any particulars," I said. "I won't even stop by the office. I'll go directly there."

"Will you be gone long?"

"Maybe forever."

I was only half joking. Television is a volatile industry, and Hunt Stromberg was a very volatile executive. He was a mixed blessing to me. It was Hunt's support that helped me sell *Gilligan's Island* in the first place. On the other hand, it was Hunt's mercurial nature that introduced me to the joys of migraine headaches.

Hunt was one of those executives — and I've met others — who believe you can only get the best from people in the crucible of chaos. If things are going smoothly, there must be something wrong. Consequently, like the three witches in *Macbeth*, Hunt was always stirring the boiling cauldron for a little more toil and little more trouble.

I hopped into my car and drove to Television City. I knew it was useless for Edna to phone and ask about "particulars" of the meeting. Nobody would tell her. After years of experience, I finally learned this was a deliberate technique on the part of network executives, at least those at C.B.S. They told a producer to come to a "crisis" meeting, but they never told him the nature of the crisis. He never knew whether it involved the script, the cast, the budget, or any one of a dozen things that could precipitate a crisis. This was calculated to panic the producer, make him vulnerable and defensive when he arrived for the meeting. His mind was supposed to resemble Stephen Leacock's man who jumped on his horse and "rode madly off in all directions."

But I was familiar with their game. There was no need to panic, I said to myself, as my mind rode madly off in all directions. Was it the script? Was it the cast? Was it the budget? I would know soon enough.

I parked my car at Television City, under the watchful, unblinking C.B.S. eye painted on the side, entered the building, and went up to the third floor to Hunt Stromberg's office. When I opened the door, I could see at once it was a major crisis.

Hunt was seated behind his desk, the window behind him. In couches and arm chairs around the room in a horseshoe were seated six top C.B.S. programming executives. It was a formidable-looking group. They were quiet and unsmiling. A few of them were friends of mine. One was a close friend. He wasn't smiling either.

Hunt indicated a chair that was awaiting me at the open end of the horseshoe. Clearly, Hunt was the judge, and the other men the jury. It was not unlike the Star Chamber proceedings of the fifteenth century. Only a little crueler.

It was definitely not a situation that called for me to say, "Hello, fellas. What's new?" A simple "Hi" was sufficient. So I said it.

"Hi."

Mr. Stromberg got right to the point.

"Sherwood, all of us here at C.B.S.," he started, indicating the others in the room, "have spent a good deal of time the past few weeks thinking about your series."

I had spent all of the last eighteen months thinking about my series. But I kept that thought to myself as Hunt continued.

"And we feel there's a real crisis."

Here it comes.

"Characterizations. It's the way you've painted your characters. We've all seen the pilot film several times, and we'd like you to hear our comments."

From the atmosphere in the room, I was looking forward to their comments like a turkey looks forward to Thanksgiving. But as long as I had to say something, I figured I might as well say something nice.

"I know you all have the best interests of my show at heart," I said, "so I'd certainly like to hear your comments."

Hunt was apparently pleased with my response. "Let's start with you," Hunt indicated the man sitting to his left, "and let's just go around the room."

The executives started ticking, clockwise.

I no longer recall which executives made which comments in which order, but I remember what was said, very distinctly. So I will simply number the executives from 1 to 6. I remember Executive #6 specifically, because he was my good friend Sol Saks.

Sol and I had very similar backgrounds professionally, both having written comedy for many years. Our wives, Mildred and Ann, were also good friends and we saw each other socially quite frequently. Sol and I were both medium height and weight. We both wore glasses, and both had brown hair. Many people thought we looked very much alike, which each of us regarded, understandably, as an insult.

There was one executive in the meeting I had never met before, or if I had, we had had very little contact. His name was Bill Froug, and he had been a writer and producer of dramatic programs before becoming a C.B.S. executive. I didn't know at the time, but Bill Froug was to become a very important part of my life in the months ahead.

Bill was one of these people who always seem to have a tan, even during the rainy season. For other people there was rain, but for Bill, somehow there was always sunshine. He was several inches taller than Sol and me, and he had a glib sort of smile that I would learn to trust less and less as time went by.

I didn't know any of the other executives in the meeting very well, except, of course, for Hunt himself.

I listened attentively as the inquisition began.

First Program Executive: "Sherwood, we all know *Gilligan's Island* is a broad comedy, so I understand the characters have to be broad. But Thurston Howell III is simply too much. There isn't anybody who's as rich as that, except maybe J. Paul Getty and Howard Hughes. And how many people in our audience know J. Paul Getty or Howard Hughes? Nobody can identify with a billionaire. It's okay to make Thurston Howell rich. Let's say he owns a few companies. Or maybe a big office building. Something like that. But jokes like having seven seats on the New York Stock Exchange, one for each day of the week, are simply ridiculous rather than funny."

I thought that joke about seven seats on the stock exchange was pretty good. Maybe I could use it some other time.

Then Program Executive #2 spoke up. "That's an interesting point about Thurston Howell III lacking viewer identification, but the character who troubles me more, as far as identification is concerned, is Ginger. Obviously, Ginger is gorgeous. We can all see that when we look at her. But why does she have to be a movie star? There are plenty of beautiful housewives in this country. Ginger could just as easily be a beautiful housewife. What terrific viewer identification! What empathy! You're looking for empathy, aren't you?"

Actually, I could have used a little of it myself, right there in that room.

Since Program Executive #2 asked his last question directly of me, I responded. "Of course I'm looking for empathy on the part of the viewer. But I don't think you have to be a cop to identify with the problems of a policeman. I don't think you have to be an M.D. to identify with a doctor. And I don't think you have to be a movie star to understand one, either."

Nobody bothered to respond to my comment. Evidently, producers, like children, are meant to be seen, not heard.

Program Executive #3: "Those observations about Thurston Howell III and Ginger are both fundamental."

All program executives agree with one another in the presence of a producer. That's an unwritten network law. I wouldn't even be surprised if it's a *written* network law.

Program Executive #3 (Bill Froug, I believe) continued: "But the character who really bothers me is the Professor. There's nothing duller than a teacher. It's too intellectual an occupation. And dull. Just plain dull. We simply have to make him more colorful."

Well, so far I had two characters that were too colorful, and one that wasn't colorful enough.

Program Executive #3 went on: "However, I'm not here just to criticize. I've got a marvelous idea for the Professor. Something that will make him more exciting, more colorful."

Program Executive #3 had dropped the first shoe. I waited for the second one to fall. It fell.

Program Executive #3: "The Professor is really a bank robber. He just pretends to be a professor!" Number 3's voice was exultant as he handed me his brilliant idea on a silver platter.

I found it hard to comprehend this suggestion. "You mean, this ignorant

Jim Backus, Natalie Schafer, Tina Louise, Alan Hale, Dawn Wells, Russell Johnson, and Bob Denver—the cast that almost got away. If the Program Executives had had their way, I'd have lost seven out of seven of the characters I'd conceived. The Howells were "unbelievable"; Ginger was too glamorous; Mary Ann was old-hat; the Professor was boring; and the Skipper's relationship with Gilligan was "all wrong." But viewer testing proved that every one of the characters was all right.

criminal merely *pretends* to be intellectual and scientific and knowledgeable?" I asked, trying to imagine John Dillinger as the Chancellor of M.I.T.

Program Executive #3: "Exactly!"

How does one pretend to be intellectual and scientific and knowledgeable if one is ignorant, I wondered.

Program Executive #3: "And being a bank robber, and on the lam, he doesn't *want* to be rescued. So when they're about to be rescued, he screws things up so that they're stuck on the island."

Program Executive #3 stopped now, presumably to accept some sort of award for his contribution. He didn't get one from me, but he got one from Program Executive #4.

Program Executive #4: "What an interesting idea! and really different! That would certainly prevent the Professor from being dull."

It would also change the whole concept and focus of the show, I wanted to say.

But before I even had a chance to open my mouth, Program Executive #4 contributed another length of rope to the lynching party.

Program Executive #4: "If you ask me, the dullest character is Mary Ann. The sweet-little-girl-next-door has been done to death. She's in every TV show. She's in every movie, and I'm sick to death of her. I'm sure the viewers are, too. I can't say that I've been helpful in coming up with an idea to improve her, like he"—indicating Program Executive #3—"did with the Professor. I don't know what to do with Mary Ann, but I know something has to be done, if you want the viewers to like her."

Four down, and three to go, I said to myself. This shouldn't take much longer. It didn't.

Program Executive #5: "There's no point discussing Mrs. Howell. She's just as unbelievable as her husband. The viewer can't identify with either one of them."

Did the executives in that room know they were talking about the same characters the audience had loved in the pilot film? The very characters who were responsible for turning the pilot into a series?

Had these men seen the audience testing? The graphs of sample audience reaction to the show and to these characters?

I knew the test results very well. *Both* sets of results. Those tests were etched forever in my memory. They were extraordinary. That's why I had gotten that congratulatory phone call from Jim Aubrey. Now these executives sitting in Hunt Stromberg's office were advising me to change the characters who sold the series.

And Alice in Wonderland thought *she* went to a crazy tea party.

The hands of Hunt Stromberg's clock now pointed to Program Executive #6, Sol Saks. Sol was the only person in that room, besides myself, who had ever written or produced comedy. He had created the enormously successful *Bewitched* and had written the pilot film for that series. He had many other outstanding comedy credits. For some reason, Sol had decided to become a program executive at C.B.S. at that time. He was their resident specialist in doctoring sick comedy series. It was now up to Dr. Saks to make a diagnosis. He was clearly on the spot.

Program Executive #6 Sol Saks cleared his throat. "*Gilligan's Island* is not exactly my cup of tea . . . " he began.

I knew Sol's predicament. He couldn't afford to disagree with all his fellow C.B.S. program executives. I also knew Sol's experience in comedy made him realize how ludicrous these other suggestions were. I would have felt sorry for Sol if I hadn't been so busy feeling sorry for myself.

Program Executive #6 Sol Saks continued: "I don't deal with those kinds of characters in my own shows, and I simply don't understand them. So I'm afraid there isn't much I can say." Apparently, Sol had opted to follow the advice made famous by Sam Goldwyn: "Include me out."

At this point, the prosecution rested.

I felt like a defendant who had just faced six district attorneys. Judge Hunt Stromberg, Jr., seemed to be wearing a black robe. The pen stand on his desk looked like a gavel.

"Sherwood," said Hunt, "you've heard all these opinions. What have you got to say?"

"Hunt," I replied, "when I came into this room I had seven Castaways on a deserted island. Apparently I'm left with just two. Gilligan and the Skipper."

"About that relationship" said Hunt, "it's all wrong. You can't have that great big Skipper browbeating Gilligan and bullying him around. Everybody's going to hate the Skipper. He's got to be nice to Gilligan!"

It was a clean sweep! I was left with no characters on an uncharted, deserted island. It seemed like a nice place for me to visit right then.

I sat there speechless, overwhelmed. Until that moment, I had never fully appreciated *The Trial* by Franz Kafka.

Finally, his honor, Hunt, said in his best judicial manner, "We've given you the benefit of our thoughts, based on a great deal of deliberation. What do you plan to do about it?"

With no conscious plan in mind, I replied, "You say you've been considering these things for weeks. I think it's only fair for me to spend some time thinking over your suggestions before I make any comments."

"That does seem fair," agreed the Judge. Everyone else immediately seemed to think it was fair, too. So the meeting broke up, and I left C.B.S. to return to Stage 2 at Studio Center and continue work on the set: the blueprints, construction, props, decorations, etc.

I didn't realize it then, but if the good Lord had given me 20 years to think of an answer to Hunt's question, I couldn't have come up with a better response.

Any attempt I might have made in his office, in that atmosphere, to defend my characters, would have forced me to make concessions. One character, probably more, would have been sacrificed in that room. I don't know whether I would have lost Mr. Howell, or Ginger, or the Professor, or Mary Ann, or Mrs. Howell, or the marvelous relationship between the Skipper and Gilligan; but a general can't fight a war without casualties. If I had undertaken battle that day, some members of that small army of Castaways would have fallen in the crossfire. It's possible I myself would not have survived. Networks much prefer compliance to defiance.

That meeting took place in 1964. I sincerely believe that meeting today would take place without me in the room. And it would result in my removal from the show due to "creative differences."

As it was, I promised Hunt I'd think it over. And I did think it over. And I'm still thinking it over.

Sometime later, an intellectual friend of mine, an architect named Neil Deasy who reads Latin for pleasure, accused me of stealing the tactics of Quintus Fabius Maximus, a Roman ruler in 200 B.C. who originated the "Fabian Policy," also known as "delaying tactics." Quintus Fabius, Neil said, devised the strategy of never meeting the enemy in battle. Instead, he kept them involved in little skirmishes so they knew his forces were ready. As a result, he was able to reign longer than any other Roman ruler at that time. He was also known as Fabius Cunctator, "Fabian the Delayer."

I told my intellectual friend I had never heard of that particular Roman ruler, and that my reading of Latin was limited to a few pharmaceutical prescriptions. But I don't think Neil believes me.

He still calls me Fabius.

Another Meeting at Mount Olympus

"Sidney?"

"Hi."

Sidney was Sidney Marshall, a friend of mine who was a well-known dramatic writer in television. We were friends, but not close friends, although I had known him for many years.

"This is Sherwood." Then I added, "Sherwood Schwartz." I didn't know how many Sherwoods Sidney knew.

"Oh, hi, Sherwood. I haven't talked to you in some time. How's it going?"

"I'm in the first year of a new series."

"That bad, huh?"

Contrary to popular belief, dramatic writers often say amusing things. Often more amusing than comedy writers.

"That bad," I answered. "Are you working on a series now? I mean, on a regular basis?"

"No. Freelance stuff. Just turned in a script yesterday. Why?"

"Well, if you're available, I'll have C.B.S. contact you about my show."

Sidney was puzzled. He knew I wasn't doing *Route 66* or *Ben Casey* or *The Twilight Zone*.

"You're doing *Gilligan's Island*, aren't you?" he asked.

"Right. *Gilligan's Island*. How'd you like to be the script editor?"

Sidney laughed. "Come on, what are you calling about?"

"I told you. Script editor on *Gilligan's Island*."

"Where are you calling from, Camarillo?" Sidney was referring to a mental institution located in the nearby town of Camarillo. I told you: dramatic writers are often amusing.

"C.B.S. wants a dramatic script editor on *Gilligan's Island*. Hunt Stromberg insists on it."

"What for? It's a situation comedy."

"I've been all through that. They tell me I know all about comedy, but I don't know anything about drama."

It's amazing how "they" always know who can write what. "They" know which writers can write comedy and which writers can write drama. By some omniscient power, "they" even know who writes soft comedy, hard comedy, one-liners, variety comedy, video tape comedy, or film comedy.

It would shock some network executives if they found out that the same William Shakespeare who wrote *Hamlet* also wrote *Much Ado About Nothing.* "They" never would have permitted that sort of crossover.

In spite of the fact that Sidney Marshall had spent many years with network executives who have this sort of tunnel vision, he still couldn't believe my phone call.

"The drama is inherent in the series," he said. "It's life and death for those Castaways. How much more dramatic can you get?"

"I've been all through that with Hunt Stromberg. I don't have time to argue with the network any longer. I have to start turning out episodes for the series."

"Exactly what am I supposed to do as script editor on *Gilligan's Island?*" Sid wanted to know.

"You mean, in addition to picking up a check every week?" I asked.

"Yeah."

"Very little. Read the scripts, make a few changes, but don't hurt the comedy."

"Is this conversation for real?"

"It's not a joke, if that's what you mean," I assured him. "It's a real offer. A dramatic offer."

Then Sid asked, "Why me? You know lots of other writers who write drama."

"Yes, but most of them have had a little comedy creep into their work. You're clean, man. I don't remember a chuckle in anything you've ever written."

"And that's how I'm getting the job as script editor on *Gilligan's Island?* Nobody's ever going to believe this."

"Then don't tell anybody."

For the next four weeks, Sidney Marshall sat in an office in the *Gilligan's Island* production wing, as script editor. He read drafts of the scripts as they were being written and rewritten. Surprisingly enough, he made few suggestions for adding to the drama, but he did add some jokes here and there. Then he left—a little richer, a little bored, and a little more bewildered than ever by network thinking.

Perhaps C.B.S. felt Sidney Marshall was responsible for the drama in the stories during that period. If so, they had never read my own outlines in my initial presentation. The dramatic aspects of *Gilligan's Island,* originally written on that white butcher paper, were the basis for virtually all the first year's episodes, and many of the following years' episodes as well.

For the time being, however, the presence of Sidney Marshall appeased C.B.S., and pre-production continued.

The lagoon was nearing completion. It had proved to be more difficult than we originally thought. One end had to make a sharp turn to indicate it was going out of view to the ocean. In addition, a great deal of special rigging—hooks, angle irons, handles—had to be sunk into the bottom of the lagoon, anticipating sight gags and physical stunts that hadn't even been written yet.

One day, as John Rich, Hal Cooper, and I were trying to work these problems out with the production people, art director, and special effects experts, another phone call came in for me from Hunt Stromberg.

"I've got a wonderful idea, Sherwood. Can you get over here right away?"

"Sure, Hunt."

It was one of the few times I was alerted to the type of news to expect. Good news from Hunt Stromberg. Or was it? One never knew what a "wonderful idea" could lead to.

At C.B.S. Television City, I learned I was going to watch the pilot film of *Gilligan's Island* with Robert Lewine, West Coast Vice President C.B.S. Television Network, and Hunt. They were the two most important C.B.S. executives on the West Coast.

These two men and I took our seats in the center row of the executive screening room. The only other person in the room was Larry Heath, the film editor. He was sitting by himself in the back row in case the film should break or some other mechanical problem should arise.

Hunt was bubbling over with excitement. "It's an absolutely wonderful notion," he was saying.

I tried to keep in mind that network "wonderful ideas" and "wonderful notions" can sometimes cause producers wonderful ulcers.

"I assume this has something to do with *Gilligan's Island*," I said—a minor jocular remark as I awaited the idea. Hunt was so excited, it passed unnoticed. Maybe deservedly so.

"It's absolutely marvelous!" said Hunt. "Right, Bob?"

Bob said, "Right."

I glanced at Bob Lewine, who seemed cheerful enough, but hardly imbued with the sort of ecstatic enthusiasm of his colleague.

Hunt was on the edge of his seat, almost quivering with anticipation before he revealed his brainstorm. "We're going to look at the pilot. Together. I want you to get the feel of this thing."

I had seen the pilot of *Gilligan's Island* at the cutting, recutting, editing, reediting, conservatively a hundred million times. However, if Hunt wanted me to see it again, with him and with Bob, he must have a reason.

"Fine," was all I could muster.

Hunt pressed the start button on the console and the three of us in that row together, and Larry Heath in the back row, started to watch the pilot film of *Gilligan's Island*. We watched for about ten minutes or so, to the point at which Gilligan goes hunting through the island jungle to see if there are other inhabitants.

Suddenly Hunt pressed the stop button. The film ceased and the lights came on in the viewing room.

"That's what I wanted you to see! Where Gilligan goes to the other side of the island."

Obviously, this was where Hunt's idea came in.

"Do you know what he finds on the other side of the island?" asked Hunt.

I knew what Gilligan found on the other side of the island. He climbed up a tree and he saw a boat which he thought might be able to rescue them. In his haste and ignorance, it turned out to be the very wrecked boat that had beached them on the island. But that wasn't the answer Hunt wanted.

"What does he find on the other side of the island?" I inquired, fearing the worst. I got it.

"A dinosaur!" exclaimed Hunt proudly.

He waited for me to share his enthusiasm. I'm afraid I disappointed him because I answered with some trepidation.

"You mean, a live dinosaur?"

"Of course!" Hunt was annoyed with me. "Gilligan is leading him on a leash. Naturally he's alive!"

"A leash?"

"Just picture it! Gilligan and his pet dinosaur! It's our answer to *Mr. Ed.*"

I hadn't even known Mr. Ed needed an answer. But all of a sudden a horrible thought occurred to me.

"You mean a talking dinosaur?"

"Don't be ridiculous! Whoever heard of a talking dinosaur!"

Hunt was offended by my question. But why a talking dinosaur is any more ridiculous than a living, breathing, walking dinosaur on a leash, is beyond me.

I was tempted to say, "Casting is going to be murder," but Hunt was far too serious about his idea to treat it with any levity.

"It's certainly very different," I admitted, "but it presents some real production problems."

"What do you mean?" Hunt asked, protectively.

"I mean, how do you keep a dinosaur and Gilligan in the same shot? Dinosaurs are enormous. If you want to see Gilligan on the television tube, all you'll see is a piece of the dinosaur's rear leg. And if you want to see the dinosaur, Gilligan will look like an ant on television." I wanted to add, "And over the shoulder shots will be murder," but I didn't.

The simple logic of my argument gave Hunt pause.

"What do you think?" he asked Bob.

None of us can remember why the whole cast was on stepladders in the lagoon. Perhaps it was the episode when they thought the island was sinking. For a while, in meeting after meeting at "Mount Olympus," it seemed that the whole series was sinking in a quagmire of executive decisions.

"Sherwood's got a point there," Bob responded. "I think we have to be careful with the size of the dinosaur. Maybe only thirty-five feet or so."

"Thirty-five feet?" Hunt seemed crestfallen at such a small dinosaur.

I sneaked a look back at Larry Heath. His eyes were ping-ponging back and forth between these two executives as they discussed the length of the dinosaur. His eyes had a kind of glazed, bewildered expression. The sort of expression the Egyptians might have had when they saw the Red Sea open.

"How does that sound to you?" Hunt asked me.

I have had very little experience filming dinosaurs. I had no idea whether thirty-five feet was large, small or medium. I only knew I wanted no part of a dinosaur on *Gilligan's Island,* Mr. Ed or no Mr. Ed. Then I remembered something.

"Disney Studios has just perfected a process called 'Dynavision'," I told Hunt and Bob. "It has nothing to do with dinosaurs, but it may help us."

"What's 'Dynavision'?" asked Bob.

"It's a new process Disney has perfected, for superimposing lifelike animated creatures into live action film. That way we can make the dinosaur any size we want and control its actions. We won't even have to build a scale model."

"Great idea," said Hunt.

"I understand it's quite expensive," I warned.

"It may be the solution. Check it out."

After this advice, Hunt rose from his seat, as did Bob Lewine. They exited the viewing room, and I followed.

I stopped for a moment at the back row by Larry Heath, who had observed and overheard everything that had been said in that viewing room. I looked at Larry. His eyes were still moving from side to side in his head as though Hunt and Bob were still talking to each other. I decided not to interrupt Larry's thoughts, whatever they were.

The next day I phoned Hunt Stromberg and reported on my conversation with Disney Studios. Their Dynavision process was a solution, in visual terms, to the dinosaur idea. However, it was *not* a solution in terms of budget. That process was extremely expensive and would add more to the cost of each episode than the cost of the episode itself.

Mr. Stromberg was very disappointed to hear this news. But he was content with the fact that his dinosaur idea, like many other great ideas, was defeated by economics. Hunt never again raised the topic of dinosaurs.

Oddly enough, Larry doesn't think this was the most outlandish idea he heard during those imaginative suggestion days with Hunt Stromberg. Larry's favorite was the "big finish" Hunt wanted filmed to end the pilot episode. This involved landing a plane on "Gilligan's Island." The plane door opens, and thirty midgets stream out. For some reason, Hunt thought this was a very funny big finish to the film.

Aside from the difficulty of finding thirty midgets, there was an additional problem. There was no "Gilligan's Island" for a plane to land on, even if we could afford to rent a plane. "Gilligan's Island" was a stock shot.

From John Rich's point of view, as a director, there was an even more incredible suggestion made by Hunt for a "big finish." In this idea, a helicopter landed on the nonexistent island. But it landed on the part of this nonexistent island that had quicksand. As a result, the helicopter sank slowly into the quicksand, and the blades, as they turned, screwed the helicopter right into the ground.

Even if we had an island, and even if we had quicksand, and even if we had a helicopter, and even if we could somehow rig the special effects to make the rotors on the helicopter turn as the helicopter sank from sight, the cost of that one scene would be equivalent to the cost of five or six entire episodes.

John tells me he still wakes up at night with a nightmare in which a helicopter is screwing itself into the parking lot at Television City.

18

Yet Another Meeting
at Mount Olympus

"It's about time I met John Rich," said Hunt Stromberg on the phone.
I couldn't believe it. Hunt was the man who said John Rich and I would
make such a great team. That was when he phoned me about the deal C.B.S.
was making with John; the deal, actually, they were taking over from United
Artists. I had assumed Hunt knew John well. Such was not the case. Hunt knew
about John only through his reputation.

John, as well as Hal Cooper, had been working with me in pre-production
for many weeks now. During all that time, it never occurred to me that John
and Hunt had never met. At this point three scripts had finally been accepted
as shooting scripts.

It was this fact which apparently prompted Hunt to suggest a meeting
with John to discuss the scripts and prepare a shooting sequence. This was one
of those rare meetings of which I knew the subject in advance.

Alerted now to the fact that John was meeting Hunt Stromberg, Jr., for
the first time, I decided John and I should drive to C.B.S. together. I wanted
to brief John Rich a little about Hunt Stromberg.

First, let me brief you a little about John Rich. As I've indicated before,
John is a very talented director. He not only gets all the comedy values out of
the script, he adds to them. He puts it all up there on the screen.

That's enough to ask of any director, except one who's about to have his
first meeting with Hunt. Especially the John Rich of 1964. At that time, John
had little patience with beating about the bush. If you asked him a direct question, you got a direct answer. Circumlocution was not his strong point.

I knew John very well. I also knew Hunt very well. I would be driving a
lit match to a meeting with a stick of dynamite. A stick of dynamite with a
short fuse.

Hunt Stromberg, Jr., was an executive who took himself and his position
very seriously. You could disagree with Hunt, but never directly. His ideas—
and some of them were pretty wild, as I've already described—had to be considered. They could be discarded, for some "legitimate" reason, but they could
never be arbitrarily dismissed. I had dealt with other executives who demanded

that sort of reverence. It's not easy, but it's part of a producer's job. It's what I call "respect for office." It was a working arrangement.

John hopped in my car, and we drove from Studio Center to C.B.S. Television City in Hollywood to our meeting with Hunt. On the way, tactfully as I could, I presented the problem to John. He was a little surprised. Perhaps a little annoyed, too.

"What the hell! I've been in a lot of meetings with a lot of executives."

"I know, but Hunt is a special case. You're sometimes very direct with people, and you can't be direct with Hunt."

"Don't worry about it."

"You can disagree with Hunt," I persisted in pointing out, "but not directly. Find a way to ease into it."

"Don't worry about it," repeated John.

I still had misgivings. I felt somehow that the irresistible force was about to meet the immovable object.

"I've been very anxious to meet you," said Hunt as he shook hands with John.

"I've been just as anxious to meet you," replied John.

So far, so good, I said to myself.

"Sit down, fellas," said Hunt as he returned to his chair behind the desk. "Let's kick around the first few scripts to decide on a schedule."

"Fine," I said. "As you know, we have three final drafts, and two others are very close now."

"Let's just talk about the three final scripts," said Hunt, indicating scripts on his desk. "Jim and I"—Hunt meant James T. Aubrey—"would like to film this episode first. The one titled 'Goodbye Island'."

"Impossible!" exclaimed John.

Hunt's jaw dropped in surprise. Well, that didn't take long, I said to myself.

"What do you mean 'impossible'?" asked Hunt, in an ominously quiet voice. "It's in final draft. Are you telling me it can't be shot?"

"Of course, it can be shot," said John. "But not first. It's by far the most difficult of those three scripts. It's much better to start a series with a simpler script. So the cast and crew get a chance to work together."

Again, Hunt spoke quietly. "Jim and I both believe this is the best script. We would like it on the air first. And we would like you to shoot it first."

"We can shoot it second, or even third, and still get it on the air first," John pointed out.

Feeling a little like the Dutch boy putting his finger in the dike to stop the flood, I said, "Hunt, why don't John and I kick this scheduling around a little? There may be a way to simplify the shooting on 'Goodbye Island'."

On the surface, Hunt seemed almost amiable as he responded, "Okay." But I knew better. The little Dutch boy had had an easier chance.

Ida Lupino, who directed several episodes, is about to get dunked by the Skipper.

"Wonderful to meet you," said John, as he rose to shake hands with Hunt.

"Good to meet you, too," replied Hunt.

John and I left Hunt's office and returned to the parking lot. I don't think that meeting lasted more than a minute.

As we were getting into my car, John said, "He didn't seem very difficult."

Things are not always what they seem, I said to myself. I was reluctant to tell John what I really thought. We headed back to Studio Center.

After we got back to our offices, John left almost immediately for New York. He had some business there that would take a few days.

The next day I got a call from Bill Michaeljohn, John Rich's agent. "What the hell happened, Sherwood?"

"Why?" I asked Bill, as innocently as I could.

"John's off the show as co-producer. They're paying him off. He's through as of right now. And his directing assignments have been cut in half. He's doing the first four instead of the first eight. What the hell happened at that meeting?"

It would have taken an hour to explain what happened in that one-minute meeting. It wouldn't have helped matters anyway. As I paused to think of a reply, Bill continued.

"Not only that, Hal Cooper is off the show, too! Because John brought him in!"

It was less than twenty-four hours since my meeting at C.B.S. with John and Hunt. It hadn't taken Mount Olympus very long to hand down this new edict.

"Bill," I said, wearily, "I'm really heartsick about this. And I'm too tired to get into it right now. I'll talk to you later." I put down the phone.

John Rich's memory of those tumultuous two days differs somewhat from mine. John remembers the meeting with Hunt I've just described, but he doesn't attach the importance to it that I do.

When John was in New York, his secretary in our *Gilligan's Island* offices called him to tell him that Bill Froug had taken over his office space. John got back to Los Angeles as quickly as he could. As soon as he arrived at Studio Center, he spoke with Bob Norvett, head of C.B.S. physical production. John asked Bob to explain why someone else was in his office, why his name was off the door, and why his parking space had been moved to the far end of the area.

"The order came from C.B.S. Fairfax," answered Bob.

"Including moving my parking space?" asked John.

"Yes," Bob replied.

"Can you tell me who ordered this?"

"Hunt Stromberg," said Bob.

John phoned Hunt Stromberg and asked to see him, and Hunt agreed to a meeting that same day. A few hours later, John Rich was at the home of the gods.

"What's going on?" John demanded of Hunt. As I've indicated before, John is one director who's direct.

Hunt said, "If you don't know, I'll fill you in. We have been examining your contract, and it's outrageous. We have to pay you, and you have an associate producer who reports directly to you. You also have a percentage of the show. We can't live with this contract."

That's how John found out C.B.S. had assumed his contract, along with others, from United Artists when they moved the series production of *Gilligan's Island* to C.B.S. Studio Center.

John told Hunt how the original deal had been negotiated. Herb Jaffe, Vice President of United Artists, arranged it as insurance. Procter and Gamble, one of the sponsors of *Gilligan's Island*, knew John from *The Dick Van Dyke Show,* which they had also sponsored. They thought Sherwood Schwartz might need help on *Gilligan's Island* because he had never produced a series before.

Hunt wasn't interested in the reason for the deal. He told John he wanted him off the lot.

"You have been very rude," said John, "to me, to my secretary, and to Hal Cooper. I intend to live up to my contract. And I expect you to live up to yours. You'll have to pay me the money."

"You'll never work in this town again," said Hunt, furious.

"Just give me the money, and I'll leave," said John.

"What about the ten percent ownership?" asked Hunt.

"That's for removing my parking space," answered John. "Because of the way you've gone about this."

"One more thing," said Hunt. "Will you direct the first four episodes?"

"What happened to 'you'll never work in this town again'?"

"Did I say that?" asked Hunt.

Whether Hunt was infuriated, as I believe, by John's direct confrontation in that one-minute meeting, or whether Hunt was infuriated, as John believes, by John's contract, the result was the same: John was gone. So was Hal Cooper.

Here I was, about to start filming a new series, the first new series of my own, with the first day of shooting just two weeks away. I had just lost my co-producer and my associate producer. My executive liaison with the network, Bill Froug, the man who was supposed to help me produce the show, had a completely different idea of *Gilligan's Island* from mine and was always in my hair.

That is, what was left of it by now.

One More Meeting at
Mount Olympus

"Have a seat," offered Hunt, indicating the couch in his office.

It was another one of those command phone calls: Drop whatever you're doing and report to C.B.S. (That could prove awkward if you happened to be in the men's room at the time.) Apparently, some new crisis had developed.

Driving from Studio Center in the Valley to Television City in Hollywood, I wondered vaguely what this new crisis might concern. There were so many possible crises it was pointless to speculate. So I speculated about the pointlessness of speculation.

"Bill should be here in a minute," Hunt said. Bill was there in less than a minute. Bill Froug, that is. He was full of smiles and looking very pleased with himself as he entered the room. He sat on the same couch with me, but some distance away. Nevertheless, his manner was quite friendly.

"Hi, Sherwood."

"Hi, Bill."

Either voluntarily, or by a C.B.S. appointment Bill had become the C.B.S. executive producer to *Gilligan's Island,* the liaison between the show and the network. The presence of Bill in that assignment, voluntary or not, was a little odd because his past experience both as writer and producer had been in drama.

Apparently, Sol Saks, who should logically have been the C.B.S. liaison executive, still insisted on keeping *Gilligan's Island* at arm's length. Whatever his reasons, Sol seemed to want nothing to do with my show.

However, as I learned recently in trying to track down information for this book and corroborate certain facts, Sol remained active in the background. Bill Froug wasn't acquainted with many comedy writers. Sol knew those writers very well, and arranged meetings with them and Bill. With Bill's guidance those writers were trying to effect C.B.S. changes in the characters of the Castaways on the island.

I was unaware of any of these things at the time of this meeting in Hunt's office. Nevertheless, I had an uneasy feeling. Bill's manner was a little too friendly, considering the differences in opinions about *Gilligan's Island* we were continuing to have. Even by C.B.S. executive standards, Bill's arrogance was extreme. He persisted in trying to run *my* show *his* way.

"This is going to come as quite a surprise to you," started Hunt, as he looked at me. "Maybe even a shock."

I said nothing. I looked over at Bill. He said nothing either, but he still had that self-satisfied smile on his face, like the proverbial cat who swallowed the canary.

"I'm sure you're going to be angry," continued Hunt. "In fact, I know you're going to be angry. Sometimes networks have to do certain things to protect themselves. So I hope you'll understand."

"I don't know what we're talking about," I responded, "but I've been working with networks a long time. With this network in particular, and with you in particular, Hunt. So I'll try to understand."

"We did something without your permission, Sherwood. Without your knowledge." Hunt paused.

It was unusual for Hunt Stromberg, or Jim Aubrey, or Bob Lewine, all top-level C.B.S. executives, to devote much time to preamble. Usually, blows fell. Whatever it was, I was sure by now it was something pretty heavy. I was right.

"We had a script written by some other writers," said Hunt. "With my consent, and under Bill's supervision. The script was to reflect more accurately our thinking about the characters in your show. I'm sure you remember the meeting we had on that subject."

Apparently, the "Fabian Policy" had worked better for Quintus Fabius Maximus than it had for me.

"Bill was in charge of the new script, but he did it with my full knowledge and blessing. I want you to know that. I gave him the authority to proceed."

I looked at Bill again. The cat just sat there with the same smile. I could see canary feathers sticking out of the corners of his mouth.

Many thoughts went through my mind, as I sat there with the handle of the knife protruding from my back. First, I wasn't sure whether the network had the right to authorize a new script without discussing it with the creator/writer of the pilot. Bill Froug himself was a long-time active member of the Writers Guild, and very vocal about his union affiliation. Regardless of his opinion of my work, or his position as an executive of C.B.S., the Guild rules specifically forbid this sort of action—one Guild member undercutting another Guild member.

Forgetting the Guild rules, and what I regarded as the immorality of Bill's actions—and Hunt's, for that matter—I was faced with an alarming situation. All my meetings, all my battles to preserve *Gilligan's Island* as I believed in it, were on the chopping block now. What could I do to prevent the axe from falling?

So far Bill had not said a word. I hadn't said anything either. I wasn't swallowing canaries. I had the unpleasant taste of crow in my mouth. Hunt was the only speaker at that meeting, and he continued speaking.

"Yesterday Bill handed me the new script, the one he had supervised, and I've had an opportunity to read it. I must say, he's changed the characters the way he promised he would, and developed *Gilligan's Island* in accordance with all our thinking. That's why I've called this meeting. I wanted both of you to hear my comments at the same time."

I was reminded of the title of the episode I was preparing that week: "Goodbye, Island." What a cruel coincidence!

Then Hunt said firmly and distinctly, "Bill, why don't you leave Sherwood's fucking show alone?"

It took me a moment to grasp the significance of what Hunt had said. I looked over at Bill. I have never seen an expression like that on a man's face in my entire life. His mouth was open in a mixture of astonishment and complete disbelief—like a runner in the middle of a 100-yard dash who looks down and sees that he has no legs. He was so stunned, he apparently couldn't move or even speak.

It seemed like a good time for me to exit.

"Bye, Hunt. So long, Bill."

As I left the room, I remembered Hunt bidding me goodbye. I don't remember Bill saying anything.

Driving back to Stage 2 at Studio Center where *Gilligan's Island* was filming away, all oblivious to my latest experience on the CBS torture rack, I wondered about the meeting I had just attended. Why was I at that meeting? Why didn't Hunt simply tell Bill he didn't like the new approach? Why did Hunt risk antagonizing me by telling me the whole background? Why had he deliberately humiliated Bill in my presence?

I knew I had seen only the tip of an iceberg in that meeting. Apparently, that was all Bill had seen, too—because that iceberg had obviously slammed right into his boat. He had been even more surprised than I.

It wasn't until 1978, fourteen years later, that I would be given an explanation for that weird meeting. The explanation came from Charles Pomerantz, who handled public relations for Procter and Gamble and Phillip Morris, the two sponsors of *Gilligan's Island* in 1964. Charlie told me the sponsors had gotten wind that creative changes were being contemplated in *Gilligan's Island*. The advertising agencies got in touch with C.B.S. and said the sponsors had bought the show the way it was. If changes were made they would pull out their sponsorship.

In those years, sponsors and ad agencies still had plenty of muscle. Antagonizing two major companies who spent enormous sums of money on TV advertising was something no network was willing to risk. That was the reason, Charlie said, for the sudden reversal in that meeting with Hunt.

David Lawrence recently corroborated Charlie's story. David was with

Procter and Gamble Productions then. It's his recollection that Procter and Gamble bought the show because they liked the pilot film, and they wanted it done the way they bought it. "If you change it, we're going to drop out," they said.

In 1983, I heard a different story. This came to me from Sol Saks, but not directly. Larry Markes, one of the writers approached by Bill Froug to write a C.B.S. approach to the characters on *Gilligan's Island,* was a close friend of Sol's. In fact, it was Sol, according to Larry, who arranged the meeting between Larry and Bill.

Sol told Larry that my meeting with Hunt and Bill was originally planned as a larger staff meeting, the purpose of which was to refocus the characters the way C.B.S. wanted. If I objected, I was to be removed.

But the Nielsen rating on the first episode of *Gilligan's Island* came in on Monday. The meeting was scheduled for Tuesday. The show, based on that first rating, was clearly destined to be a hit. Hurried phone calls to the C.B.S. staff cancelled the full-scale meeting, and resulted in the meeting I described with Hunt Stromberg and Bill Froug.

In the future I will probably hear still other theories or tales. Back in 1964, however, I was unaware of any of these explanations. I simply was happy to leave the meeting with my concept and characters intact.

Strangely enough, Bill Froug remained the C.B.S. executive liaison between *Gilligan's Island* and the network. Since his contribution had been so thoroughly discredited in our meeting with Hunt, why did Hunt keep him on in that capacity? Why? Were "they" simply trying to drive me crazy?

I was reminded, with some justification, of a quote from Euripides, a writer some twenty-four hundred years earlier. "Those whom the gods would destroy, they first make mad," he said.

Euripides. I wonder what network he wrote for?

Always Be Nice
to Your Script Editor

"I'm really happy to be working with you," said Bill Davenport.

"So am I," said Charlie Tannen.

"I'm delighted you guys are here," I answered.

Davenport and Tannen were joining my show to become script editors on *Gilligan's Island*.

With John Rich, Hal Cooper and Sidney Marshall gone, I was saddled with the double responsibility of being the producer and the script editor at the same time. This, coupled with continuing meetings at C.B.S., meant I was working 36 hours a day, ten days a week.

In the first year of a new series, the characters are not really known to writers who are at work on episodes for that series. As a result, a considerable writing burden falls on the script editors and the producer. Even on a series that's been on the air for several years, there's rewriting, but nothing compared to the first year.

Scripts go through four, five, as many as ten rewrites before they're filmed. Even then, it's the pressure of time that finally forces the issue, rather than the fact that the scripts are perfect when the cameras start to turn.

It was natural for me to welcome Bill Davenport and Charlie Tannen with open arms. I had never worked with Bill personally, but he was considered an excellent comedy writer by the many mutual friends we had. I didn't know Charlie Tannen at all, but if he was Bill Davenport's writing partner that was good enough recommendation for me.

It may have even been Bill Froug who suggested Davenport and Tannen as script editors on *Gilligan's Island* because Froug was still my C.B.S. liaison executive. If that were the case, it was something of a surprise, because I might well have chosen Bill Davenport as my script editor myself.

Davenport turned out to be a valuable addition, and took a great deal of the rewriting pressures off me while he was on the show. Unfortunately, I can't say the same for his partner, Charlie Tannen. Tannen had a stiff, bristling moustache and a personality to match. He and I operated on very different wavelengths and we weren't able to communicate. Other writers who were working on scripts found the same thing true of Tannen. He could be very obstinate and had a difficult time contributing in writers' meetings. However, with help from Davenport in the script area, things went better for four or five weeks.

Then one day I found out something I never knew about Davenport. He failed to show up for work on a Monday. I phoned his house.

"Mrs. Davenport?"

"Yes," she answered.

"Bill didn't show up today. I wonder if anything's wrong."

It was with great embarrassment that Mrs. Davenport continued the conversation.

"I guess you don't know about Bill's problem," she said. "It's very hard for me to tell you this, because I know Bill loves working with you on *Gilligan's Island*."

I didn't know what Mrs. Davenport was talking about.

"What's wrong?" I asked. "Perhaps I can help."

"I don't think so," Mrs. Davenport replied.

I was now beginning to detect tears in her voice as she continued.

"Bill is an alcoholic."

"I've never seen him take a drink," I said. "I've never even detected liquor on his breath."

"He goes for weeks at a time without a drink," she said. "Then he goes on a drinking spree. He's been drunk for three days now."

"I'm sorry to hear about this, Mrs. Davenport. Bill's been a big help to me on the show."

"He knows that, and that's why he's so ashamed of himself. He knows he's let you down." She was sobbing now. "That's what makes it so hard for me to talk to you."

"Don't worry about that. Do you have any idea when he'll be ready to work? I mean, is it days, or weeks, or what?"

"That's the big problem, Mr. Schwartz. I don't know. The last time this happened, about two months ago, he promised if it ever happened again he would go to a sanitarium for rehabilitation. That's where he is now."

"In a sanitarium?"

"Yes. In Westwood. He kept his promise. We admitted him there yesterday."

Stories about alcohol, and other drug problems, in the entertainment field were not new to me. There are enormous pressures in an industry where behavior is largely based on fear and insecurity. All sorts of chemical crutches are used. Writers, directors, producers, actors, executives, feel the need of these stimulants to help them face each new day. I was truly sorry to hear that Bill was part of this group. However, I had to look at the situation realistically. I was responsible for producing a weekly series.

"How long will he be in the sanitarium, Mrs. Davenport?"

"I'm really not sure," she replied. "I know it'll be at least three weeks. Maybe more."

As I thought about the implications of this, she continued.

"I'm sorry, Mr. Schwartz. I'm really sorry." She was crying openly now.

"I'm really sorry, too."

There was nothing more for me to say.

I was left with Charlie Tannen as my script editor.

As I've indicated, communicating with Charlie was a problem for me as well as for the writers who were working on scripts for the show. I felt it was more sensible to work out Charlie's commitment to the show by letting him write a few original scripts. Meanwhile, I had gotten my second wind, so to speak, thanks to Bill Davenport, and I took up the added burden of script editor again.

There's a fascinating story, following the adventures of Bill Davenport after he placed himself in that sanitarium in Westwood. During his rehabilitation there, Bill met an attractive young woman, Joan Harris, at the same sanitarium who was trying to conquer some other illness. She had been admitted about a week before Bill.

Romance sometimes rears its head in strange places. There, in that sanitarium, two people who suffered from different problems began to share their troubles. As the days went by, they began to share each other.

The relationship blossomed into a whirlwind courtship. When Bill's inamorata was released from the rehabilitation center a week before Bill's turn to exit, Bill decided he couldn't live without her. When Joan was released, Bill went A.W.O.L. He climbed over the wall of the sanitarium so he could join her.

Bill and Joan eloped to Las Vegas, where they were married. They both overlooked the rather important fact that Bill had a wife and three kids back in Los Angeles. I have no idea what the new Mrs. Davenport's familial obligations were.

The reason I know this story is because Bill invited my wife and me to a wedding reception at the Beverly Hilton Hotel in honor of his new bride.

Mildred and I were surprised by the invitation. As far as we knew, Bill was married to a woman in Los Angeles and was still in that sanitarium in Westwood. Nevertheless, having received it, we went to the reception.

We were amazed to find that the reception party had taken over what seemed to be an entire floor at that magnificent hotel. It was a very elegant affair. There were more waiters and hotel personnel in formal attire than there were guests. Mildred and I both wondered about this extreme exhibition of affluence. We knew Bill couldn't afford such a lavish affair.

His new bride could, however. She was an affluent woman—indeed, an heiress, whose family was worth many millions.

It only goes to prove once again the truth of the Richard Lovelace poem:

Stone walls do not a prison make,
Nor iron bars a cage.

Evidently the same holds true for rehabilitation centers.

This bizarre story about my script editor could only have a more bizarre ending. It did.

A few weeks after that wedding reception, I was working on a script for *Gilligan's Island* at C.B.S. Studio Center. I looked out the window just as a chauffeured limousine drove up outside the building where Bill had been my script editor.

A few moments later my secretary buzzed me and said Bill Davenport was here and would like to see me for a minute. I wondered why this *nouveau riche* writer was mingling with us common folks again.

Bill came into my office, and after we shook hands and exchanged "hellos," Bill said, "I just dropped by to see how my show is doing."

"What do you mean 'your show'?" I asked.

"Well," answered Bill, "*Gilligan's Island* is sponsored by my wife's company. She happens to be an heiress in a family that manufactures one of their products. So while I left here as your script editor, I've returned as your sponsor. So let's keep those ratings up there, Sherwood, old boy."

Bill said it with a twinkle and a smile. But he was telling the absolute truth. Seven weeks ago Bill had been my script editor. Now he was my sponsor.

In this land of Hollywood make-believe, I don't think any writer would dream up an ending like that. It's too unbelievable. Yet that's exactly what happened.

Speaking of unbelievable endings, after that wild escapade, Bill straightened out his tangled marital situation, stopped drinking and has been clean and sober for over fifteen years. He returned to writing as staff writer and script editor, and he's justifiably proud of the fact that he was able to win his battle with alcohol. And he's found, he says, that "it's easier to write in a vertical position than horizontal."

21

Life on the Stage

"I've just read the first three scripts, and I want to know what I'm doing here," demanded Tina Louise.

I've spent so much time describing meetings with executives and script problems, it may seem these are the only functions of a producer. That's not true. They are important areas, but there are equally, if not more important, duties in producing.

Many pages ago I said it's the characters on the screen to whom the viewers must relate. It's impossible to underestimate the importance of stars on a TV series. They are the reason the viewers tune in each week; to see "her," or "him," or "them."

It follows, therefore, that one of the producer's main concerns is his cast, especially the permanent cast—actors and actresses who are in the show every week. In the case of *Gilligan's Island* that meant all seven Castaways, because every actor and every actress were in every episode.

That's why it was so upsetting to me when Tina walked into my office and said what she did. I honestly didn't know what Tina meant.

"You didn't have to take me out of a Broadway play to do this series," Tina continued, "Anybody could have done this part."

"That's not true. You're tall, beautiful, with a gorgeous figure and red hair. And you have that wonderful innocent sexiness. That's Ginger, and that's you."

"But I'm hardly in these scripts. This isn't the show they described in New York."

"The show *who* described?"

"The people in casting at C.B.S. These scripts don't remotely resemble the series they promised me."

I was afraid to ask the next question because I had a hunch I knew the answer. Nevertheless, I asked anyway.

"What did they tell you?"

"They told me *Gilligan's Island* was a show about a movie star," said Tina. "A movie star who is cast adrift on a desert island with six other people."

I know casting directors sometimes have to exaggerate a little in order to negotiate a deal. Exaggeration is one thing, but total distortion is something else.

No wonder Tina was upset. If what she was telling me was true, she had every right to be furious when she read the first several scripts. They featured Gilligan and the Skipper. The other parts were evenly divided—Thurston Howell III probably a little more evenly than the others.

I did my best to calm Tina. In the first place, I apologized for whoever had described *Gilligan's Island* in that manner. Then I explained as tactfully as I could that in a show titled *Gilligan's Island* the major star would logically be Gilligan. Since Gilligan worked most closely with the Skipper, naturally a lot of scenes would involve them. They would be "heavy" in every episode. However, in each episode, it was my intention to feature one of the other Castaways in the main plot. That's the way *Gilligan's Island* was designed.

It was just coincidence, I told her, that the first few scripts didn't feature the character of Ginger as much as the others. The next script might feature Ginger, or perhaps the script after that. The "starring" role would rotate from Tina to Jim Backus, to Natalie Schafer, to Dawn Wells, to Russ Johnson. It all depended on which writers got to final draft with which script. The character of Ginger would certainly be the focal point of many stories, I assured her.

"That still doesn't make *Gilligan's Island* a series about a movie star who's cast away on a desert island with six other people," insisted Tina.

"I agree," I said. "They were wrong to describe the show that way. Just give me a chance to prove Ginger is very important in this series."

"Another thing," added Tina, "I don't like this wisecracking, brittle humor for Ginger. I want to be more like Marilyn Monroe and maybe something like Lucy. I talked to Jim Aubrey and he agrees with me."

"So do I," I replied. It had been immediately obvious to me that casting Tina Louise had altered the original concept of Ginger. That concept was in keeping with the girl whom Tina had replaced. Tina shouldn't, actually couldn't, play the part that way. Tina was definitely in the Monroe mold. I was already at work on Ginger's character in all the scripts in preparation, modifying her dialogue and actions in that direction.

When Tina left my office, she was only slightly mollified, but at least I had prevented her from getting on the next plane back to New York.

I tried to track down the person who had misrepresented the show in order to convince Tina to leave a featured role in a Broadway show to "star" in *Gilligan's Island*.

It couldn't have been Ethel Winant. She would never resort to that kind of overselling in order to cast a role, no matter how important it was. I knew Ethel too well to believe that.

I spoke to a few other people in casting at C.B.S. West Coast and East Coast. All I got was:

"Not me."

"Not me."

Tina Louise breaking up on the set at one of Jim Backus' ad libs.

"Not I."

There's always one college graduate in the crowd.

No one would accept the responsibility for that phony sales pitch.

Then it occurred to me, why did it have to be somebody at C.B.S.? It could have been her agent who had exaggerated her role to make the deal more attractive to Tina. If so, who would ever admit anything to me?

Gilligan's Island tropical fruit: a bunch of grapes, a peach, and half a watermelon. *(Courtesy of the Stephen Cox Collection)*

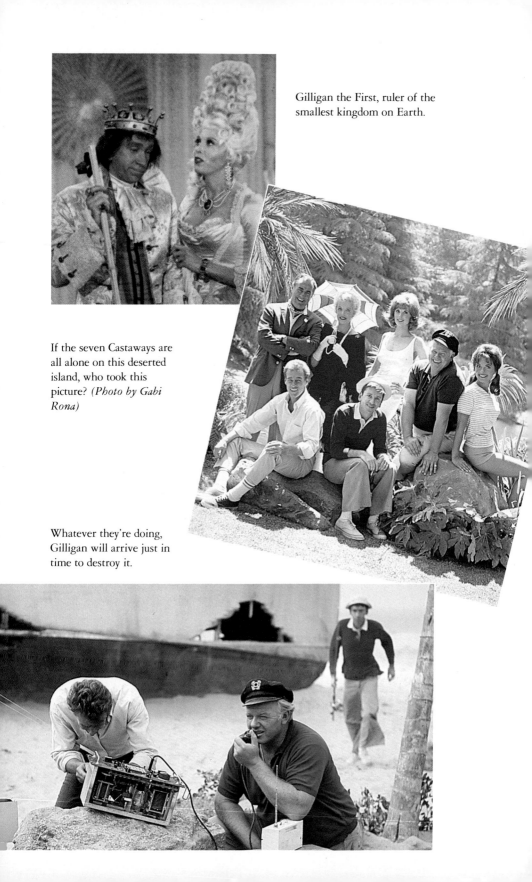

Gilligan the First, ruler of the smallest kingdom on Earth.

If the seven Castaways are all alone on this deserted island, who took this picture? *(Photo by Gabi Rona)*

Whatever they're doing, Gilligan will arrive just in time to destroy it.

The Skipper looks pretty happy for a captain in command of a shipwreck. *(Courtesy of Jim McHugh)*

Bob Denver and his son Patrick. You can tell this scene wasn't being filmed, by the lit cigarettes. Gilligan's was a nonsmoking island. *(Courtesy of Jim McHugh)*

Mr. Howell reminiscing about his favorite Swiss bank accounts. *(Courtesy of Jim McHugh)*

Mrs. Howell's favorite color is red. Mr. Howell's favorite color is green—as in money. *(Courtesy of Jim McHugh)*

The Professor's amazing button-down shirt; washed 886 times without losing a button.
(Courtesy of Jim McHugh)

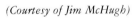

(Courtesy of Jim McHugh)

Gilligan and the Skipper in the Howell mansion: as out of place as two navy beans in a bowl of caviar.

The Skipper looks like he's had too many of Mary Ann's coconut cream pies.

The Odd Couple: The Lean and the Queen.

Mary Ann dressed as a bride, and Gilligan (surprise!) dressed as Gilligan.

(Courtesy of Jim McHugh)

Gilligan is all wet, as usual.
(Courtesy of Jim McHugh)

This photo shows the camera crew, the technicians, and the entire area at Paramount where we shot the footage of the floating hutful of Castaways.
(Courtesy of Jim McHugh)

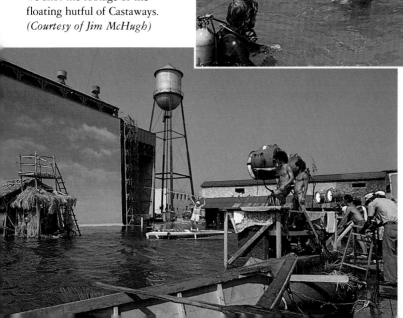

I will never forget these
wonderful people...

...And neither will
millions of viewers

Sherwood Schwartz

This in-memoriam page appeared in *Variety* and *The Hollywood Reporter* in May 1991. Jim Backus, Alan Hale, and Natalie Schafer all passed away within a two-year period.

Captain Queeg never found out who ate the strawberries either.

The rest of the cast seemed completely happy — even Natalie Schafer, who had had no interest whatsoever in doing a TV series. After her agent submitted the pilot script of *Gilligan's Island* to her, she felt it didn't have a chance to become a series, so she agreed to do the role of Mrs. Thurston Howell III. Her motives were simple: as Natalie herself puts it, "to get all that money and a free trip to Hawaii besides."

In February 1964, Natalie was in Puerto Vallarta, Mexico. Her mother was very ill at the time. A telegram arrived for Natalie. She read it and started to cry.

One of her friends asked, "Is that about your mother?"

Natalie answered, through her tears, "Worse. The pilot sold."

Once in the series, however, Natalie, too, took an active interest in her part. After the first few episodes, she quietly approached me about the role. It was evident that in my anxiety to beef up Jim Backus' part — the guarantee I had given in order to attract and keep him — I was failing to pay as much attention as I should to *Mrs.* Thurston Howell III. Natalie carefully pointed this out to me, and with good reason. I wasn't taking full advantage of her abilities as a comedienne. After that, Mr. and Mrs. Howell shared the limelight more equally, becoming a sort of a comedy team instead of a comic and a straight "man."

I also gave Natalie the same assurance I had given to Tina, and to the rest of the cast, about the rotation of episodes featuring the five Castaways. They all knew that Gilligan and the Skipper were the principal characters, and they accepted this as the modus operandi of the show. In fact, they all began to look forward to each new script as the one in which they would be the "star."

It was difficult to balance this rotation exactly because some scripts needed many rewrites, while others were ready more quickly. Some episodes, for budget reasons, were shot back-to-back. This, too, upset the rotation I promised the cast.

Fortunately, the Castaways were a relatively amiable group — particularly when compared to other shows where one hears horror stories about co-stars who won't even talk to each other. Or shows where one actor won't go onstage until "the other" actor is already there. Or shows rampant with jealousies over billing, or footage, or money. Sometimes there have been actual fistfights. Not only between male stars, but female stars as well. None of these things were true on the set of *Gilligan's Island*.

It wasn't paradise, but what is?

Some of the performers were more gregarious than others, like Alan Hale and Jim Backus. They were at their happiest, between takes, telling stories and jokes. Both of them loved an audience for their anecdotes, and Natalie Schafer, Dawn Wells, and Russ Johnson, as well as members of the crew who weren't busy at the moment, were delighted to listen to Alan and Jim who were wonderful storytellers. Alan Hale was his own best audience. He not only enjoyed listening to the laughter of his audience, he laughed just as hard as they did when he told a story.

Natalie Schafer could give as well as receive, and she often regaled the others with her own stories about show business. Those stories began with her days on the Broadway stage several decades earlier. We never knew exactly how many years earlier, because Natalie refused to divulge her age to anyone.

All the stars had to get physical exams before the series started. It's customary procedure on all films, feature as well as television. In the course of Natalie's exam, the doctor asked her how old she was. Natalie asked, "Have you ever examined me before?"

"Yes," said the doctor, "several times."

"Well," answered Natalie, "just keep putting down the same number."

Bob Denver and Tina Louise weren't as outgoing as the rest of the cast, and spent a good deal of time to themselves. Not with each other, though. There was always some coolness between Bob and Tina. It related to their roles in the show.

Bob always felt there was no place on *Gilligan's Island* for the sexy image that Tina represented. He felt it was an unnecessary ingredient in the character mix. Since *Gilligan's Island* was a comedy show, he didn't think sex was essential in our microcosm.

By nature, Bob is an introspective, shy, almost solitary individual. He's the exact opposite of the foolish, bumbling Gilligan he portrays so convincingly. Bob is highly intelligent, very well coordinated; a skilled, remarkably talented actor. He's also very sensitive. Underneath his thin skin are raw nerves, easily irritated.

Differences of opinion between Bob and me, which occurred from time to time, always had to be settled on intellectual and logical terms. Bob knew my door was always open to him for any sort of complaint, and he appreciated that. Later he was to work with producers without my open-door policy, the kind of producers who simply issue orders and don't deal with actors as people. Bob resents that kind of authority bitterly. Especially executives at networks and production companies who have never had direct contact with the filming process. He doesn't think they understand his problems. Most of them probably don't. But Bob and I have worked together many times on many other projects, always with great respect for each other.

Tina, like Bob, is introspective. But she isn't shy. Not at all. On more than one occasion, Tina made various wardrobe changes right on stage in front of cast and crew in order to save time, wearing little, if anything, underneath.

Like Bob, Tina is also a private person. Not in the same way, however. Tina's privacy has a kind of a once-removed quality, as though she has other things on her mind. At least that was my interpretation at the time.

For example, one day she was very dissatisfied with one of her scenes in the show. I went to her dressing room to discuss the scene with her. At some length, I explained the reason for the scene and why it was necessary for the plot.

When I was all through, Tina asked me, "Can I have my dressing room painted white? I hate this gray color."

I didn't know if she had accepted my explanation, or whether she had even heard anything I said. But I had her dressing room painted white – and she did the scene as written.

Later on, Tina explained her behavior. She saw very quickly that she was going to lose the argument about the scene, so she simply shifted to a different topic. She dismissed one point she couldn't win, and moved on to another point she hoped she could.

After *Gilligan's Island,* Tina had a real character identity problem. She loved the fact that the character of Ginger had made her a famous star, recognized not only in the United States, but worldwide. However, she resented the fact that the audience accepted Tina Louise as Ginger, and Ginger as Tina Louise. That kind of identification caused her a great deal of aggravation. Long before Tina played Ginger, she was a member of Actors' Studio, with dreams of an important dramatic career. *Gilligan's Island,* which made her an important TV star, became a roadblock to that career.

The other Castaways all made use of their characters after the show went off the air. Most of them still make appearances on theatre stages billed as "Mary Ann from *Gilligan's Island,*" or "Bob 'Gilligan' Denver," or "The Skipper from *Gilligan's Island.*" Russ Johnson is delighted to be identified as the Professor, and Jim and Natalie were equally happy to be recognized as Mr. and Mrs. Thurston Howell III.

But not Tina. She has fought the "Ginger" label ever since the prime-time series ended in 1966. She even refused to do the *voice* of Ginger for the two Saturday morning animated series based on *Gilligan's Island.* Tina declined a large sum of money to appear as Ginger in the enormously successful two-hour movie, *Rescue from Gilligan's Island.* She likewise declined all offers for any subsequent *Gilligan's Island* films.

These refusals were not easy for Tina. Each request was very tempting to her, and only rejected after a great deal of soul-searching.

I've spoken to Tina frequently about this. She always seemed to be on the verge of capitulating to the lure of money and the ego-seduction of doing the role that made her famous. But each time, at the last moment, she changed her mind. She simply has a fear that if she ever identifies herself with Ginger again, she will lose all chance to play other types of roles, dramatic or comic.

In 1982, *Good Morning America,* the David Hartman Show, was doing a series of reunion shows with old TV series. Much to my surprise, and, I'm sure, the other Castaways, Tina agreed to appear with the rest of the *Gilligan's Island* cast. Payment was minimal.

Tina Louise, as Ginger, the role she created so beautifully, found herself typed after the series ended.

Perhaps it was because of her daughter, Caprice, whom she adores. Caprice has been watching the reruns of *Gilligan's Island*. She loves the show and she adores her mother as Ginger. Maybe it was Caprice who was responsible for Tina's decision to appear, at long last, with her old friends on *Gilligan's Island*.

Or perhaps it was the following incident.

Tina was having dinner at Guiseppe's, a fine Italian restaurant in Los Angeles. A woman approached her table, apologizing for interrupting Tina's meal. However, this lady was just leaving the restaurant and explained there was something she wanted to tell Tina. Tina has always been gracious to fans, and she encouraged the woman to talk.

The lady told Tina that her husband had died recently. He had cancer, and his last few months were agony. His favorite television show had been *Gilligan's Island,* and his favorite star was Tina Louise. He asked for video tapes of certain shows which featured Tina, such as the episode in which she played a nurse and sang "I Want to Be Loved by You" to Gilligan, and the episode with Phil Silvers in which she played several different parts. There were a few other favorites, too. During his last few months he played those tapes over and over. He said it was the only thing that helped ease the pain. The lady thanked Tina for bringing such comfort to her husband when drugs didn't even seem to help.

When the woman left the restaurant, Tina stared after her for a few moments. Goosebumps were running up and down her spine as she realized how much her characterization of Ginger on *Gilligan's Island* had meant to someone she had never seen and never met.

When Tina told me this story, I advised her to multiply that experience by many thousands. I believe she finally came to understand the full impact the stars of a TV series like *Gilligan's Island* can have on viewers.

If Tina was at one extreme in her reaction to her role on *Gilligan's Island,* Alan Hale was at the other extreme. Alan gloried in his identification with the Skipper. He loved the show. He loved the character. To all intents and purposes, Alan *became* the Skipper. His bright blue short-sleeved shirt and captain's cap brought him instant identification all over the world, and he rejoiced in it. He never tired of signing autographs and chatting about *Gilligan's Island.*

Alan's dedication to the show, right from the start, was unbelievable. An unforgettable example came at the end of the second season, during our "wrap party." That's a Hollywood tradition when a film is completed, or a TV series "wraps" shooting for the season. Alan was his usual self, mingling with the cast and crew, spreading jokes and sunshine everywhere he went.

As Alan and I exchanged a few comments at the party, he said, "Thank goodness we finished shooting. Now I can take care of my arm."

"What's the matter with your arm?" I inquired.

"Oh, I broke it a few weeks ago," he answered.

I couldn't believe it. For the last several weeks Alan, as usual, had been doing all kinds of physical stunts with his little buddy, Gilligan.

"How could you lift Bob Denver, and haul all those coconuts and do all those other things with a broken arm?"

"It wasn't easy," Alan admitted. He pointed to his right arm near the elbow. "It hurt like heck. I used my left arm mostly."

"You better take care of that right away."

"I'm going to the doctor right from the party," said Alan.

Something occurred to me. "How did you break your arm?" I asked.

"When I fell out of the tree in that episode three or four weeks ago," Alan answered. "I was supposed to land on some mattresses. I hit okay with my body, but my right arm went off the pads and hit the stage."

"My God, that's concrete!"

"Yeah, I know," said Alan ruefully.

"You should have told me about this right away," I said to Alan. "Our company is insured for things like that. We could have held up production for a day or two and gotten a cast for your arm. We could have written it into the script. We could have made the bandage look like the Professor had made it from some burlap and vines."

"Why go through all that trouble?" Alan wanted to know. "We only had a couple of shows left. Now I'm going to see my doctor."

"Your own doctor?" I asked.

"Yeah. Sure."

"Alan, this happened during filming. Let me call the insurance company and make arrangements. We can pay for the doctor and—"

That was as far as I got.

"You've got enough problems, Sherwood," Alan said. "Don't you worry about this."

"But—"

Alan was waving goodbye to everyone at the wrap party. With his left hand.

Alan Hale's consideration for others is a way of life for him. It was that warmth and gentleness I saw in his face when I looked across the restaurant that day, a few weeks before we shot the pilot in 1963. That massive teddy-bear quality is absolutely genuine. I know, because Alan and I have spent time together in more serious moments.

I've been interested in Children's Hospital, Los Angeles, for a number of years, thanks to Mrs. Mary Duque. As far as I'm concerned, Mrs. Duque is the patron saint of Children's Hospital. Every so often, if I can coordinate a visiting day at the hospital with her, I spend an afternoon there with a TV star whom I know well enough to ask. We go from room to room, spending a few minutes with each of the children.

It's actually a very disturbing several hours for us because we see children who are involved in distressing types of therapy. Youngsters a few years old are on respirators, dialysis machines, and other ominous-looking equipment. Your heart goes out to these innocent little children.

Nobody is gentler and kinder than Alan Hale with young people. And, or course, nobody is better loved by children than the Skipper from *Gilligan's Island*.

I'll never forget one particular room where a young boy about eleven had just arrived from recovery. He had had a kidney removed, and was just starting to stir as he came out of anesthetic.

Alan and I were uncertain whether we could visit the room, and even the nurse wasn't sure. However, the doctor waved us in. Alan and I were at the foot of the lad's bed as he began to open his eyes. When his vision started to clear, he looked at Alan in disbelief. His eyes suddenly opened wide, and his face filled with wonder. In a voice that wasn't much more than a whisper he said, "Skipper?"

I wondered briefly at that moment whether that young boy thought he had died and gone to *Gilligan's Island*. But Alan, as usual, knew exactly the right thing to say. "That's right, son. The Skipper is here with you. Everything's going to be fine now."

"That's good," murmured the boy. A smile appeared on his lips and spread across his face, and he closed his eyes.

"We have no medicine that's anywhere near as good as that," the doctor said to Alan Hale. "You've already put him two days ahead of schedule."

"That's what we're here for," said Alan, as we moved on to the next room.

I've visited hospitals with other stars of *Gilligan's Island* and *The Brady Bunch,* shows where I've become very close to the performers. I don't think enough stars understand how very special they are. And what wonders they can accomplish.

People, young and old alike, don't know writers or directors, or producers. They know stars. As the doctor himself said, there's no medicine that can take the place of a personal visit from a star, whether TV, film, football, baseball, or any other star in the sports or entertainment world.

Many performers do spend time visiting hospitals, convalescent homes, adoption homes, rehabilitation centers, and even juvenile halls and prisons. I applaud them for that. It takes up their time, and the sights aren't always pleasant. But I'm sure many more celebrities would participate if they fully understood the special medication they supply for people of all ages who are going through temporary or chronic problems.

Alan Hale was not the only performer on the *Gilligan's Island* stage dedicated to the show. One Sunday I got a phone call at home from Jim Backus. He was due to shoot a scene Monday afternoon. "Can you rewrite that scene so I can do it sitting down?" Jim asked.

I was familiar with the scene Jim was talking about. I was puzzled. "Do you think we can make it funnier that way?"

"No, no. It's just that I have to have a little surgery Monday morning," said Jim, mentioning a part of his anatomy located directly behind his lap.

"We don't have to do that scene Monday afternoon, Jim. I can shift your scenes to Tuesday, or maybe even Wednesday."

"Absolutely not," said Jim. "My scene is scheduled for Monday and I'm going to do it Monday."

"That's silly," I insisted. "We'll be shooting in that same area of the stage Tuesday and Wednesday. It's no trouble for me to shift the schedule."

"I insist," was Jim's reply. "I already bought an air cushion for me to sit on. That's why I want you to rewrite the scene so I can sit down."

"If that's what you want, okay."

"That's what I want," said Jim.

"I'll have some Preparation M on the set for you," I said.

"You mean Preparation H."

"No. Preparation M," I answered. "Thurston Howell III would find money more soothing."

"Oh, that's a good one, by George," said Jim. "And I've got enough money to *buy* George."

Then Jim gave me his famous Mr. Magoo laugh and hung up.

He did the scene as scheduled, Monday afternoon. Sitting down.

Many years later, we did a two-hour film special for N.B.C., *The Harlem Globetrotters on Gilligan's Island*. Jim Backus was quite ill at the time. After a while, it became obvious that Jim would be unable to do his traditional role of Thurston Howell III in the film.

I refused to recast the role with anyone else. Nobody could play Thurston Howell III like Jim. Besides, it would have been a terrible blow to Jim, psychologically, for him to be sitting home watching TV and seeing someone else playing Thurston Howell III.

Instead, we rewrote the script to bring in an heir to the Howell fortunes, Thurston Howell IV. This part was played by David Ruprecht. David did a wonderful interpretation of Jim's Howell characterization, without trying to do an imitation of Thurston Howell III.

Jim phoned me near the last day of shooting and said he felt well enough to come in and do a few lines. Could I find a way to work Thurston Howell III back into the script?

Old soldiers may fade away, but actors, real, thoroughbred actors, never do. When the curtain goes up, they want to be on stage.

I quickly added Jim to an existing scene at the end of the film, with the excuse that Thurston Howell III had just returned from a trip visiting one of his many enterprises. Jim's part was very short, only four or five lines. But I'll never forget the stage that day, when Jim appeared as Thurston Howell III.

Jim was thin and shaky as he crossed into the scene to do his part. He was obviously very weak, but even under those conditions he managed to "take stage" and dominate the scene in his own Thurston Howell III fashion.

After he finished his few lines, I looked around the stage and saw tears in the eyes of many people in the cast and crew. Some of them who had been with the show for many years were crying openly.

As Jim turned to leave with Henny, his wife of many years, there was such thunderous applause that it turned into an ovation. Tears still in their eyes, everyone stood and applauded, until Jim was forced to stop on his way to the exit. He turned back to face them and waved kisses to his many friends. I saw tears in Jim's eyes, too. Then Thurston Howell III left the stage.

I was very happy to say Jim managed to check the progress of that illness, Parkinson's disease. He appeared in several feature films and TV shows after that day in 1981. He and Henny had a book published in 1985 about his illness, *Backus Strikes Back,* and they published another one in 1988, Jim's autobiography, *Forgive Us Our Transgressions.*

Henny Backus, Jim Backus' wife, as a native queen, trying to convince Gilligan to become her son-in-law.

What about the other Castaways? Were they as dedicated as Jim?

On the coldest day, when all the Castaways had to go into the lagoon in one of the scenes, guess who was the first to jump into that uninviting, chilly water?

Natalie Schafer, that's who. With her ever-present parasol over her head, Natalie would lead the charge of the other six Castaways into the lagoon. There wasn't anything in the script Natalie refused to do, whether she was called upon to take a fall, sink into quicksand, or swing from a tree.

Did I say Natalie never refused to do anything? That's not quite accurate. There was one thing Natalie absolutely refused. In fact, she was so adamant about it, she had the clause inserted in her contract. That clause reads as follows: "In this series there shall be absolutely no closeups of Natalie Schafer above the waist."

Apparently, Mrs. Thurston Howell III was never to be found guilty of having a wrinkle.

Away from the set, Natalie and Jim Backus were very close friends.

Natalie was also a good friend of Henny, Jim's wife. And she loved to joke about the remarkably close relationship between Jim and Henny.

In addition to being Jim's wife, Henny practically ran Jim's life, advising him on career moves, what he should have for breakfast, and what tie to wear. They never had any children, and Henny, in many ways, treated Jim as one. She took full charge of everything he did.

One day Jim told me he had gotten a role in a feature film, and in the movie he was playing the President of the United States. I told Natalie Schafer about this, and she immediately exclaimed, "Good God, that means Henny is running the country!"

Everybody in the cast was dedicated to the show, above and beyond the call of duty.

Assume you're an actor in a scene with a lion. The lion is supposed to remain on the bed while you tiptoe to the door and exit. Assume further that you have rehearsed that scene several times, and each time the lion has remained peacefully on the bed while you make your exit.

Now assume that the cameras are rolling, and as you start to exit, the lion, instead of remaining peacefully on the bed, leaps for you as you start toward the door.

That's exactly what happened to Bob Denver in one of the episodes of *Gilligan's Island*. The only thing that saved Bob's life is the fact that the bed wasn't bolted to the floor. As a result, when the lion made his leap toward Bob, the lion's back legs pushed the bed backwards, removing the force from his jump. Because of this, the lion's leap fell short of Bob by about two feet.

The trainer moved in instantly, and grabbed the lion. Bob wasn't even scratched. Nevertheless, he had come within inches, literally, of being crushed beneath a 400-pound lion.

Assume this happened to you. How long would it take to get you back on the bed with the lion again? Would *never* be long enough?

Bob Denver said "Okay, one more time. And keep the bed loose, in case he jumps again."

The next take was good, and the show proceeded as scheduled.

Despite his initial reserve, Bob did often join in the fun with the rest of the cast. For instance, one day Alan Hale and Jim Backus, both devoted golfers, got into a heated discussion about who could drive the ball farther. They each had their golf clubs in their cars, and during lunch break they went out in the backlot, near a ravine, past the parking lot. Bob went along, as did a few other members of the cast and crew to witness the competition. Alan and Jim each drove three or four balls as far as they could into the ravine.

Nobody would climb down into the ravine to verify the winner, and Alan and Jim each claimed victory.

"My ball went at least ten yards farther than yours," insisted Alan.

"How dare you insinuate you outdrove me," countered Jim in his best Thurston Howell III voice. "After all, I'm a Harvard man."

Meanwhile, Bob had a private little chat with one of the C.B.S. guards.

The guard came to the set after lunch and asked who won the big driving match.

"I did," claimed Alan.

"I did," argued Jim.

"Well, whoever won," said the guard, "drove the ball across the ravine and right through the windshield of a Cadillac in the parking lot. The guy wants six hundred bucks for a new windshield."

"He won by twenty yards," claimed Alan.

"I did like heck! He outdrove me a mile," argued Jim.

*

It took Tina Louise a little longer than the others to warm up to the crew and the rest of the cast. In fact, it took a scene in one of the shows to prove Tina had a sense of humor before the chill began to thaw.

Tina had to do a shower scene in a makeshift island shower stall, and Tina insisted she wanted to do the scene in the nude. The bamboo shower door would hide her from the shoulders down, so the camera wouldn't actually show anything except her head, shoulders, legs, and feet.

Word had gotten around that Tina was going to strip once she got into the bamboo booth. The shower was just a bucket of water that tipped over when a cord was pulled. The bamboo stall had no top on it.

Just before the scene, every electrician, every carpenter, every grip, had some reason to be up on the catwalks above the set. There must have been forty-five men up there, waiting for that shower scene to start.

Tina walked on stage in her sarong-type bathing suit, and into the shower stall to do the scene. She never looked up. While ninety eyes stared down from above, Tina undid the sarong and whipped it off.

There was another sarong underneath!

Tina flashed a smile up at the men and made a shame-on-you gesture. The rest of us howled with laughter as the men scurried down from the catwalks.

What surprised me the most about Tina was her willingness, even eagerness, to deglamorize herself. This was particularly true in dream sequences we did from time to time in *Gilligan's Island*.

In one dream sequence, Cinderella was played by Natalie Schafer, and Tina was one of the wicked stepsisters. Tina wanted the makeup man to go as far as he could. He went further. She was the ugliest looking stepsister you ever saw, with warts on her face, a huge crooked nose and blacked-out teeth. She made Margaret Hamilton's "wicked witch of the West" look like Snow White.

Tina played one scene with a rubber cap so she'd look bald; another scene where she was covered with feathers; and one where she was covered with mud. In another show she played a dual role in which she was the plainest Jane possible, with no makeup, an awful hairstyle and clothes to match. She loved doing parts like that.

As a producer, there was only one real continuing problem I had with Tina.

Obviously, every performer fights for attention on the screen. When you're competing with the broad physical comedy of Bob Denver and Alan Hale, and the witticisms of Mr. and Mrs. Thurston Howell III, it's natural to use whatever ammunition you have to get the audience's attention.

Tina had plenty of ammunition. She played most of her scenes in her light beige V-neck gown. Somehow, between rehearsals and the time the camera rolled for actual takes, that V was always mysteriously slipping down to reveal more cleavage. From time to time I would get a phone call from the director of that episode asking me to come to the stage and make a decision. This was among my pleasanter duties as the executive producer: to gaze at Tina's bosom and decide whether or not there was too much cleavage.

One day, I was called to the stage again for this purpose. I took one quick look. The Alps were clearly in evidence.

I said, "Tina, we'll have to do that scene over. You better stop yanking down the front of that dress."

Tina denied any such action. "It's just the way I'm built," she pouted. "After all, I'm not a boy."

"I know you're not a boy," I said. "The audience knows you're not a boy, too. Even the censor knows you're not a boy. But he's not going to permit that much cleavage."

"I just can't help it. That's the way the dress fits me."

"Okay. Then leave it that way. When you see this scene on the air you'll find out you're 'voice-over.' The camera will be on the other people, and we'll hear Ginger's voice."

That's the last thing actors or actresses want to hear—that their film footage will be left on the cutting room floor. They want their faces to be on the screen, not just their voices.

"I don't know what's wrong," said Tina. "I'm not showing anything that everybody hasn't seen a million times before. On every TV show."

Nevertheless, she hiked the shoulders of her dress up a few inches so that some of the cleavage disappeared. It was still evident that Tina Louise was very much a girl, but I was satisfied we wouldn't have a problem with the censor.

One day, having solved a cleavage crisis with Tina, I returned to my office and continued work on the rewrite of next week's script. I hadn't been working more than fifteen minutes when I got another call from the stage. A new crisis had developed. I left for the set.

"What's wrong with these hip huggers?" Dawn Wells asked. She was

Considering the fact it was a deserted island, the castaways had plenty of company. That's cinematographer Richard Rawlings, Sr., with his cap on and his back to the camera; camera operator Dick Duval, also with his back to the camera; Dick Williams operating the boom microphone; and Danny Buck, the Gaffer. Hidden in the foliage are Scotty McKuen, Buddy Taylor, Dick Johnson, Lily La Cava, Keester Sweeney, and a whole host of grips, electricians, decorators, carpenters, painters and special effects men.

dressed in hip huggers and a halter top, leaving her midriff bare. The top of her hip huggers just came to her navel, leaving it exposed.

In those years, C.B.S. had what was referred to as the "Intermittent Navel" rule, concerning female navels. I'm sure the other networks had the same rule. Barbara Eden in *I Dream of Jeannie* on N.B.C. had to paste a jewel in her navel. The harem outfit she was wearing would have revealed her navel on a permanent basis, instead of intermittently.

According to the "Intermittent Navel" regulation, it was okay if a female navel appeared and disappeared. Permanent view of a female navel was *verboten*. On the other hand, you could stare at a male navel all you wanted. That seems to me a clear violation of the equal rights principle. But I didn't make the female navel rule. I just had to see it was obeyed.

"Just raise those hip huggers a little bit," I said to Dawn. "Up to here." I drew a line just above her navel.

"Everyone has a navel," Dawn pointed out.

"Everyone has other things we can't show on television," I replied.

Very reluctantly, Dawn hiked her hip huggers up about an inch.

"Now let's see you walk," I suggested.

Dawn Wells walked.

As she walked, her hip huggers moved up and down. Sometimes you saw Mary Ann's navel and sometimes you didn't. Peek-a-boo.

"That's okay now," I said.

"I still don't see what difference it makes," said Dawn.

"Neither did Tina," I answered.

Dawn continued the scene, still a little piqued over the commotion caused by the innocent-looking little dimple in her abdomen. I returned to my office, and resumed work on the rewrite.

That night, when I got home from the studio, Mildred asked me, "How did work go today?"

"It was very rough, dear," I answered. "Between Tina's tits and Dawn's belly button, I didn't have a moment's peace."

I was lucky to escape with my life.

*

Audience identification of actors with the characters they play on the TV tube is amazing. When *Perry Mason* was in its prime, Raymond Burr addressed the Bar Association, as though he himself were an attorney. When *Marcus Welby, M.D.* was at the top in the ratings, Robert Young addressed the American Medical Association.

The same sort of fate befell Dawn Wells. Dawn will be the pretty little sweetheart who lives next door as long as she lives, sincere and innocent, the eternal virgin.

The question Dawn is asked most frequently is, "Why didn't you ever get married to Gilligan?" Nobody ever asks, "Did you and Gilligan ever make out?" That would be an unthinkable question to ask sweet Mary Ann.

Dawn Wells appears in stage plays in many cities all over the country. When she does, she's frequently asked to speak at local high schools and colleges. Whenever she talks to the youngsters, they treat her as though she's their age. Dawn Wells lives in a Mary Ann time warp. She'll be nineteen years old if she lives to be a hundred.

Despite this daring sexy scene—with Gilligan and Mary Ann separated by only a palm frond—their relationship was perceived by viewers as the ultimate in innocence.

Recently, Dawn told me what happened in a Texas high school when she was speaking to the class. The teacher left the room for some reason during Dawn's remarks. As soon as she was gone, those girls started asking Dawn questions about sex, drugs, religion, death, bigotry, etc.

They still viewed Dawn as a contemporary, frozen in time by the magic of reruns. They wanted to know what would Mary Ann do in a case like this? How would she react in a case like that? They freely discussed the most intimate topics with Dawn just as though she were one of their own classmates. But all those kinds of questions stopped when the teacher returned.

"It's amazing," Dawn said to me. "Those young girls didn't discuss those topics with their own mothers or their teachers, but they felt they could confide in me. I'm still Mary Ann, I guess."

But even Mary Ann is in for a shock once in a while.

Last year Dawn Wells was appearing in a theatre, in a play, *The Owl and the Pussycat*. When she finished her performance, there was a soldier waiting to see her in her dressing room. He had a bouquet of flowers. He said, "I just had to meet you, Miss Wells," as he handed her the roses.

"Isn't that sweet of you," said Dawn, as she took the flowers. "Did you like the show tonight?"

"Oh, yes," said the serviceman. "But those flowers aren't from me. They're from my father. He used to love you on *Gilligan's Island*."

After the shock passed, Dawn thanked the young man for the bouquet. She was so numb from that "compliment," she didn't even feel the thorns as she grabbed the stems.

Russell Johnson, in some ways, had the most difficult role in the show. While everyone else was colorful and funny, either physically or verbally, the Professor had to carry the plot in believable fashion. That's what made him such a necessary character in *Gilligan's Island*, and that's why Russ Johnson made such a wonderful Professor.

Very often, Russ would be called upon to make some scientific explanation; sometimes geological, sometimes botanical, sometimes anthropological, sometimes chemical. All this scientific information had to be imparted to the other Castaways in multisyllabic words. Very often they were highly technical, involving chemical equations or mathematical formulas, which made them very difficult to pronounce. Once they were in the script, however, Russ Johnson was determined not only to memorize them, but to pronounce them correctly.

Sometimes I'd be on the stage when Russ was struggling to say words that looked good on paper, but simply couldn't be spoken. I'd try to make changes in his dialogue, changes that wouldn't hurt the meaning in any way. Russ wouldn't hear of it. He insisted on doing his dialogue exactly as written.

As a practical joke, one day I wrote a phony speech for the Professor which wasn't really intended to be used in the show. I filled it with so much technical, polysyllabic verbiage that it had no meaning, and the combination of letters rendered it unfit for human pronunciation. I thought we'd have a laugh about it the next day on the stage.

Instead, when I got there, Russ was doing the scene, and by God, he had memorized that entire half page of meaningless words absolutely correctly, pronouncing every single syllable. Not only that; he spoke the gibberish with authority.

Actually, the laugh was on me. The cameras weren't even rolling. Russ Johnson was just showing me he could learn anything that anybody wrote.

Some years later, a TV channel in Philadelphia tried an audio-television experiment on an educational network. The experiment involved different learning techniques with children, using *Gilligan's Island* as the test case.

Dr. Terry Borton linked W.K.B.S. (TV) and W.U.H.Y. (FM). Steve Baskerville, on radio, narrated video clips of experiments the Professor had done in different episodes of *Gilligan's Island*. For example, the way he had recharged a rundown battery in the radio, using two different metals and sea water as a conductor; or the way he made glue from sap, or glass from sand.

Leonard Belasco, the associate director and producer of this project, compared the results with a separate test of 260 comparable Philadelphia school children. There was a "distinct correlation" between the amount learned and the number of hours of *Gilligan* video they watched. The educators found that students learned the information almost four times as well from their friend, the Professor, and the *Gilligan's Island* video clips, then they did from their regular teachers.

The result didn't come as any surprise to me.

Recently, I asked Russ Johnson what was his most vivid recollection during those early years on *Gilligan's Island*.

Russ didn't hestitate a minute. He described one morning when he was being made up behind the cyc, which formed the backdrop of the *Gilligan's Island* stage. (Keester Sweeney, the makeup man, had his dressing rooms in that area.) Keester was applying the makeup to Russ's face when Russ looked in the mirror and saw a tiger behind him. A real, live, big tiger! It was some distance away, but it was coming toward Russ and Keester!

Russ knew a tiger was supposed to be on the set that day. In fact, he could hear the trainers calling to the tiger on the other side of the cyc. Somehow, the tiger had wandered off the stage and gotten behind the cyc and was heading toward the makeup table.

Russ said he was never so frightened in his life. There was no leash on the huge animal, and he knew the trainers were on stage near the camera, calling to the tiger.

"Don't be alarmed, Keester," said Russ to the makeup man, "But there's a tiger about 40 feet away, and he's walking right toward us."

"A tiger?" asked Keester, as he turned to look.

"Don't turn. Don't look. Just keep putting my makeup on," said Russ. "Make believe nothing's wrong."

"You mean, there's just a tiger? No trainer? No chain? No nothing?"

"Just a tiger."

By this time, the tiger was only about ten or fifteen feet from the makeup table. (Russ said, "His paws looked as big around as a pizza.")

Russ and Keester were so frightened, they both actually stopped breathing. The tiger continued walking toward them. Then he passed by, brushing so close his whiskers touched Keester's legs. He continued past them, circled the cyc, and went on stage to his trainers.

("I was limp," said Russ, "and Keester was even limper.")

"Are you okay?" Russ asked Keester.

"Yeah, I'm okay," said Keester.

"This experience with the tiger hasn't affected you in any way?"

"No," answered Keester.

Russ pointed to the mirror and said to Keester, "Then how come you put my makeup on in stripes today?"

Keester did a double take as he examined Russ' face. Then he started to laugh as he realized Russ was only kidding.

*

During the twenty-six years after the pilot film of *Gilligan's Island,* the Castaways, except for Jim Backus who battled with Parkinson's disease, were blessed with extraordinarily good health. Even Jim's illness seemed to be arrested in 1984. Then, in 1989, incredibly witty Jim Backus lost the fight, and his inimitable voice was stilled, the voice which had created the persona of Mr. Magoo and Thurston Howell III.

The following year, 1990, generous, warm Alan Hale, the Skipper, sailed away on his final "three-hour tour."

Then, the traditional rule of three, which is such a superstition in show business, took away colorful, elegant Natalie Schafer in 1991. I like to think Mrs. Howell joined Mr. Howell in some grandiose heavenly mansion.

In the space of little more than two years, the world was deprived of three of its favorite entertainers, and I lost three very close friends.

A full-page memoriam appeared in *Variety* and *The Hollywood Reporter* on May 1, 1991.

Gilligan's Island Hits the Airwaves, and Vice Versa

Gilligan's Island is a television series that never should have reached the air this season, or any other season.

> Hal Humphrey
> *Los Angeles Times*

It's difficult for me to believe that *Gilligan's Island* was written, directed and filmed by adults. . . . It marks a new low in the networks' estimate of public intelligence.

> Terence O'Flaherty
> *San Francisco Chronicle*

It's impossible that a more inept, moronic or humorless show has never appeared on the home tube. . . . *Gilligan's Island* are two words I vow never to use again.

> Rick DuBrow
> *United Press International*

Gilligan's Island is quite possibly the most preposterous situation comedy of the season.

> Jack Gould
> *New York Times*

Judging from the opening episode there was some difficulty in seeing how far to make this one joke (?) go as far as one episode. . . . *Gilligan's Island* would appear to have little future if initialer is any indication whatsoever.

> Dave Kaufman
> *Variety*

I couldn't believe *Gilligan's Island* was anything but a bad accident. . . . It's positively the worst new program in a season full of mediocre entrees.

> Cynthia Lawry
> *Oakland Tribune*

Without a doubt, *Gilligan's Island* is the stinkeroo of all time.... I have a feeling the cannibals will get them pretty soon.
> Fred Storm
> *San Francisco News Call Bulletin*

The nonsense that transpires on *Gilligan's Island* may stir up some laughter if you're a child, or unsober, or slightly weak in the head.
> Donald Freeman
> *San Diego Union*

Gilligan's Island can well go down in television history as being the series to most completely waste the talents of one of the biggest casts ever assembled for a half-hour comedy show.
> Arlene Garber
> *Hollywood Citizen News*

Those quotes are from some of the worst critiques that I found in an old scrapbook.

Why would I save them? Who knows? Maybe there's a masochistic tendency in me somewhere — perhaps the same perversity that's present in all people who work in the arts and put their efforts on public display.

I didn't even remember saving those notices. I found them when I was rummaging through my closets for data and information in writing this book.

Actually, *Gilligan's Island* has been the subject of so many derogatory jokes and comments over the years, I myself was brainwashed into believing it had been universally condemned when it first hit the air. Therefore, I was somewhat surprised to find, in that same old scrapbook, the following quotes:

The biggest surprise on C.B.S., which premiered six new shows this week, was *Gilligan's Island* ... a half-hour comedy on Saturdays which has come up with an excellent comedy team in Alan Hale, Jr. and Bob Denver.
> Terry Turner
> *Chicago Daily News*

Gilligan's Island came in smiling with a merry melody, glamour, and drenched with tropical sunshine ... nautical nonsense that promised gags, gals, guffaws.... Even viewers who expected something heavier than breezing entertainment must have stayed with the show from here in.
> Ed Omstead
> *Hollywood Reporter*

Gilligan's Island is a delightful spoof on castaways, and a fun show.
> Alan Rich
> *Valley Times*
> Los Angeles

Gilligan's Island is a series which focuses light heartedly on the problems of an odd band of Fridayless Robinson Crusoes ... [who] land on a desert island. There, with a long supply of wild gags, they face life undaunted. *Gilligan's Island* is cleverly contrived, preposterous and often quite funny.
                                                        CNS
                                                        San Jose Mercury News

The best of the lot appears to be *Gilligan's Island.* . . . The sad thing is that the best shows are hampered by bad time slots. *Gilligan's Island,* for example, will be aired Saturday nights—traditionally a bad time for situation comedies.
                                                        Larry Rummel
                                                        Phoenix Gazette

My dollar says the series should be a winner. It (*Gilligan's Island*) may turn out to be a sort of way-out Robinson Crusoe.
                                                        Eve Starr
                                                        Inside Television

However, I'm not implying there was an even balance between positive reviews and negative reviews. Most of them were dreadful. Jim Backus referred to them as "character assassinations." Many of them rivaled the notices posted by *The Beverly Hillbillies,* a series previously considered by critics the absolute nadir of television programming. As Donald Freeman wrote, "next to *Gilligan's Island, The Beverly Hillbillies* shapes up as advanced Noel Coward."

The week Mr. Freeman wrote this, by the way, *Gilligan's Island* had been on the air for several months and was in third place in the National Nielsen ratings, tied with *The Fugitive.* He was understandably at a loss to account for this. "How do you explain hula hoops?" Mr. Freeman asked.

It's simple, Mr. Freeman. People liked them.

Obviously, I'm not quarreling with a critic's right to state his judgment about whatever he's reviewing, whether a television program, theatrical film, stage play, art show, concert, opera, or ballet. That's what he's paid to do. It's his obligation, in fact, to his paper or magazine. It's also his obligation to the public that reads the review to get an objective opinion.

However, I didn't create, write, and produce a TV show to please critics— or, as you've already read, network executives. I created, wrote, and produced a show to please two judges: myself and the public.

It's a relatively simple task to produce a show that will appeal to a few dozen critics. Their opinions and tastes are pretty obvious and fairly well known. It's a lot more difficult to produce a show that will appeal to 25 or 30

million people of all ages, all backgrounds, all races, all colors, and all creeds.
That's the number of viewers you needed in 1963 every week to have a hit TV
series.

Gilligan's Island quite obviously pleased me, or I would not have gone
through the agonies I've described in getting it on the air. Just as obviously,
Gilligan's Island appealed to the public, or it would not have become such an
immediate success as well as a long-lasting hit. What difference, then, you may
ask, did the opinion of a few critics make?

It made a great difference. Not to me personally. Certainly not to the
ratings. But as the producer, I had to deal on a practical basis with the
devastating fall-out of their reviews: on the cast, on the network, on the sponsors, on the writers, directors, my associates, and even on my friends.

The effects of those first reviews were very far-reaching. *Gilligan's Island*
became the whipping-boy for all of television. Thanks to the critics, it began
to be fashionable to epitomize the worst of TV by using *Gilligan's Island* as
a basis for comparison. Comics used it as the butt of jokes, whether they personally liked the show or not. Knocking *Gilligan's Island* became a popular indoor sport.

Hardly a week went by without a derogatory gag from Johnny Carson, or
some other talk show host. It became the classic name used by comedy writers
searching for ways to insult TV.

Strangely enough, none of these jokes and insults made the slightest dent
in the popularity of *Gilligan's Island*. For all I know, constant repetition of the
name may even have helped.

The only serious damage to *Gilligan's Island* by the defamatory press was
the effect on William Paley. Mr. and Mrs. Paley moved in very high social
circles, with cultured friends in the arts, politics, business and national affairs.
Mr. Paley was very sensitive to critics' reviews of C.B.S. shows, as though it
were criticism of his own taste, which he prided himself on as being impeccable.

I'm told Mr. Paley was simply embarrassed to have "that show" on his network after what the critics said. He was also annoyed by the jibes he took from
his friends at cocktail parties.

As a result, Mr. Paley exempted *Gilligan's Island* from the standard C.B.S. programming policy in those years, that of keeping a hit show in
the same time period season after season. C.B.S. did that with *I Love
Lucy, Gunsmoke, Red Skelton, The Defenders, Ed Sullivan, Andy Griffith*,
etc., etc. Yet *Gilligan's Island*, which climbed into the top ten the first year,
was moved, in its second year, from Saturday at 8:30 p.m. to Thursday, 8:00
p.m.

Again, it climbed back into the top ten, a little more slowly this time as
viewers had to find it. Then once again in the third year, *Gilligan's Island* was
moved—from Thursday at 8:00 p.m., to Monday at 7:30 p.m.

Again, it won its time period, but this time it failed to climb to the top ten of the ratings. However, it accomplished what C.B.S. wanted. *The Monkees,* on N.B.C., on the basis of audience testing and analysis, was supposed to become a major runaway hit. That never happened. It was on at 7:30 on Monday opposite *Gilligan's Island. Gilligan* was the work-horse that provided safe lead-ins for other C.B.S. shows that followed.

I'm convinced that better reviews would have allowed *Gilligan's Island* to remain at 8:30 Saturday, where it had skyrocketed in the ratings. That would have added at least two more years to the life of the show. As it was, a viewer needed a road map to follow the path of *Gilligan's Island* from year to year: different nights, different times.

Yet, it was difficult for me to blame the critics.

The pilot episode, which showed the arrival of the Castaways on the island and established each of their characters, wasn't the first show on the air. I *wanted* it to be first. In addition to establishing concept and characters, it was the film that had sold the series in those extraordinary audience tests.

I reshot the scenes that included Ginger, the Professor, and Mary Ann, because those three roles had been recast. I edited them into the pilot film, which I scheduled as the first episode. Then C.B.S. decided to release another show first — an episode in which they try to escape from the island.

It was wrong, I insisted, to start the series with the Castaways trying to rescue themselves. First, I maintained, the viewers should know who they were and how they got there in the first place. But there was no way I could persuade C.B.S. They simply exercised their "creative control" and aired "Two on a Raft" as the first episode, the episode I had scheduled as second or third. Their final "discussion" with me was very simple: They didn't include me in the meeting when the programming decision was made.

For those interested in knowing what happened to the pilot film, it was the twelfth episode, aired December 19, 1964. It became our Christmas show. I wrote some additional scenes in which the Castaways considered their blessings during the holiday season. After all, they were alive and well; they hadn't been lost at sea; there was still a good chance they'd be rescued. By means of flashbacks, I was able to incorporate about 75 percent of the original pilot film in that Christmas episode.

But how were the critics, and the entire television audience for that matter, supposed to know my scheduling problems? *Are* they supposed to know my problems?

Of course not. They're supposed to tune in to see the show and judge it strictly on the merits of what appears on the tube. That's what I do as a TV viewer. And I, too, would have been puzzled by the first episode of *Gilligan's Island,* if I were part of the television audience.

In the pilot episode of *I Dream of Jeannie,* Larry Hagman, an astronaut, parachutes onto a desert island. He finds an old bottle and when he opens it, out pops the genie, Barbara Eden. In that pilot film, the astronaut's inability

"Two on a Raft" episode, with the Skipper battling the winds, the waves, the sharks, and Gilligan.

to convince his superiors about the genie, and Barbara Eden's antics, were all clearly established as the basis of the series.

The same was true for *My Favorite Martian*. In the pilot episode, the audience saw Ray Walston arriving on Earth in his disabled spacecraft. The pilot film established his connection with Bill Bixby, who became his "nephew," and the ground rules for the series were carefully established.

In another TV series of mine, *The Brady Bunch*, I used the pilot film to set the concept of two separate families becoming one new family. I showed the wedding with the mother and her three daughters, and the father with his three sons. It was aired, very sensibly, as the first episode, and illustrated the type of stories future episodes would deal with.

This logical foundation for a TV series was laid in many other pilot films, both comedy and dramatic. Unfortunately, I was unable to convince C.B.S. to do the same with *Gilligan's Island*. Whether this would have made any difference to the critics and their reviews is something I'll never know.

What disappointed me most about the reviews on *Gilligan's Island* is that none of them noticed the theme of "social microcosm." Admittedly, the philosophic aspects were subliminal, buried in the broad comedy. But they were there. I had hoped somebody somewhere would notice. Nobody did. At least, no reviewer that I recall.

No, that's not quite true. There was one exception: the same Donald Freeman who had ripped into the show in his column in the *San Diego Union*. Mr. Freeman said, "*Gilligan's Island* sensitively probes man's moral and spiritual isolation in satirizing the futility of money and machine in primitive society." He then smugly concludes with, "If you believe that, you're getting pretty soft in the head."

But it's all right there, in the various episodes. I wonder whose head is soft.

Over the years, term papers, essays, and theses at colleges and universities, started to explore the philosophic content in *Gilligan's Island*. In each case, I was amused that the student writing the critique had "discovered" the social microcosm. Each was certain this aspect was accidental. No such philosophic thought, they believed, had ever been intended on the part of the creator.

One of these papers, with the imposing title — "*Gilligan's Island*: A Socio-Political Allegory of Our Time," was written by a student at U.S.C. In his preface, he says, quite explicitly, "While, in all likelihood, producer-creator Sherwood Schwartz never intended *Gilligan's Island* as anything more than an entertaining situation comedy, the program may also be subject to explication in the following more contemplative light."

Mr. Bruskin, who wrote this very serious analysis of the concept and characters of *Gilligan's Island,* was astounded to learn that the use of the phrase "social microcosm" was in the original 1963 presentation. Other authors of similar papers in TV courses in various colleges were equally amazed to learn I knew about the social content in my show, and that the seven characters were carefully chosen after a great deal of thought.

Incidentally, some of those college papers carried *Gilligan's Island* a lot farther than I intended. One thought I was advocating a communistic society as the answer to man's problems. Another thought I was advocating anarchy. Still another suggested the answer was my "egalitarian society." Another felt *Gilligan's Island* demonstrated socialism.

However, any thoughts of "meaning" hidden among the coconut palms and bamboo huts on *Gilligan's Island* were the least of my problems when the show made its debut on television. After the initial reviews appeared, Bob Norvett, head of production at C.B.S. Studio Center, was alerted to ready Stage 2 for dismantling. C.B.S. had a pilot film in preparation; they were going to film on the *Gilligan* stage. Twenty-four hours after *Gilligan's Island* was born, it was already in intensive care.

That's when something interesting happened: The opinion of the critics bumped head-on into the opinion of the public.

Saturday night at 8:30, had been a death trap for one comedy show after another on C.B.S., including *The Phil Silvers Show* the prior year. Nobody could dent *Lawrence Welk* on A.B.C. That show had been a fixture in that time period since 1955. But in 1964, when *Gilligan's Island* appeared on C.B.S., Lawrence Welk failed to win his time period for the first time.

Gilligan's Island followed the very strong *Jackie Gleason Show* on C.B.S. In a matter of weeks, *Gilligan* not only held the entire *Jackie Gleason* lead-in, but added to it, passing Gleason in the ratings. It moved relentlessly higher, heading for the top ten.

The reviewers were just as relentless in their criticism. If anything, they attacked the show more viciously as the ratings rose. The fact that the viewers seemed to love *Gilligan's Island* infuriated them; perhaps they thought the viewers were trying to prove them wrong. The viewers, of course, weren't trying to prove anything. Viewers were simply watching what they liked to watch.

People who want to see a Broadway play have to spend $75 or more for a pair of tickets. If there's dinner involved, and a babysitter, that's $150 for the evening. Those people pay very close attention to what Broadway critics say before they spend that kind of money. As a result, Broadway critics have a life-or-death effect on plays when they open.

Taking your family to the movies is far less expensive. Film critics have, accordingly, less of an effect on the life of a movie. Good press is important, but not crucial to the success of a film.

Television, on the other hand, is free. You can take your whole family to see a television show for nothing. And if you don't like that show, you can press a button and take them all to see another show. And another show. Until you find one you like. Thus, while television critics may have a major effect on nervous network executives, sometimes on sponsors, and sometimes on the personnel of the show itself, their effect on the viewer, except in very rare cases, is minimal.

Perhaps there were more brutal critics of *Gilligan's Island* than Hal Humphrey of the *Los Angeles Times,* but that's the paper I used to read every day. Hardly a week went by without some derogatory comment about *Gilligan's Island*. Even if he wasn't reviewing television shows that day, he would find some way to drag an insult in by the heels, sometimes completely out of context to his topic.

I had never even met Mr. Humphrey and couldn't understand the reason

The official Castaways photo. Thousands upon thousands of these were sent to Gilligan's Island *fans all over the world — who loved the show in spite of the critics.*

for his unceasing assault. It was as though I were only producing the show to torment Hal Humphrey. Finally I decided to invite him to lunch and see if I could find the cause of his severe case of "Gilliganitis."

Mr. Humphrey accepted my invitation, and we had lunch in late December, 1964, at a restaurant called Frascotti, then located on the corner of Sunset Boulevard and Crescent Heights. The day was warm and beautiful. We sat outside on the patio. After a minimum of small talk, I asked him, quite frankly, why he continued to knock *Gilligan's Island*, even when he wasn't actually reviewing it, or anyone in it.

"Because," he answered. "I think *Gilligan's Island* is an absolute waste of the airwaves."

His answer was not surprising. But I was determined to find out why his comments about *Gilligan's Island* were so vicious and so continuous.

"I'll readily admit," I said, "that our first episode on the air must have been a little confusing."

"I don't think 'confusing' is the proper adjective," Mr. Humphrey responded, with a bit of an edge.

"Perhaps not," I said, determined to be as agreeable as possible. "Lately we've done some episodes that were considerably better."

"That's distinctly within the realm of possibility."

It seemed Mr. Humphrey was much the same in person as he was in his column. I ignored the barb. "Did you see 'Wrongway Feldman'?" I asked. "Hans Conried was a long-lost pilot they found on the other side of the island."

"No," he replied. "I didn't see 'Wrongway Feldman'."

"Or 'Home Sweet Hut'?" I inquired. "That was an episode concerning the importance of combined effort: 'United we stand, divided we fall'."

No, he hadn't seen that one either.

"How about 'President Gilligan'? That episode dealt with problems facing a democracy. Or 'The Big Gold Strike'?" Those episodes, in addition to being funny, had a little something to say.

No, Mr. Humphrey hadn't seen those.

"Perhaps I can screen one or two of them at your convenience," I suggested. "Either at our studio, or at your office, if you have screening facilities there."

"No, I don't think that's necessary," replied Mr. Humphrey.

I wondered which episodes had caused those comments in his column. "Can you tell me which episodes offended you so much?"

"The first one was all I needed," said Mr. Humphrey.

I was surprised. Apparently, he had seen only the first episode.

"You mean, all your remarks about *Gilligan's Island* are based on that first episode?"

"Not exactly," admitted Mr. Humphrey. "All I saw was the first five minutes. That was good enough for me."

I could scarcely believe it. This man sitting across from me, calmly having lunch, had seen the first five minutes of a new series. On the basis of that not-even-birds-eye view he was subjecting it to a barrage of continuing insults in his daily column.

Somehow we finished our lunch. Mr. Humphrey thanked me for the invitation and left. He had no desire to see any of the episodes I mentioned. If I read his intentions correctly, he had no thought of ever viewing the show again. Yet I suspected the caustic remarks would continue. They did.

I must admit that critics, as a group, mystify me. They seem to act as though the writer, director, actors, and producer put together their collective talents just for that particular critic's approval. They view things on an intensely personal basis.

This is my favorite caricature drawing of the cast of Gilligan's Island. *It appeared in many TV supplements, including the L.A.* Herald-Examiner, *when the series debuted in 1964.*

Their opinions, therefore, are reflective of a certain person, born in a certain environment, with a certain education, certain predetermined likes and dislikes, and certain genetic traits. Why do they assume they speak for hundreds of other people in a theatre? Or millions of viewers in television-land?

I'm sure critics understand that their columns are written to appeal to as many readers as possible in their publications; not to a few dozen special readers. Otherwise they'd lose their jobs. Why don't they understand that's the identical aim of the shows they criticize?

Obviously, they have a right to their opinion. But that's all it is. An opinion. Why do they become so incensed when the public disagrees? It's as though there's something holy about their opinion, as opposed to the opinions of others.

George Bernard Shaw said, "A drama critic is a man who leaves no tern unstoned." Apparently, Shaw, who had been a drama critic himself, had been stung by a reviewer when he wrote those words.

The fault I find with critics is their failure to take into account the *intent* of the entertainment. If a play is intended for an audience on Broadway, it should be criticized, quite properly, on that basis. A feature film is screened at thousands of movies houses, and aimed at an audience of millions. It should be criticized on that basis.

The aim of television is to please millions of viewers in millions of homes in every part of the country. The aim of an 8:00 series is different from the aim of a 9:00 series, and far different from the aim of a 10:00 series. The target demographics at different hours indicate very different audience mixes. Therefore, it seems to me, the intent of a TV series should be given some consideration by TV critics.

I take some comfort in a poem by Arthur Guiterman:

The Stones that Critics hurl with Harsh Intent
A Man may use to build his Monument.

A Captain Should Go Down
with His Own Ship

"What am I doing here?" asked David Harmon.

"I sent for you," I said.

"Why?" asked David.

"You're a writer, aren't you?"

"Yeah. But I'm not a comedy writer."

"That's your opinion," I replied.

I had never worked with David Harmon before, but I had served with him on the board at the Writers Guild. He was very witty and very quick in those meetings. I knew that David had written many TV shows, but always in the adventure genre—westerns, police stories, etc.

However, I also knew from those shows that David had written the *funny* episodes of those adventure stories. In fact, some of them were hilarious episodes, despite the fact that they were labeled drama.

David didn't consider himself a comedy writer *per se* because he didn't write traditional straight line/punch line jokes. He thought only those writers who wrote situation comedies and variety shows were comedy writers. David himself wrote funny situations, funny ideas, and funny character dialogue, but not formula-type jokes.

David Harmon was a comedy writer, but didn't know it.

"Well, maybe you know something I don't," said David. "I thought my agent made a mistake when he said you wanted to see me about a script for *Gilligan's Island*."

"No mistake," I said. "I think you'd be very good for this show. Unless, of course, you're not interested."

"I don't even know what the show's about," confessed David. "Ruth and I have been out of the country for a month, and we haven't seen any of the new shows. My kids love it. All three of them said it's the funniest new show this season. About a bunch of people stuck on an island."

It's amazing how kids can sum up two years' work in nine words. But that was *Gilligan's Island* all right: a bunch of people stuck on an island.

"Tell me about the show, so I can start thinking," said David.

As I started to describe the show to David, Jack Arnold came into my office. Jack had arrived that morning to start preparation for next week's show, which he was going to direct. I had never met Jack before that day. He was a very good friend of Hunt Stromberg's, but more importantly, as far as I was concerned, he was an excellent director.

Jack Arnold was remarkably flexible. Most directors stay pretty close to one field — comedy, or westerns, or adventure. Jack had directed a certain type of monster picture, *Creature from the Black Lagoon,* that was to spawn a whole new generation of monster films. Yet Jack Arnold also directed *The Mouse That Roared,* with Peter Sellers, a hilarious film that was to bring international comedy acclaim to both Peter Sellers and Jack Arnold.

He had also produced a few TV series, one of them *Mr. Lucky.* While *Mr. Lucky* was an adventure show, it also had a great deal of humor.

When Jack walked in, he and David Harmon both did a double-take.

"Jack!" exclaimed David.

"David!" exclaimed Jack.

Jack and David embraced each other.

"What the hell are you doing here?" asked Jack.

"What do you mean, what am I doing here? What the hell are you doing here?" David responded.

"I'm directing next week's show," said Jack. "I just arrived this morning to start preparing. It's great to see you, luv." (Jack had spent some time in England. He called everybody "luv.")

"You look great, Jack," said David. Then, in answer to Jack's original question: "I'm here because Sherwood thinks I'm a comedy writer."

Finally I broke in. "I gather you two men know each other."

"Slightly," said David.

"David has written some of the funniest scripts I've ever directed. Every time we needed a comedy episode on *Mr. Lucky,* the only writer I would use was David."

"And all these years I thought I was writing drama," David said, with a shrug.

Jack and I both laughed.

Within minutes, it seemed like the three of us had been working together for years. It was that kind of instant rapport.

Jack told me I'd be lucky if I could get David to write scripts for *Gilligan's Island.* David told me I was lucky to have Jack Arnold directing. They were both right. On that day in mid–November — it might have even been my birthday, November 14 — the sun rose twice.

Jack Arnold, after one or two directing assignments, fell in love with *Gilligan's Island,* and it with him. He soon became the semi-permanent director. David Harmon, after writing a few scripts, came aboard *Gilligan's Island* as the script editor. Thanks to these two gentlemen, I was able to take time off to breathe once in a while.

Jack Arnold (third from right), who directed over 30 episodes of Gilligan's Island, *and I (with tie), with the cast on the set of "The Friendly Physician" episode.*

The ratings on the show were wonderful, and getting better every week. The show itself was improving, too, as the Castaways became more and more familiar with their characters and their relationships. This was due in part to their own experience, in part to Jack Arnold, and also in part to better scripts as the writers learned more about the show.

I had a script editor with whom I could communicate. No matter how poorly written a first draft was, a page-by-page meeting with David Harmon would straighten out 90 percent of the problems.

I could finally see a light at the end of the tunnel. Sometimes, they say, the light at the end of the tunnel can turn out to be a train heading in your direction. Although I didn't know it at the time, there were *two* lights heading toward me, one right after the other.

Jack Arnold came to me one day and said, "I'm going to make a phone call, and I want you to be there when I make it." He sounded serious.

"What's it about?" I asked.

"Just listen to my phone call," said Jack. "You'll hear for yourself."

I was curious. I knew machinations went on behind producers' backs. It came with the territory. There was more than a bit of C.I.A. at C.B.S.

The producer always has the same problem. If he concerns himself with things going on behind him, he can't do the job that's in front of him. He has to worry about scripts, dailies, the stage, the schedule, the budget, etc. He can't spend all his time looking in the rearview mirror. As a consequence, he exposes his back to the slings and arrows of outrageous executives.

Jack sought out a quiet, unoccupied office, and I followed. Obviously, it was a conversation he didn't want anyone else to overhear. I must admit I was very intrigued by the mysterious way in which Jack was proceeding with this phone call. He dialed a number.

"Hunt Stromberg, please. This is Jack Arnold."

Jack motioned me to step closer so I would be sure and hear the conversation he was having. He also wanted to be certain I could hear it was Hunt Stromberg to whom he was speaking.

I don't like that sort of thing. It's like listening on an extension. But Jack's insistent manner made it obvious this phone call was being made precisely for my benefit. I moved closer and listened.

I distinctly heard Hunt's voice at the other end. I couldn't hear what Hunt was actually saying, but I heard his voice. And I could hear every word Jack Arnold said.

"Hi, Hunt. This is Jack. I want to say something, and I want to make it as clear as I can. I'm over here directing Sherwood's show. And that's what *Gilligan's Island* is. Sherwood's show.... Yeah ... yeah, I know. But that's why I'm making this call. If Bill Froug steps in to produce this show, I'll never direct another episode. If Sherwood is removed, I'll never direct another episode. It's his show, and I'm working with him. I won't work with anyone else. I'm sick of these meetings with you, and with Bill, and all the rest of the stuff that's going on. You brought me in here to see if I could help, and to tell you what's going on. Well, I'm telling you what's going on. Sherwood knows what he's doing, and Bill Froug hasn't got a clue. I have to get back to the set now. I'm directing."

Jack put the phone down. "I wanted you to hear everything I said. You can't believe what's been going on behind your back with Bill Froug and Hunt. They want to get rid of you and have Bill and me produce *Gilligan's Island*."

Before I could even question Jack further about that shocking conversation, he left for the stage. I remained there, standing near the phone, wondering about all this.

After all, I had created *Gilligan's Island,* sold the show, written it, produced it, salvaged it after it had been rejected, and managed to get it on the air. It was climbing in popularity with every passing week. What was it that I didn't have?

The answer was really quite simple. I didn't have Hunt's ear. I wasn't a company man. I didn't have an office next to his at Mount Olympus. I couldn't stop in three or four times a day and tell him what a lousy job Sherwood was doing on the show. Access. That's what I lacked. Access.

While I was sweating it out with the daily problems and myriad details that form a producer's life, Mr. Froug evidently had plenty of time for these intimate chats with Hunt Stromberg.

Later, Jack Arnold filled me in more completely about those meetings he had been forced to attend at C.B.S. with Hunt and Bill. It was Bill, in particular, said Jack, who was trying to engineer the takeover. Finally, Jack couldn't stand this espionage and talk of overthrow any longer and decided to let it all hang out in front of me. At least I would know the facts, and make my decisions based on them.

This brings up an interesting question, as pertinent today as it was then: How does a major network executive ever learn the truth?

He is never in the daily meetings with the writers of the show, so he has no way of knowing which writer contributed what. He can't tell, personally, how important the script editor or producer is to the writing or rewriting. He is seldom on the stage to see how the producer and director handle the crew or the cast. He is virtually never in an editing room to see the kind of guidance a producer gives the film editor to control the pace and mood of a show.

A major executive in television, or in any other business, is invariably insulated from the activities of his employees who are several steps removed. What he learns is invariably told to him by his own lower-level executives, any or all of whom have their own axes to grind. At the least, it's to their benefit to exaggerate their own importance to the show to which they're assigned. It's natural for them, consciously or unconsciously, to diminish the contribution of the other creative elements.

In the case of *Gilligan's Island*, according to Jack, Bill Froug had come to him with the scheme that he and Jack eliminate me completely, and jointly produce the show—a show which was already high in the ratings, and obviously destined to become a great success.

Recently, Sol Saks told me, "Bill Froug thinks you hate him."

I corrected Sol.

"Sol, you mean Bill Froug thinks I have every reason to hate him. I haven't spoken to Bill since the day he left the show, so he can't know how I feel."

It's a common human practice to attribute to others emotions we ourselves would feel under the same conditions. I believe psychologists refer to this as emotional transference.

"Anyway," repeated Sol, "he thinks you hate him!"

"I don't hate him," I answered. "I don't intend to send him gifts on his birthday, but I don't hate him. I don't even think his actions were deliberately meant against me personally. He was doing what he thought was his job."

Actually, I have a perverse sympathy for people like Bill, executives whose major aim is to please their superiors. They don't necessarily do what they think is right or wrong. They simply do what they believe their boss would like them to do, and think what they believe their boss would like them to think.

This problem exists not only in television, but in any bureaucratic

We had a number of guest stars on the show. Sterling Holloway made an appearance as a prisoner who corresponded with the Castaways from his cell via homing pigeon.

environment. In government, for example, subordinates sometimes commit immoral acts in carrying out orders of their superiors; orders sometimes unspoken, and sometimes unintended. In our own country, administrations have been occasionally toppled by this misplaced loyalty to president rather than to country.

Did Bill Froug do what he thought was right, or what he thought Hunt Stromberg wanted? The reason for his actions made little difference to me in 1964. The thing that counted was the terrible effect it had on my life when I was fighting to preserve my show.

Following Jack's disclosure of the cloak-and-dagger operation, I had only one course of action: I had to phone Hunt and discuss this matter openly. However, before I could call Hunt, the second light at the end of the tunnel ran smack into me. In the nature of a phone call from my agent.

"Hi, Woody."

Only three people called me "Woody," all three from my days in Armed Forces Radio Service: Rosey, my agent; Lester Linsk, another agent; and Lloyd "Skippy" Shearer, a writer who later became the editor of *Parade* magazine.

It was George Rosenberg on the phone. In spite of the fact that Rosey hadn't liked the show and had refused to represent it, he considered himself my friend. I considered myself his friend, too. Differences of opinion shouldn't destroy twenty-year friendships.

"Hi, Rosey."

"Woody, I just took you off the show."

I couldn't believe my ears. Rosey and I had never discussed any such thing. I had broken my back for months now and for the first time things were beginning to run smoothly. Except, of course, for the plot against me I had just learned about.

"What do you mean, you took me off the show?"

"I just called business affairs at C.B.S., and told them I'm taking you off the show. I don't like the way you look. You look like a fucking zombie, and I'm not letting you take any more punishment."

I'm sure the aggravations with United Artists, Jim Aubrey, Hunt Stromberg, Bill Froug, scripts, and the sixteen-hour-a-day, seven-day-a-week work I had been doing for four months must have taken their toll on me physically. Maybe I did look like "a fucking zombie." Nevertheless, taking me off the show was a hell of a big decision for an agent to make without consulting his client.

"Get back on the goddamn phone," I said. "Call C.B.S. Business Affairs and tell them you made a mistake."

"I just called them and took you off. They'll think I'm crazy."

"You are crazy, if you did this without talking to me first. This show is going to be a tremendous hit."

"The way you look, it's not worth it. You're going to have a nervous breakdown."

"I know you think this is for my good, Rosey, but I'm not going to have a nervous breakdown. Maybe I would have without Jack and David, but not now."

"Jack and David who?"

"Jack Arnold and David Harmon, two guys who have really turned things around for me. Just get on the phone and call C.B.S."

"What'll I tell them?"

"Tell them anything you want. You had no right to do this in the first place. Tell *that* to Business Affairs."

Then I had an idea.

"Never mind, Rosey. I'm calling Hunt about something else. I'll cover this with him, too."

"What are you calling Hunt about?" Rosey wanted to know.

"It's too much to explain." Besides, at that moment I wasn't exactly thrilled with my long-time friend and agent, George Rosenberg.

"Sorry, Woody."

"Okay," I said, as I hung up.

But it wasn't okay. Shortly after that, I dismissed Rosey as my agent. But not as my friend. I appreciated his concern about my well-being. As an agent, however, he had acted rashly and precipitously, making a decision like that strictly on his own.

I faced what I knew would be a very difficult conversation with Hunt Stromberg. In fact, I decided to make that phone call from home. I didn't want any interruptions, any emergency calls from the stage, or anything else to disturb this phone call. The conversation with Hunt would be difficult because I hoped that when it was over, we would still be working together.

The first part of my phone call was relatively easy. I clarified that the George Rosenberg call to C.B.S. Business Affairs was made without my authorization, without my knowledge. Then came the hard part.

I discussed the Jack Arnold/Bill Froug situation; the fact that Jack Arnold had told me about Bill's plan to remove me from the series and share producing credit with Jack, a plan that apparently had Hunt's blessing. Hunt didn't deny that.

I reminded Hunt about my past ten years with C.B.S.: *The Skelton Show, My Favorite Martian,* and now *Gilligan's Island.* Three different C.B.S. shows in the top ten. How could that be repaid by this underhanded plot to remove me from my own show?

Hunt admitted I was certainly very important to those three C.B.S. shows. He reminded me, however, that he was the executive "instrumental in instigating and/or furthering these assignments." He insisted he was my "greatest admirer." It was his belief, Hunt said, that I had *asked* to be removed from the show as its producer. That idea must have come either from Rosey or from Bill Froug.

My own complaints to Hunt about producing *Gilligan's Island* concerned interference from his network executives. It was increasingly difficult to fend off attempts to change my concept and characters and get the show on the air every week. What I wanted was relief from interference, not release from my job as producer.

Mildred had been in the room with me while I made that call to Hunt.

"You know something," she said, in some surprise, "you're sweating."

I was unaware. I felt my head. I was sweating, all right. I never sweat. Maybe after two sets of tennis, just a little. Ordinarily, not at all. I guess that phone call was even more difficult than I thought it was.

Or maybe I really was close to a nervous breakdown. Because I did something then that was very uncharacteristic of me. With a promise from

Hunt that the network pressures would cease; with four final scripts ready for shooting; and with preliminary ratings indicating *Gilligan's Island* would become a success, my wife and I left the city. We went to Palm Springs, without leaving an address or phone number.

What straw was it that finally broke this camel's back? It came when, with immediate problems alleviated (if not solved), I finally read my contract with United Artists.

During the making and the selling of the pilot film, I had had little time, and frankly, little interest in the contracts I was signing. I assumed, since they were sent to me by my own agent, they must be okay. There should be a song about that called, "It Ain't Necessarily So."

I had never sold a show before, and as various documents were sent along for my signature, instead of hiring my own attorneys, I simply asked Rosey if everything had been okayed by his attorneys. Rosey always assured me that they had been. It was only later that I discovered that Rosey's answer referred to the legal aspects of those documents *as they applied to Rosey's agency.*

I was unaware then, and many writers are unaware today, that it is in fact illegal for an agent's attorney to read a contract from the standpoint of the client. They read it from the standpoint of the agency. Otherwise, there's a possibility of conflict of interests. This was never explained to me by anybody, and I was shocked when I realized how many ridiculous terms I had agreed to and how many different clauses I had approved.

To give one example: I found that the director, Rod Amateau, was receiving 50 percent more royalty on every episode of *Gilligan's Island* than I. That really staggered me! I had created, written, produced and recut the version of the pilot which sold it. Rod had directed the pilot film, and his version had been rejected. Yet his royalty was 50 percent higher than mine.

I also learned from some of these documents that there was even a dispute over who had created the show. I had registered the presentation, characters, and story outlines with the Writers Guild long before United Artists was involved. In addition, the credits clearly stated on every episode of *Gilligan's Island* every week that it was "created by Sherwood Schwartz." Yet United Artists claimed somehow, in certain clauses, that they had "created" it.

Perhaps this could all be traced back to Rosey's original belief that *Gilligan's Island* was a hopeless idea for a series. Maybe he would have taken better care of my interests if he had any faith in the show.

In any case, I was furious when I learned about some of the small print in agreements and contracts and various documents. I felt I had been raped.

That's when Mildred and I left for Palm Springs. I was incommunicado to any executive at United Artists with whom I had ever had any previous contact. In other words, I would not speak to Dick Dorso, Frank Reel, Norman Glenn, Dixon Dern, Herb Jaffe, etc., etc. I communicated this information to my attorneys. Yes, Virginia, I was now smart enough to engage my own attorneys, the law firm of Schiff, Hirsch, Levine and Schreiber. Specifically, Barry Hirsch. My attitude was, as Paddy Chayefsky was to phrase it many years later, "I'm mad as hell and I'm not going to take it anymore."

This action on my part, coupled with sudden concern over a pilot film which was the only one they finally sold that year as a series, spurred United Artists to action. Through Barry Hirsch, they asked if I would talk to Howard Gottfried, a young attorney who had recently joined United Artists in New York. I said I would, since Mr. Gottfried had not been party to any agreement or discussions re *Gilligan's Island*.

Mr. Gottfried flew to Los Angeles and drove to my incommunicado address in Palm Springs. He understood my anger. He listened to all my complaints, and agreed on behalf of United Artists to make certain concessions in my contract with them. Then I returned to *Gilligan's Island* to produce the show.

Meanwhile, Hunt, true to his word, replaced Bill Froug. Instead, my new C.B.S. liaison executive to *Gilligan's Island* was a gentleman named Stan Kallis.

Stan proved to be just that—a gentleman, a knowledgeable gentleman. He said his aim was to be as helpful as possible in communicating my thoughts and desires to C.B.S., and theirs to me. That was Stan's aim, and he proved to be right on target.

Later, Stan was replaced as C.B.S. liaison by George Cahan, an equally responsive executive. In fact, George was particularly helpful because he was a very good director. Several times he stepped in and solved critical production problems in that capacity.

During that first difficult year, Phil Sharpe stopped by my office late one afternoon. Phil was an old friend of mine. We had written the *I Married Joan* series together. We often spent time talking at the end of a day. Phil was a particularly well-informed man, with a vast knowledge of literature, especially nineteenth-century English authors. I think he could quote everything Samuel Johnson ever wrote.

Phil was producing another first-year show for C.B.S., and had nearby offices in the same building at Studio Center. He was the writer/producer of *The Cara Williams Show*. He had fought the same interminable battles with the network for awhile that I was going through on *Gilligan's Island*—battles of concept and characterizations. Finally he had succumbed to the pressure. He took what he felt was an easier way out. He acceded to one demand after another from the network executives, and also from his star. He made all the changes they requested. It was the only way, he felt, to preserve his sanity, and still get the episodes on the air.

That particular afternoon, Phil came into my office, had a drink, and talked for a few minutes.

"They cancelled my show today," Phil said, with a sigh.

"Sorry, Phil."

There isn't much you can say.

When a show is cancelled, it's not the network's fault, or the star's fault. After all, they made hundreds of wonderful suggestions. It's the producer's fault. He's the one who has caused the show to sink.

Phil raised his glass in a toast, a toast to a bitter lesson he had learned. Then he said something I have often quoted, to those of us who are called upon, whatever our position, to defy authority in order to preserve our own integrity.

"A captain," said Phil, "should go down with his own ship."

24

Send Help Before It's Too Late

November 21, 1964

Dear Castaway:

This Castaway Kit is our way of reminding you that you have a date with Bob Denver, Alan Hale, Jim Backus, Natalie Schafer, Tina Louise, Russell Johnson and Dawn Wells tonight, Saturday, November 21, to attend the *Gilligan's Island* shipwreck party at CBS Studio Center, Stage 2, at 7:00 P.M.

Remember, only *attending* press may participate in our onstage treasure hunt for two round-trip U.T.A. French Airline tickets to Tahiti . . . a chance to get away from it all. If you're the lucky hunter, we vow not to send our press releases after you.

Dress at the party is strictly informal in beachcomber, shipwreck or island style.

See you Saturday.

Best regards,

Jim Hardiman

JWH:gc

That's the letter that went from Jim Hardiman, Director of Press Information for C.B.S., to ladies and gentlemen of the TV press in various cities across the country.

That letter accompanied a "Castaway Kit," a survival package enclosed in burlap, which contained "essentials" for surviving on a desert island: two stale bagels, labeled "Sherwood Schwartz hardtack"; a small bottle of water, dehydrated to save space; a noisemaker (a small transistor radio) to scare natives; some snakebite antidote (a small bottle of Canadian Club); chewing gum; toilet tissue; two sticks to rub together to start a fire; a crude map of Manhattan Island, with the caption "there's no way to get there from here";

some earrings and beads to woo the natives; and a carton of Phillip-Morris cigarettes (*Gilligan's Island* was sponsored by Procter and Gamble and Phillip-Morris).

There was also a pièce de résistance for attending members of the press. They could take part in an onstage treasure hunt for two round trip tickets to Tahiti, on the U.T.A. French Airline.

This "Shipwreck Party," as a previous telegram to members of the press indicated, was to "join us in celebrating our good fortune in the ratings sweepstakes." The ratings on *Gilligan's Island* had moved steadily higher from the opening week. It was in twenty-seventh place in mid–November in days when there were over a hundred shows on the air. It never took a backward step on its way to the top ten. That's something it achieved about a month later.

When the invited press arrived at C.B.S. Studio Center, they were transported to Stage 2 in a "lifeboat," a large whale boat on wheels. The *Gilligan's Island* set, on Stage 2, looked like a tropical island to begin with. We added some extra palm trees and flowers to make it really festive. We also added a large island bar, made from bamboo and palm fronds. Drinks were served in simulated coconut shells. All sorts of delectable Polynesian food had been prepared. Later on, there was entertainment by beautiful Polynesian dancing girls, and dancing to island music.

The two round-trip tickets to Tahiti were hidden onstage. Hints to their whereabouts were supplied by the Castaways themselves: Bob Denver, Alan Hale, Jim Backus, Natalie Schafer, Tina Louise, Russell Johnson, and Dawn Wells. After a quick search of the premises based on those hints, the "treasure" was won by Dick Kleiner, a syndicated Hollywood columnist.

It was really a great party. Jim Hardiman and his staff did a wonderful job. So did Charlie Pomerantz, the public relations representative for Procter and Gamble and Phillip-Morris. Dress was very informal, as were the food and the atmosphere, and everybody had a marvelous time.

Rick DuBrow, United Press International, refused to come to the party when he received his invitation. He wrote, "Could it (the invitation) be a subtle vengeful dig hinting that the power of the pen cannot compete with practical cynicism in judging the mass public taste? Is it good old California hospitality? Frankly, I don't care what it is. Nuts to you, *Gilligan's Island*. I'm going sailing Saturday, out where the wind is cool, fresh and clear."

Mr. DuBrow evidently felt, from this and other remarks, that the party was designed to soften the hearts of the critics and the points on their pens. It was less a celebration of the ratings, he felt, than an unsubtle attempt to influence the critics.

Actually, it was a terrific celebration. And let's hear it for the independence of the American press! Nobody was influenced. Those critics who disliked the show before the party, disliked it just as much after the party. Well, maybe not Dick Kleiner, who won those two round-trip tickets.

As the weeks went by, the ratings continued their climb. Aside from the satisfaction we all enjoyed doing a show which was obviously bringing pleasure and entertainment to so many millions of people, the ratings meant something else. All interference from the network ceased. Whether Mount Olympus still felt I was right or wrong about the characterizations, they let me alone. The audience loved what they saw on C.B.S. at 8:30 on Saturdays.

Some people not only loved it, they *believed* in it—as I was to learn one day when I got an unusual phone call.

"Mr. Schwartz," said my secretary, Edna, on the intercom, "Commander Doyle is on the phone."

"Commander Doyle?"

"Yes. United States Coast Guard," she answered.

I didn't know Commander Doyle of the United States Coast Guard, and I couldn't imagine what he wanted. But I'm very impressed by people like generals and admirals and commanders, considering the fact that I myself spent my Army career as a corporal.

I pressed the lighted button.

"Commander?"

"Mr. Schwartz?"

"Yes."

"This is Commander Doyle, United States Coast Guard."

"What can I do for you, Commander?"

"I understand producers are very busy people, but I wonder if I could have an appointment with you."

"Producers are busy people, Commander, but I'll be happy to meet with an officer in the Coast Guard. Especially since I'm on an island these days."

The Commander chuckled at this. "I guess I could tell you about this on the phone," he said, "But I don't know whether you would believe me. I'd rather show it to you."

I couldn't imagine what the commander was talking about, but I put my secretary on the phone with him, asking her to make an appointment at the first opportunity.

A few days later the commander showed up at my office.

"I must say I was intrigued by your phone call," I said as he sat down in a chair near my desk.

The commander was in uniform. He was in his early forties, and looked very much an officer in the United States Coast Guard.

"Well, like I said on the phone, I didn't think you would believe this unless I showed you."

"Showed me what?"

"These," Commander Doyle replied as he took a batch of envelopes from his pocket and placed them on my desk.

"Telegrams," I said, still wondering.

The Skipper is telling someone about the shipwreck. Unfortunately, the someone turns out to be Gilligan.

"Right. Just read some of 'em."

I read a few. Some were addressed to Hickham Field in Honolulu, some to Vandenberg Air Force Base, and some to other military bases. While the wording varied from one telegram to another, they all said substantially the same thing:

> For several weeks now, we have seen American citizens stranded on some Pacific island. We spend millions in foreign aid. Why not send one U.S. destroyer to rescue those poor people before they starve to death.

These telegrams weren't jokes. They were serious wires from concerned citizens—*adult* citizens.

Lajos Egri, in his classic book *The Art of Dramatic Writing*, refers to the importance of the audience's "willing suspension of disbelief." This was the most extreme case of suspended disbelief I ever heard of. Who did these viewers think was filming the Castaways on that island? There was even a laugh track on the show. Who was laughing at the survivors of the wreck of the S.S. *Minnow?* It boggled my mind.

For those social scientists who don't believe television has an effect on viewers, I offer the foregoing as evidence.

I'm not implying there were thousands or even hundreds of telegrams. There were perhaps fifteen or sixteen. But if some adults, even a few, believed *Gilligan's Island* was real, just think of the effect other shows on television have—shows portrayed with much greater emphasis on reality, shows that deal with violence, sex, drugs, and crime. Those shows have enormous impact on the impressionable. Especially the dramatic shows, where, very often there is explicit detail in the commission of a crime, or the enactment of a rape. What effect does that have on the sort of viewing audience who thought *Gilligan's Island* was being broadcast live?

I've read some surveys that reached the conclusion that TV is actually an outlet for the viewer's violence. The viewer, according to these surveys, realizes that television isn't real, and TV is simply acting out his fantasies for him. The killing he sees on television shows obviously isn't actual killing, because the same actor reappears on other shows.

How does this equate with the killings we see on that same television set on the news programs every night, before and after the "entertainment" killings? The news killings are certainly real. How are some of those psychologically disturbed, or borderline viewers supposed to distinguish the "real" from the "unreal" killings? Or the "real" from the "unreal" crimes? Or the "real" from the "unreal" use of drugs? Or the "real" from the "unreal" rapes? What constitutes fantasy-release? And what acts as a stimulus to a small percentage of viewers?

I've read surveys taken in prison, where over 50 percent of the inmates said they used techniques learned on TV shows in the commission of their crimes: murders, bombings, robberies, etc. They had used the step-by-step preparations they saw on television programs. As far as they're concerned, TV shows are "how-to" shows to demonstrate criminal methodology.

If you want to know how to wire dynamite with the best kind of detonator to make the best type of bomb to suit your purpose, some program is bound to show it. Then you can put it on a video cassette, and run it in slow motion so you'll be sure to get it right.

If you want to know the proper way to "shoot" drugs, or snort coke, or take a real deep drag on grass, you can learn that on television, too. You can also learn about poisons and the best way to administer them. You can find out how to purchase illegal firearms, and the best way to prevent tracing them. If you're interested in raping someone, you'll find out the wonderful odds in in your favor of getting away with it—and what type of defense your attorney should use. You can learn all these things, and more, without leaving your living room.

I'm not advocating censorship to eliminate the problem of reaching the wrong person with the right information. That's contrary to the First Amendment, the right of free speech—a right I fervently agree with.

I *do* believe, however, in some *self-imposed* censorship on the part of writers and producers. It seems to me that's part of the *responsibility* that goes along with the First Amendment. To paraphrase Justice Oliver Wendell Holmes' famous declaration, "Free speech doesn't give you the right to shout fire in a crowded living room."

In the battle for ratings, it's easy to succumb to the temptation of sensationalism. A two-hour TV film titled *I Was a Nude Teenage Prostitute Until I Found Lesbianism Through Drugs* will get a certain number of viewers. But that's bastardizing the medium.

Television shows have a tremendous influence on the viewer. I don't even think that point is debatable. In fact, it's self-contradictory to claim television doesn't influence the viewer. That's the whole purpose of commercial television.

Sponsors spend over two billion dollars annually to influence the viewer with their commercials. That's how they sell their products. The higher the ratings, the better the commercials, the more money the sponsor makes. There's no doubt about the correlation, or the sponsors wouldn't be spending billions of dollars on TV.

It's preposterous to argue that only three commercial minutes out of every thirty have an influence on the viewer; that the other twenty-seven entertainment minutes don't count. People are influenced to some degree by everything they read, everything they hear, and everything they see. Most of all, everything they see on television.

In fact, television *makes* an event a reality to the viewer. They're not convinced about a happening until they see it on TV—whether it's a war, an earthquake, an epidemic, or a two-headed horse. I heard a commentator on radio say one day, after a news bulletin, "I guess you people won't believe that until you see it on television tonight."

The thought of those telegrams Commander Doyle showed me that day has always remained with me. Television is a mass medium. There are over 120,000,000 sets in use. And there are all sorts of people watching—including people who believe exactly what they see. It seems to me a great opportunity for producers to accentuate the positive in those viewers, instead of inspiring the negative.

End of chapter.

End of soapbox speech.

25

Pratfalls and Philosophy

"Can you please tell me Mrs. Howell's maiden name?"

I squinted, blinked my eyes open, and shook my head to try to clear it. It was 6:00 a.m., and I had no idea who was on the phone.

"Who is this?" I asked.

"That's not important," she answered. "I have to know Mrs. Howell's maiden name. There's a trivia contest on a radio station here in Kansas City."

I reminded my caller it was two hours earlier in California than it was in Kansas City. She had awakened me, I pointed out.

"Sorry about that," she said, cheerfully. "But I have a chance to win $100. What was Mrs. Howell's maiden name?"

I asked the caller how she had gotten my number, which is unlisted.

"That's not important," she said, annoyed. "Someone else is going to win that prize if I don't hurry."

"That's too bad," I said, without sympathy. "I don't even know Mrs. Howell's maiden name."

"Aren't you Sherwood Schwartz, the creator, writer, and producer of *Gilligan's Island?*"

"Yes."

"How can you possibly not know the answer to a simple question like that?" she demanded.

"Look, lady, there were a hundred episodes of *Gilligan's Island,* and I did that show a long time ago, and I don't remember everything in every episode. And goodbye."

"Isn't there someplace you could look it up real quick? I haven't got much time."

"Goodbye," I said again, and hung up.

Mildred was staring at me sleepily as I put down the phone. "What was all that about?"

"You'd never believe it," I answered. "Go back to sleep." But has any wife ever gone back to sleep when her curiosity is aroused? I had to explain the whole stupid conversation. Then Mildred went back to sleep.

But me? Could I go back to sleep? Of course not. I could only lie there in bed wondering about Mrs. Howell's maiden name.

Trivia contests on radio are apparently very popular. I had received other trivia phone calls about *Gilligan's Island* from various parts of the country. Also trivia calls about *The Brady Bunch*. In every case there was actually a correct answer to those trivia questions. I was sure there was a correct answer to this question, too. What *was* Mrs. Howell's maiden name?

Finally, curiosity got me out of bed. I went into the den, where I keep bound volumes of radio and TV scripts I've written and/or produced. Feeling like a fool, at 6:30 a.m., I started looking through the *Gilligan's Island* books for Mrs. Howell's maiden name.

It wasn't in the original presentation. It wasn't in the "bible" containing the description of the seven characters either. Yet her maiden name had to be somewhere. I was sure of that.

Feeling more and more foolish, I began to think of various episodes where that name seemed likely to appear. At the same time I was getting angry with myself. What was I going to do with this information when I found it? I couldn't give it to the lady caller from Kansas City. I had hung up on her twenty minutes ago.

Then I suddenly remembered! There was an episode in which the Castaways heard on the radio that the minister who married Mr. and Mrs. Howell didn't have the proper credentials in the state where the wedding took place. As a result, all the marriages he performed there, including Mr. and Mrs. Howell's, were null and void. When Mrs. Howell learned that, she refused to live "in sin" with Mr. Howell, and he had to move out of their hut.

I was sure it was in that episode, "Mr. and Mrs.?" (written by Jack Gross, Jr., and Michael R. Stein), that there was reason to mention her maiden name. I checked the volume containing that script, and there it was! On page 9, scene 11, episode #74, was Mrs. Howell's maiden name!

Wentworth!

"Lovey" was Miss Eunice Wentworth!

That episode was one of many in which I believe I fulfilled my promise to Dr. Frank Stanton to mix a little philosophy with the pratfalls, a little social comment with the slapstick. Most of that particular show was devoted to broad comedy: Mr. Howell being forced out of his own hut, and commandeering Gilligan and the Skipper's hut; attempts by the other Castaways to help Mr. Howell win Lovey's hand again; and the very farcical wedding sequence, on a raft in the middle of the lagoon with the Skipper, as captain, able to perform the ceremony "at sea," and with Gilligan serving as best man.

There were lots of pratfalls. But there was also social comment. About respect for the institution of marriage. Not only by the Howells, but by the other Castaways as well. It was implicit in their attitudes.

There wasn't any obvious preaching about the sanctity of marriage vows. No lecturing or moralizing. But it was, nevertheless, the accepted view on

Nehemiah Persoff, an exiled dictator, takes over Gilligan's Island *and makes Gilligan his puppet ruler in this dream sequence from the "Little Dictator" episode.*

Gilligan's Island that matrimony itself was not to be treated lightly, no matter how broad the comedy that surrounded it.

Other issues in social, moral, ethical, and political fields were treated in similar fashion; underneath all the whipped cream and icing, there was usually something solid to chew on.

The subject of democracy as a form of government was addressed in five or six different episodes. One of them, "Gilligan Goes Gung Ho" (written by Bruce Howard), illustrated the abuse of power in a democracy when the person in command is unaware of the responsibilities of office. In this case it was Gilligan who was put in charge while the Skipper was gone for the day.

Gilligan almost wrecked the entire community because he didn't know how to interpret or administer the "official rules" he was given. He became completely dictatorial as he exercised the power of office.

A more complicated story about democracy was the subject of "The Little Dictator" (an episode written by Bob Rodgers and Sid Mandel). Nehemiah Persoff was the guest star who played "The Little Dictator."

Mr. Persoff was the dictator of a Central American country whose regime had been overthrown. Instead of executing him, a compassionate firing squad decides to dump him on a small uninhabited island where he can live out his days by himself. The island turns out to be "Gilligan's Island." The ex-dictator quickly learns it's not uninhabited—there are seven Castaways.

The former dictator knows only one form of government: dictatorship. Thanks to his revolver, he quickly changes the administration of the island from democracy to tyranny. In order to win their democracy back, the Castaways have to stage a revolution to overthrow the dictator.

There was plenty of slapstick in this episode, including a very imaginative dream sequence in which Gilligan sees himself as a puppet ruler. In the dream Gilligan is an actual puppet and Persoff, the dictator, the puppeteer who pulls the strings and manipulates Gilligan to do his bidding. But in spite of all the physical comedy and fun, the serious theme was quite evident: Sometimes you have to fight for democracy in order to preserve it.

In the blend of pratfall and philosophy I like to use, the theme of irony was a frequent visitor to *Gilligan's Island*. It was the basis for at least eight of the episodes. One of these, "X Marks the Spot" (which I wrote with my brother Elroy), was a supreme case of irony.

In this episode, the Castaways become very excited about the possibility of rescue when planes fly overhead, obviously checking out their island. They are convinced someone has discovered their presence on the island, and without doubt, a rescue party will soon be dispatched to save them.

There is great joy on the island until they hear, on their radio, that the Pacific Command has been searching for a small uninhabited island to test the explosive power of a new missile. It gradually dawns on them that their island has been chosen to be wiped off the face of the earth! The very plane they thought was targetting them for rescue actually makes them a target for destruction!

This really dramatic story was told in broad slapstick style. In fact, when the missile lands on the island, it fails to detonate immediately, and Gilligan rides it like a bucking bronco, hoping to head it off the island and into the sea. That comedy sequence was about as farcical as you can get—yet the story and theme of the show were actually very dramatic.

Similar irony is experienced by Thurston Howell III in the episode entitled "The Big Gold Strike." Mr. Howell would like nothing better than to be rescued. He also would like nothing better than to leave the island with a large cache of gold they have discovered. So he tries to do both: he hides the gold on the raft they have built to escape the island. The weight of Mr. Howell's gold sinks the raft, preventing it from sailing on the only perfect tide that would have taken them into the shipping lanes. Thus Mr. Howell and the other Castaways discover that not only can you not take it with you, it can even prevent you from going.

Episodes titled "Angel on the Island," "Three to Get Ready," and "The Pigeon," among others, all tackled themes dealing with the ironies of life. As in all the episodes of *Gilligan's Island,* these stories were told in broadly comic terms, with their serious comment well below the surface. Children, of course, saw only the fun. Others, who believe in the advice "seek and ye shall find," did manage to detect substance beneath the froth. We received many letters from adult viewers recognizing this point.

Personally, I've always been fascinated by the problems of human communication. Misunderstandings between people, as well as misunderstandings between nations, may turn innocent remarks into insults, and gestures of friendship may be interpreted as acts of war.

A case in point is "Music Hath Charms" (written by my brother Al Schwartz and Howard Harris). In this episode, Gilligan learns to play a crude drum, fashioned of island materials. This inspires Mrs. Howell to cultural activity, forming an island "symphony orchestra" with the Castaways playing various percussion instruments made of coconuts, hollow logs and bamboo.

As they rehearse these island instruments, the sound of their "symphony orchestra" drifts to a nearby island, where natives interpret the "hostile" sounds as a threat of war. In order to prevent an attack upon themselves, the natives decide to attack the island where, they think, preparations are underway to start a war with them.

Many wars are started with just such misunderstandings. And they often result in adopting "first-strike" measures.

"Two on a Raft" (written by Fred Freeman and Larry Cohen), the first episode of *Gilligan's Island* to air, used this same basic theme. So did "Where There's a Will" and "Smile, You're on Mars Camera."

Other important philosophic themes appeared in episodes of *Gilligan's Island.* "Home Sweet Hut" (written by Bill Davenport and Charles Tannen) illustrated the importance of "united we stand, divided we fall." "St. Gilligan and the Dragon" (written by Arnold and Lois Peyser) may well have been a landmark show: Airing in 1964, it dealt with the female Castaway's right to have an equal voice with the men. Male and female opinions were equally important.

The episodes I've noted were not the only ones that dealt with some substantive thought. They are simply illustrations of the kinds of social statements scattered through many of the episodes of *Gilligan's Island.*

Thanks to its very concept, "Gilligan's Island" used stories that were a complete departure from usual situation comedy. There were no episodes about "the boss coming home to dinner," or a "problem with the new neighbors," or "who dented the fender," or "the family vacation," or "the bad report card." *Gilligan's Island* had no cars, no stores, no schools, no phones. It was like no show the audience, or the critics, had met before. That may be the reason it delighted the viewers, and nonplussed the critics.

A few years ago, at a cocktail party, I met a professor of the University of Southern California. He teaches TV courses to students majoring in television. The professor told me he always devotes part of one lecture to me and to *Gilligan's Island*. He considers it, he said, the most imaginative series in television. He told me that in the years to come, it will be looked upon as the equivalent of *Alice in Wonderland* to the television generation.

Even though it was a cocktail party, he seemed quite sober when he said that.

I must confess I was quite flattered.

"Whatever Happened to *Gunsmoke?*"

"Congratulations, Sherwood. *Gilligan* has been renewed for next season."

"That's good news, Mike."

"Just make sure those seven Castaways are funny for another year."

"Okay. I'll keep doing it till I get it right."

Mike chuckled.

Mike Dann was the new President of Programming at C.B.S. There had been a purge of top-level executives by William Paley and Frank Stanton in early January, 1965. In one dramatic weekend, Jim Aubrey was removed from office, along with Hunt Stromberg.

There were all sorts of rumors at that time about the reasons for the sudden shake-up in the high command. However, I have no personal knowledge of the truth of any of those allegations, so it would be pointless to repeat any of that "information" here. Besides, it had little to do with the future of *Gilligan's Island*.

The net result of this purge was a new hierarchy at C.B.S., with Jack Schneider, Tom Dawson, and John Reynolds in top positions, and Mike Dann the new head of programming. On the West Coast, Bob Lewine was replaced, and Perry Lafferty became Vice President C.B.S. Television City, an office that now included development as well as current programs. This initiated a top-level management that was more reasonable to deal with, and eliminated much of the pressure and chaos of the previous administration.

There was an enormous difference between Mike Dann and Jim Aubrey in just about every way. Physically, the two men were quite different. Jim was tall and lean; Mike was shorter and stockier. Their personalities were just as opposite. Jim always appeared to be negative and acerbic, ready to impugn whatever was under discussion. Jim used what is sometimes referred to as "positive negativism." In contrast, Mike was cheerful, optimistic, and interested, always ready with encouragement and support. Jim was cool, even cold, in his relationships with other executives, producers, and performers, even major stars like Jack Benny and Danny Thomas. Mike was much warmer with the people with whom he worked.

No matter how serious a meeting might be, Mike would always keep things in perspective by injecting a friendly remark, or telling the latest joke he had heard. He took his job seriously, but not himself. His attitude clearly indicated we were in the entertainment industry, not in an operating room where the patient's life was at stake.

As a simple example of this: One day in 1965 Mike was visiting C.B.S. Studio Center, where *Gilligan's Island* was being filmed, along with other C.B.S. series. He stopped for a few minutes at various stages and producers' offices to say hello to his "C.B.S. people" and exchange a few words on a personal basis. This sort of friendly social call would have been completely out of character for his predecessor.

When Mike dropped by my office, I was out, either in a meeting somewhere or in an editing room. Mike strolled into my office, grabbed a pencil and scribbled a note to me. A copy of his note is on the next page. I've included it only to give an insight into the man. He hadn't read a script. It was just his way of saying "Hello. Sorry I missed you." Again, this sort of pleasant byplay would have been unthinkable coming from Jim Aubrey.

At any rate, it didn't come as a great surprise when Mike phoned to tell me *Gilligan's Island* was being renewed for a fourth year. During the three previous years, we had been moved from one night to another, and one time period to another, and we had always beaten our opposition in the ratings. Just as important to the network, since we were always an early prime time series, we had always delivered an excellent lead-in to the show that followed.

After the phone call from Mike, the first thing I did was call the cast. They were elated by the news. I took my Castaways to a celebration lunch, and we all looked forward to another exciting year of filming.

I had already presented new ideas for the fourth season to C.B.S. — Perry Lafferty on the West Coast, and Mike Dann, John Reynolds, and Tom Dawson. They were enthusiastic about my proposals for more frequent use of guest stars. I had also suggested, if the ratings started to fall, to rescue the Castaways, and turn "Gilligan's Island" into a hotel complex, using Thurston Howell III's millions to finance the venture.

I shared these ideas with the cast. They were delighted with them, and even happier at the prospect of another season at higher salaries. Two of them even bought new homes. Dawn Wells and Russ Johnson each purchased lovely houses in the San Fernando Valley, Dawn in Tarzana, and Russ in Studio City.

Then something odd happened—or rather, *didn't* happen. It didn't seem odd for several weeks; then I began to wonder. Mike Dann had phoned to tell me *Gilligan's Island* was on the 1967 fall schedule. But I hadn't gotten confirmation from C.B.S. Business Affairs. That's what actually makes a renewal official.

I knew there was always some delay in notification from Business Affairs. Many legal papers had to be signed. Sometimes new arrangements were negotiated between network and production company. In addition, Business from the desk of:

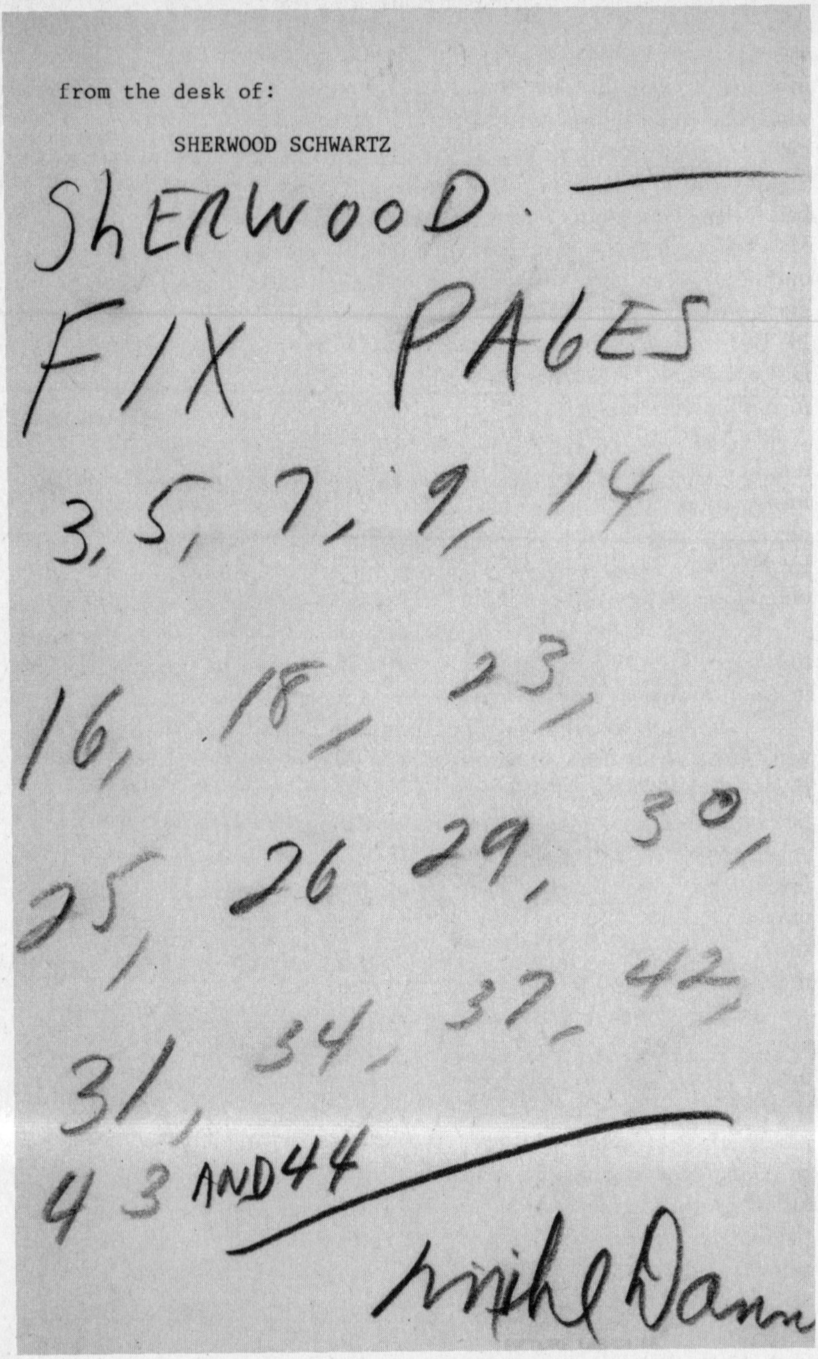

SHERWOOD SCHWARTZ

SHERWOOD.

FIX PAGES

3, 5, 7, 9, 14

16, 18, 23,

25, 26 29, 30,

31, 34, 37, 42,

4 3 AND 44

Mike Dann

Mike Dann's "friendly hello."

Affairs liked to wait until the last possible moment for practical reasons. There was always the possibility of a major star in a series becoming seriously ill, or involved in a scandal of some kind. Unexpected developments occurred sometimes to change the network's mind about renewal. I understood all these factors—but when the delay persisted, I became a little uneasy.

Then I got a strange phone call from Jim Backus in New York. Jim was back East appearing in a television special emanating from a theatre in Manhattan. While he was in New York, Jim had a meeting with Perry Lafferty, one of his very closest friends. Mr. Lafferty, Vice President West Coast Programming, was in New York for the final program schedule meetings for the 1967 season, with Mike Dann, John Reynolds, Jack Schneider, and Tom Dawson. Perry congratulated Jim on *Gilligan's Island*'s renewal for the following year.

That same day, Jim had lunch with Earl Wilson, the entertainment columnist for the *New York Post*. Earl Wilson was a friend of Jim's, and more importantly, his column was perhaps the most influential one in show business. Jim had the rare opportunity of giving Earl a really last-minute exclusive. He told Earl that Perry Lafferty had just confirmed that *Gilligan's Island* was officially renewed in the final scheduling meeting of the year.

It was a good lunch for both of them. Jim was in wonderful spirits thanks to the renewal of his show, and Earl had a hot-off-the-press story for his column. So far so good.

Then came the strange part of the call. That evening, Jim said, he met with Perry Lafferty again, and Perry told him that the show was suddenly off the fall schedule. Perry said he was still very busy in meetings at C.B.S., but he wanted to correct the information he had given Jim that morning.

Jim was very upset for two reasons. First, obviously, was the loss of his favorite character, Thurston Howell III. Secondly, he had given incorrect hot-off-the-press news to his friend, Earl Wilson. He called Earl to try to stop the story, but it was too late. His column had already gone to press. His friend Earl might not be his friend any more.

Jim's call to me was to ask what I knew about this latest development—and I knew nothing. I had received no further word from C.B.S. after the original call from Mike Dann telling me we were renewed for another year.

I never found anyone at C.B.S. who would tell me exactly what happened. I have had to put the story together from bits and pieces. Some of these pieces came from Mike Dann, some from Perry Lafferty. Some came from two other sources, who even at this late date, refuse to tell me the entire story. Apparently, no one wants to take the blame, personally, for making the suggestion that knocked *Gilligan's Island* off the air, when it had every reason to be renewed.

As near as I can determine, this is what happened: First, *Gilligan's Island*, as both Mike Dann and Perry Lafferty had stated, was actually in the final 1967 schedule put together by the program staff.

Gilligan's Island *often featured dream sequences. In this dream, Gilligan was a bullfighter—the first fight in which the bull was the favorite.*

For many years, in February and March, Mr. and Mrs. William Paley vacationed in the Bahamas, where Mr. Paley maintains a magnificent estate on Lightford Key. It was the ritual, in those years for Mr. Paley, in the Bahamas, to be given the final program schedule for the coming season for his approval. Obviously, Mr. Paley was in continuing contact with his program executives, but the official schedule was always submitted to him this way.

In 1966, *Gunsmoke,* after a long, illustrious television career, was no longer blazing the trail. At one time it had been number one in the ratings for four consecutive years, but it had fallen from the top twenty-five in 1966. Even worse, its demographics indicated it had one of the oldest viewing audiences of any show in television, a negative sign for advertisers.

Another dream sequence, the Skipper's favorite dream: a harem filled with Mary Anns.

For these reasons, the final schedule for 1967, sent to Mr. Paley on Lightford Key, did not include *Gunsmoke*. It was, at long last, dropped from the C.B.S. schedule.

Mr. Paley was furious. *Gunsmoke* was his favorite show of all time. Not only in television, but even on C.B.S. radio. It was also Mrs. Paley's favorite show.

Mr. Paley called Mike Dann in New York demanding to know, "Whatever happened to *Gunsmoke?*" He told Mike the proposed schedule was absolutely unacceptable without *Gunsmoke*. Somehow they would have to juggle the schedule and make room for *Gunsmoke* for the 1967 season.

Mike Dann and his program associates, including Perry Lafferty, went back into emergency session to find some way to insert *Gunsmoke* back into the lineup. Somebody in that meeting—and nobody will tell me who—came up with the following solution to their dilemma: Why not try to find a new audience for *Gunsmoke*? Instead of the senior citizen viewers at 10 p.m. Saturday, maybe an early evening hour would attract youngsters?

Somebody in the meeting then pointed out the fact that the C.B.S. affiliates had shown great resistance to buying a show called *Doc* at 8:00 on Monday. It was a new half-hour situation comedy scheduled to follow *Gilligan's Island* airing at 7:30. Both the program department and the sales

Gilligan's Island's remarkable history in prime time TV, chronicled in an ad which appeared in the Hollywood trade papers in 1966.

department could please the affiliates by dropping *Doc*, and also please Mr. and Mrs. Paley by scheduling *Gunsmoke* on Monday.

The only thing that stood in the way was *Gilligan's Island*. There would be room for the hour-long *Gunsmoke* if *Gilligan* were cancelled along with *Doc* and *Gunsmoke* scheduled at 7:30. They knew this wouldn't bother

Mr. Paley. *Gilligan's Island* had been out of favor with him ever since the critics had castigated the Castaways.

As the program department anticipated, eliminating *Gilligan's Island* and *Doc* in favor of *Gunsmoke* delighted Mr. Paley. As far as I know, that was the only change Mr. Paley requested in the fall schedule that year. In a sense, *Gilligan's Island* was an innocent bystander in the shoot-out at the C.B.S. corral with Marshall Dillon.

Actually, the move was a brilliant one from the standpoint of *Gunsmoke*, as well as C.B.S. The early hour did indeed give *Gunsmoke* an entirely new viewing audience. In 1967, it leaped back into fourth place in the National Nielsens and stayed in the top ten for the next five years.

From the standpoint of *Gilligan's Island*, however, that fateful question from Mr. Paley—"Whatever happened to *Gunsmoke*?"—stranded our Castaways on that tiny desert isle forever.

No, not quite forever. Because of what happened some years later.

Big Julie Rolls the Dice

"Don't you think I should be getting some money by now?" I asked my attorney, Barry Hirsch, in 1971.

"Let's look into it," said Barry.

In 1971, *Gilligan's Island* had been out of prime-time television since the 1967 season. The series had immediately moved into syndication, where it was stripped five times per week. TV channels in every city, big and small, were clamoring to show it, and more than three dozen countries overseas were beaming *Gilligan's Island* to their viewers in a wide assortment of dubbed languages. It was quickly evident that *Gilligan's Island* was destined to become an enormous hit in syndication. Maybe even more popular than it had been in prime time.

In spite of the extraordinary success of the series in worldwide syndication, the word "profit" had never crept into any communication from United Artists. Because they provided the deficit financing, they owned the actual negative, and they were the distributors of the series in syndication.

Since I was the producer of the series, and very familiar with the budget on every episode, I knew there was very little deficit financing involved in filming *Gilligan's Island*. It seemed to me after four years of constant reruns, domestic and foreign, that the series should have turned the financial corner and gone into profit. This was naturally important to me because I was a profit participant, along with C.B.S., Phil Silvers, and John Rich.

When we "looked into it," as Barry Hirsch suggested, I bumped heads with the hard reality of what has become known in the entertainment world as "creative bookkeeping."

Remember the classic crap game in *Guys and Dolls,* the marvelous Broadway musical? That crap game, the big climactic scene, takes place in the sewer below Broadway. "Nathan Detroit" and his floating crap game have been floating from place to place to evade the police. They try to hold the game everywhere, including the back room of the "Save-A-Soul Mission." Even there, the police are hot on their trail. Finally, ingenious Nathan Detroit comes up with the idea of going down. Going way down. Into the sewer.

One of the key participants in this vitally important crap game is "Big Julie" from Chicago. He has arrived in town with a big bankroll. When it's Big

Julie's turn to roll the dice, it's easy to see why he always wins. In the first place, Big Julie insists on using his own dice. In the second place, his own dice are blank. No dots. Big Julie has had them removed, but he tells the other gamblers he knows exactly where the dots used to be.

Big Julie is a big guy, and he's got a suspiciously big bulge inside his left-hand jacket pocket. Nathan Detroit, Harry the Horse and the others are too afraid to object. Better to lose your money than your life.

When Big Julie rolls out his blank dice, he announces that his point is 10, a 6 and 4. He distinctly remembers the dots. Everyone in the sewer knows he's going to make his point. And he does. After a few rolls, Big Julie announces another 6 and 4. Then he quickly rolls a 7, and an 11. It's not unlike shearing a flock of sheep. Their wool is gone before they can say "baaa."

What has "Big Julie" got to do with *Gilligan's Island?* Plenty. In the entertainment field, the major film producers are very much like "Big Julies." It doesn't matter whether it's Universal, or Paramount, or Warner Bros. or Fox, or, in the case of *Gilligan's Island,* United Artists.

Very often, the star, and/or the producer, and/or the creator, and sometimes the director of a TV series has a profit position. In the event that series becomes a hit and goes into profit, the crap game starts. "Big Julie," the studio, rolls the dice. That's only fair. Because it's the major studios who supply the deficit financing to make the series in the first place. So far so good.

The problem arises, just as it did for the crap players in *Guys and Dolls,* when the profit participants see the dice. They're blank. Only the studio remembers where the dots used to be. In fact, they have staffs of accountants and attorneys and an entire business affairs department whose major purpose is to remember exactly where the dots on the dice used to be.

On a regular basis, usually annually or semiannually, the studio announces to the other participants in the game the result of all the rolls of those blank dice. The other players have to accept the accounting from the studios, or challenge them to show proof for every roll of the dice.

At some film studios the accountants are more creative than the writers and the producers. Hence, the industry-wide use of the term "creative bookkeeping." Some of the expenses may be simply figments of imagination on the part of someone in business affairs or accounting, trying to score Brownie points with management.

If you accept the facts and figures as provided by the studio, you simply wait for the day when "Big Julie" announces that you're "in profit." That day may never arrive. Or when it does arrive, your great-great-grandchildren may benefit.

On the other hand, if you want to challenge the statements from the studio, it becomes very expensive. You have to hire special accountants to audit the company's books. I use the word "special" because very few accounting firms are equipped to examine facts and figures involving hundreds of television channels in the United States, plus all the foreign channels in every country where the series has been syndicated.

If you had to invent a name for an accounting firm that specialized in that kind of audit, a firm with the wisdom of Solomon and the ability to put their finger on any suspicious-looking number, could you come up with a better name than "Solomon and Finger"? Well, that's the name of the best-known accounting firm in the field of entertainment audits, Solomon and Finger. And that's the firm I used.

Naturally, you need attorneys, too. How else can you legally obtain the information the accounting firm needs? In order to gain access to the books *behind* "the books," attorneys have to file a complaint, and proceed to discovery, with depositions, interrogatories, and even longer words, for which they charge you by the syllable. The Freedom of Information Act doesn't apply to film studios. Extracting information from them is like pulling teeth from a sabre-toothed tiger. And with every yank the cost continues to rise.

Auditing fees and legal fees multiply faster than rabbits. You can bet your bottom dollar — and that's the one you finally spend — that the studio can afford a long, drawn-out legal action better than you can. Their legal defense against your action doesn't cost anything. Their accounting personnel and attorneys are part of the company. They're the big bulge in "Big Julie's" left-hand jacket pocket.

Then what if the unthinkable happens? What if the audit reveals the studio's statements have been absolutely and completely accurate? If that happens it would undoubtedly find its way into the *Guinness Book of Records*. But what if? Then all your money and time and effort would be for naught.

It's that "what if" that discourages lawsuits by profit participants. There's no assurance you can prove your case. And that's the reason there are relatively few audits, and even fewer lawsuits. As time goes on and expenses mount, most legal actions that are started dissolve into grumblings, mutterings, and ulcers.

Fortunately, I had created another successful TV series, *The Brady Bunch*. My earnings in that second hit series provided the funds to carry on my audit and legal battle on *Gilligan's Island*.

In 1974, after four aggravating, time consuming, expensive years, the case of *Gilligan* versus creative bookkeeping was settled without going to trial. Attorneys for both sides reached a settlement which was satisfactory to United Artists and to me.

This experience led me to the formation of Schwartz's Rule, which states that every creator/writer/producer needs two hits: the second one to provide the money for the lawsuit on the first one.

28

Gilligan Gets Animated

"Why don't you tell me your problems?" suggested Lou.

No, Lou was not my psychiatrist. In spite of the wear and tear on my psyche in my chaotic adventures in producing *Gilligan's Island,* I had somehow managed to get along without benefit of couch counseling.

Lou was Lou Scheimer, one of two partners who owned Filmation Associates. Filmation is one of the largest producers of Saturday morning animated shows on television. The other partner in Filmation Associates, since retired, was Norm Prescott. The three of us, Lou, Norm, and I, were meeting in 1971 in their large office at Filmation Associates, on the corner of White Oak and Sherman Way in Canoga Park.

Lou and Norm were a rare partnership, absolutely equal in every way. Even the video logo on all their shows insured this equality, with the names Scheimer and Prescott rotating in a circle so that neither one was first and neither one was second. Office space couldn't be differentiated either, because they both shared the same office. Their desks looked identical, too. I didn't actually count them, but they even seemed to have the same number of pencils in their pencil holders.

Physically, however, Lou and Norm are far from identical. It would be hard to find someone identical to Lou Scheimer outside of the National Football League. Lou's about 6' 5", with weight to match. Norm is taller than average, but you can never tell that until Lou leaves the room.

Lou and Norm had called me several times about doing an animated version of *Gilligan's Island* for Saturday morning television. I was reluctant, and after several phone calls I decided to meet with them and explain.

It was easy to understand Lou and Norm's enthusiasm for the project. Because of the tremendous appeal the *Gilligan's Island* prime-time series held for youngsters, they were convinced it would be relatively easy to sell an animated series based on my seven Castaways. I agreed with them. I thought it would be an easy sale, also. But I had two reservations. That's what the meeting was all about.

The first reason was purely creative. I have always been in awe of the special world of imagination possessed by children. All of us, except for an occasional Lewis Carroll or Doctor Seuss, seem to lose that facility for fantasy as

GILLIGAN'S PLANET

Opposite: *Cartoon cast of* The New Adventures of Gilligan, *the animated series by Filmation Associates.* Above: *When the Cartoon Castaways finally managed to get off the island, they were shipwrecked again, this time on a faraway planet. Thanks to Gilligan, of course.*

we grow older. If animation could capture that unique imaginative quality of a child's world, I thought that would justify a Saturday morning version of *Gilligan's Island*. It would have to be creatively different from the original film series. In my view, it would be pointless to take the same locale, the same characters, and the same stories, and simply animate them in order to sell another show.

I had seen a number of Saturday morning animated series derived from successful film series which were simply cartoon versions of the films. I didn't feel they were a contribution to the creative process in television. Since *Gilligan's Island* was quite imaginative to begin with, that meant an animated version would have to be that much more inventive.

Although I respected both Lou Scheimer and Norm Prescott, I told them I would be uncomfortable unless I could be closely connected with the project. I wanted a hands-on supervisory capacity with the stories, scripts, and even the drawing boards in any *Gilligan's Island* animated series. Lou and Norm both assured me that they understood my creative problems, and they said they would welcome my participation. The more the better.

My second reason really had nothing to do with Lou or Norm, or animation *per se*. It was based on the phenomenal success of the film series in syndication. I was convinced there was a good chance the original series might be reactivated in some form in prime time. In fact, I had two different ideas for prime-time series based on *Gilligan's Island*. And I was quite sure I could reassemble the same cast. The question that continued to plague me was, "Would a Saturday morning animated series kill my chances to sell a new film series based on *Gilligan's Island?*"

Obviously, Lou and Norm couldn't help me with this problem. They understood why it might cause reluctance on my part. But this was a decision that I, and I alone, would have to make. I decided against it.

In 1972, Lou and Norm and I discussed it again, and I decided against it. In 1973, I decided against it for the third time.

By 1974, I began to doubt that I could sell a new *Gilligan's Island* series in prime time. In fact, in 1974 I tried to sell a two-hour TV film called *Rescue from Gilligan's Island*, with no success. Two of the networks, N.B.C. and A.B.C., said they weren't interested. The third, C.B.S., said it was *"absolutely not interested."*

Meanwhile, the original series, after eight years in syndication, was breaking all sorts of records in reruns. To insure that performance, I began to think an animated version on Saturday morning might be good promotion and publicity to maintain continuing interest in the syndicated series.

I told Lou and Norm at Filmation about my new decision on an animated *Gilligan's Island* series. They were delighted. And they sold *The New Adventures of Gilligan* to A.B.C. for the 1974/75 season.

As they had promised, Lou and Norm made sure there were plenty of inventive ideas in every episode. The animated films became a creative wellspring for all sorts of interesting creatures and natural phenomena. In addition, we made certain that each episode contained some worthwhile moral for youngsters.

In 1982, I developed another animated series called *Gilligan's Planet*, based largely on Lou Scheimer's idea. In this series, the Professor on *Gilligan's Island* manages to reconstruct a spacecraft that had been aborted by N.A.S.A. and had landed on their island. All the Castaways crowd into it, expecting to contact N.A.S.A. and return to civilization. Unfortunately, the spacecraft goes back into space and lands on an uninhabited tiny planet far removed from Earth. The Castaways are still cast away, but instead of an island somewhere in the Pacific, they are cast away on a little planet somewhere in space.

Is there a possibility of another animated series? Like *Twenty Thousand Leagues Under "Gilligan's Island"*?

As Mr. Howell would say, "Heavens to Jules Verne, why not?"

A Funny Thing Happened on the
Way to the Men's Room

"Do you know the question I'm asked most frequently?" asked Betty Lou Peterson.

In 1973, when Betty Lou Peterson phoned me from Detroit, she was the editor of the Question and Answer column of the TV Sunday Supplement in the *Detroit Free Press.* As far as I know, she still is the editor of that column.

I was sure I knew the answer to Ms. Peterson's question back in 1973, but I asked her anyway. "What question are you asked most frequently?"

"'Whatever happened to those Castaways on *Gilligan's Island*?' I get that question once or twice every week."

"I'm not exactly surprised," I confessed. "For the past few years I've had calls from TV editors in Jacksonville, Boston, Salt Lake City, and a number of other places telling me the same thing. Then they always ask me, 'Why do people keep asking that question'?"

"I guess I'm standing in the same line," said Ms. Peterson with a smile in her voice. "That's what I want to know, too."

"I can't tell you for sure. But I can give you my opinion."

"Okay. I'm sure you have the best opinion there is on that subject. What is it?"

"Well," I answered, *"Gilligan's Island* has been repeated in syndication so often, many people have seen the same episodes over and over. They begin to believe they might have missed the episode when the Castaways were rescued. Then they begin to wonder if there was such an episode. Then they write a letter to the TV editor of their paper asking whatever happened to those Castaways."

"What *did* happen, Mr. Schwartz?"

I told Ms. Peterson what I told the other TV editors who called me: that there was no rescue episode because I was sure there would be another season of *Gilligan's Island.* If I had known we were going to be off the schedule in 1967, I might very well have produced a final episode in which they were rescued.

There was no point in going into detail with Ms. Peterson, or the other

211

editors, about *Gunsmoke* and Mr. Paley's demand that Jim Arness ride again. The simple fact was that no rescue episode was ever written or produced.

After that phone call from Ms. Peterson at the *Detroit Free Press* I began to think about all those letters to all those TV editors asking the same question: "Whatever happened to those Castaways on *Gilligan's Island?*" If that many people were interested enough to make that the number one question, I thought, maybe viewers would like to see a two-hour TV film that answered that question.

At that time in TV history, reunion shows, as they later came to be called, were unknown. Nobody had done a TV reunion movie of an old TV series, as far as I knew. I don't think anyone had even tried. But the more I thought about that idea, the better I liked it.

I typed a five-page outline for a two-hour TV film movie, *Rescue from Gilligan's Island.* I had meetings at C.B.S., N.B.C., and A.B.C. about this project. N.B.C. said, "No." A.B.C. said, "No." C.B.S. said, *"Absolutely not!"*

Heartened by this enthusiastic response, I presented the same outline to the same three networks in 1975. N.B.C. said, "No." A.B.C. said, "No." C.B.S. said, *"Absolutely* not!"

Meanwhile, I was still getting phone calls from TV editors.

Fortunately, there's a constant turnover in executive personnel, so there are almost always new faces at the networks. Why not try those new faces? I went to N.B.C. I went to A.B.C. I went to C.B.S. N.B.C. said, "No." A.B.C. said, "No." C.B.S. said, *"Absolutely* not!"

Then I remembered a story from my childhood: "The Little Engine That Could." About the little engine and the way it was struggling up the hill, trying desperately to make the grade. The little engine said, "I think I can, I think I can, I think I can, I think I can." And finally it made it! By sheer persistence it finally climbed up to the top of that hill.

I remembered that charming little story from my childhood and I said to myself: *that charming little story is a bunch of bull!* Sometimes the Little Engine just can't get over the hill!

So I put away that outline of *Rescue from Gilligan's Island,* and worked on other projects.

One of the projects was a variety show called *Uptown,* which I developed and wrote with my son, Lloyd, with whom I frequently write and produce. We developed the concept in 1977. Mike Rollens, an agent at I.C.M. (International Creative Management), had been an executive at N.B.C. at the time and was very interested in *Uptown* when he was at the network. However, he had met with high-ranking opposition to *any* variety show, because variety formats had been notoriously unsuccessful for several years. *Uptown* was a concept variety show, very different from anything that had been done, but it was a "variety" show and Mike couldn't get it off the ground at N.B.C.

This is the Skipper's hat with which he used to hit Gilligan. When the series ended in 1967, Alan Hale had his hat bronzed and gave it to me as a gift. It's one of my most treasured mementos, but may soon be contributed to the Smithsonian Institution.

In 1978, Mike left N.B.C. and became an agent at I.C.M. He still loved the concept of *Uptown* and wanted to represent it as an agent.

All of this background leads up to the most important word in show business: timing. It's more important than talent. It's more important than writing. It's more important than performance, ability, hard work, or connections. It's more important than anything.

You don't believe me? Follow me through the stages by which *Rescue from Gilligan's Island* was finally sold as a two-hour TV special; a special that achieved a 52 share in the National Nielsens and also was the highest-rated entertainment program the first week it was aired, in October 1978. It remains one of the highest-rated TV films of all time.

Step number one in this extraordinary example of timing was a casual decision on my part to break a habit of long standing. It has always been my practice to send scripts by messenger to studios, to stars, to agents, etc. I somehow feel it adds a little more significance to the project than sending it by mail. And I never deliver scripts personally. Whatever the reason, whether it's ego or affectation, or some other unconscious or subconscious motivation, I simply never deliver scripts myself.

That day, March 8, 1978, I picked up the copies of the variety show *Up-town* from Alert, a printing company on 3rd Street that always did my scripts, and headed home in my car. On the way to my house, I had to pass I.C.M. on Beverly Boulevard. As I approached the building that houses that huge talent agency, I said to myself, it's really foolish to go home with the scripts and then call a messenger to bring them back to I.C.M. In fact, it was late afternoon. I might not even get a messenger until the following day, and Mike Rollens wanted this revision as soon as possible. I decided to break with custom and hand-deliver the scripts to Mike at I.C.M.

I didn't have an appointment with Mike, so I wasn't surprised when I didn't find him in his office. I did find several secretaries in an outer office who apparently serviced various executives in the wing of the building where I found Mike's office.

"Is one of you Mike Rollens' secretary?" I asked the ladies.

"I am," replied a perky young woman. "I'm Dodie Drake."

"Hi. I'm Sherwood Schwartz. Is Mike in?"

"No, He's away at a meeting. Was he expecting you?"

"No. I promised him these scripts today. May I leave them with you?"

"Sure. I'll see that he gets them."

"Thank you."

I put the scripts on Dodie's desk, and turned to leave.

"By the way, are you the Sherwood Schwartz who created *Gilligan's Island?*"

"Yes. Did you watch that when you were a little girl?"

Dodie beamed at my slicing ten years off her age.

"Thanks. I watched it when I was a teenager." Then she added, "Do you mind if I ask you a question?"

"Not at all."

"Whatever happened to the Castaways? Did I miss an episode when they were rescued?"

I smiled at the inevitablity of that question. "No, you didn't miss an episode. We never did a show where they were rescued. As a matter of fact, for years I've been trying to sell a two-hour film called *Rescue from Gilligan's Island.*

"I think that's a wonderful idea," Dodie said.

"It's too bad you're not running a network, Dodie. I think *Rescue from Gilligan's Island* could get a 50 share."

"Maybe more," said a voice behind me.

I turned to see who was speaking. I saw a man in his early forties, dressed in a dark suit with a conservative tie. He looked like an executive, and that's exactly what he was.

"I'm Bob Broder," he said. "Are you Sherwood Schwartz?"

"Good guess," I answered.

"Not much of a guess, judging from the last part of that conversation."

Then Bob added, "I'm serious. I really think a two-hour special rescuing those Castaways will get better than a 50 share."

"Well, that makes three of us, Dodie, you and me," I said.

Dodie broke in to introduce us. "Mr. Schwartz, Mr. Broder is in charge of packaging for I.C.M."

"I'd like to represent that property, if it's available," said Bob.

"It's available," I said, "But it's only fair to tell you I've been trying to sell it for four years."

"I'd like to try," Bob said. "Who do you work with here?"

"Mike Rollens," I answered.

"Would you like him to handle this?"

"Fine."

"Good. I'll talk to him and he'll be in touch. Now I have to go. I was on my way down the hall to the men's room when I overheard your conversation. And I really have to go now or—"

"For God's sakes, go! Before you float away."

Bob Broder hastened down the hallway to the men's room. I said goodbye to Dodie, left I.C.M., got in my car and went home.

The next morning, March 9, I got a phone call from Mike Rollens. "What's all this about a two-hour film called *Rescue from Gilligan's Island?*"

I explained to Mike how I had met Bob Broder at I.C.M.

"Bob's really excited about this project," said Mike. "We ought to get together as soon as possible."

A few hours later I was back at I.C.M. in Mike's office. I showed Mike my outline of *Rescue from Gilligan's Island*. Mike was just as enthusiastic about the idea as Bob Broder had been.

As a matter of fact, prior to our meeting, Mike had made some phone calls. He learned that Aaron Cohen, the executive in charge of TV specials for N.B.C., was in town. He was setting up a series of meetings with producers on Monday, March 13. Mr. Cohen was leaving the following day to return to New York, where he had his offices. For Mr. Cohen's convenience, the meetings were being held in his room at the Beverly Hills Hotel. Obviously, Mr. Cohen's schedule was pretty tight, but Mike was able to squeeze a meeting in for us at 11:15 a.m. that Monday.

Paul Klein was the head of programming for N.B.C. at that time, although Fred Silverman was due to leave A.B.C. and join N.B.C. in June. Nobody believed Fred Silverman and Paul Klein would work together because two chiefs can't sit in one chair. But at that moment in history it was still Paul Klein's schedule. If Aaron Cohen liked the idea, and submitted it to Paul Klein, Mike felt we had a good chance because N.B.C. needed product.

I met Mike Rollens in the lobby of the Beverly Hills Hotel at 11:00 Monday. We chatted about the project for a few minutes. Then we met with Aaron

Cohen on a little balcony outside his room. It was a beautiful day, and we sat around a small table on the patio in the warm California sun.

Mike thanked Aaron Cohen for having this meeting on such short notice.

With this preliminary over, I spoke about the idea for a two-hour *Rescue from Gilligan's Island.* Because of executive changes at N.B.C. during the past few years, I had never before discussed *Rescue from Gilligan's Island* with either Aaron Cohen or Paul Klein.

I outlined the basic story to Aaron; how the hurricane hits *Gilligan's Island;* how it washes the huts out to sea; how this disaster turns out to be a blessing in disguise; how they're spotted by the Coast Guard. The second half of the "rescue" show would deal with adventures of all the Castaways upon their return to their former lives before they took that cruise on the *Minnow.*

Aaron Cohen listened attentively to the outline, interrupting a few times with questions. He seemed genuinely interested, but without any overt enthusiasm. However, it was clear from his attitude that he was sufficiently intrigued that he would discuss the project with Paul Klein. Mike and I left the meeting feeling we had made a good, well-received presentation.

After some meetings, there's such excitement you know the project is about to take off. There are other meetings where there's so little interest you know it's due for a crash landing. Then there are others which seem noncommittal. I tend to be conservative after meetings. I felt the meeting with Aaron Cohen was in the third category, non-committal.

I was wrong. It was committal. Very committal. On March 16, at 3 p.m., three days after my meeting with Aaron Cohen at the Beverly Hills Hotel, I had a phone call from Paul Klein advising me that we "had a deal"; a two-hour film for N.B.C., *Rescue from Gilligan's Island.* In fact, since Paul, too, suspected it would get an extremely high rating, he wanted it to kick off the N.B.C. season, in September or October.

After four years of trying to sell *Rescue from Gilligan's Island,* I was in the right place at the right time. Because Lloyd and I wrote a project called *Uptown;* because I decided to deliver the scripts myself; because Mike Rollens wasn't in his office; because Dodie Drake asked me "Whatever happened to those Castaways on *Gilligan's Island;* because Bob Broder had to go to the men's room; because Mike Rollens arranged that last-minute meeting with Aaron Cohen; and because Paul Klein needed two-hour shows for the N.B.C. schedule. All those pieces had to fit into the puzzle in the right order to sell *Rescue from Gilligan's Island.* It was all timing.

On October 17, 1978, when ratings were announced for that week, I sent a telegram to Bob Broder:

THANKS TO YOUR KIDNEYS, "RESCUE FROM GILLIGAN'S IS-
LAND" GOT THAT 50 SHARE, AND MORE.

30

Rescued After Fifteen Years

"That sounds wonderful," Bart Farber said, when I called New York to tell him the news about *Rescue from Gilligan's Island*.

Bart Farber was Vice President of Television for United Artists. I phoned him after Paul Klein called me to confirm the N.B.C. decision to make a deal for the two-hour film based on my outline.

As a result of my 1974 settlement of my lawsuit with United Artists, United Artists, Gladasya Productions (Phil Silvers' company), and I had agreed to share, in certain proportions, any shows derived from the *Gilligan's Island* series. In fact, the animated series *The New Adventures of Gilligan* with Filmation had been based on the formula devised in that settlement. When I phoned Bart to tell him about the pending deal with N.B.C., I also informed him that attorneys for I.C.M. and my own attorneys were in the process of negotiating a license fee with N.B.C.

Bart said he would be out on the West Coast in a week or two and we could discuss United Artists' participation at that time. He was concerned about the N.B.C. license fee, vis-à-vis the budget. There was no proposed budget at that point, because there was no script. Any budget would have to be based on the five-page outline, the roughest of estimates. Executives at major studios are reluctant to work with guesstimates instead of budgets.

Perhaps I should take a moment to state the difference between a license fee and a budget. The license fee is the amount the network pays the producer to "license" his product for one or two showings of his film on their network. The budget is the amount of money the project actually costs. If the license fee is higher than the budget, the producer has a profit — rare. If the budget is higher than the license fee, the producer has a deficit — common.

You might ask, why would anyone produce something at a guaranteed loss? If there's a deficit, why bother? There are two main reasons.

In the first place, the loss may be temporary. Future runs in syndication may wipe out that deficit and put the producer into profit. That's the carrot on the end of the stick that makes the donkey keep moving. Sometimes right off the cliff. Many millions of dollars have been lost in the mistaken belief that syndication will prove to be the bonanza that will turn those deficits into dollars.

Obviously, that result does occur occasionally. That's the reason people take risks. But I once read, and I have no reason to doubt it, that your odds at winning in the casinos in Las Vegas are better than your odds when you make a pilot for a new TV show. Or, in this case, of making money, aside from a salary, in producing a two-hour TV film.

The second reason writer/producers will make a film they believe will lose money can be summed up in one word: passion. Persons who are deeply involved creatively with a project get carried away by enthusiasm, love, and dedication. The "business" people with whom they deal approach the same project from a realistic, dispassionate, dollars-and-cents viewpoint.

Ideas motivate the creative community; profits motivate the investment community. Of course, as with all generalities, there are exceptions on both sides of this rule. Sometimes profits motivate the creative community, and sometimes ideas motivate the investment community. Just remember, if exceptions occurred most of the time, *they* would be the rule.

Actually, it's a logical system of checks and balances. If creative people were allowed to proceed without any reins on their fiscal responsibility, projects would collapse financially. On the other hand, without the inspiration and originality of the inventive people, projects would fail creatively.

That's what makes the entertainment industry so interesting. Commerce and creativity are not only strange bedfellows, there's a constant struggle for the best position on the mattress.

I was certain United Artists would join me in *Rescue from Gilligan's Island* and undertake the deficit financing, just as they had done in the series. After all, *Gilligan's Island* not only wiped out the series deficit in syndication, it had become one of the most profitable ventures in United Artists' history. Besides, a two-hour *Gilligan's Island* special, with all the network promotion and publicity, would surely benefit the syndicated series. I considered United Artists' participation a certainty.

Rescue from Gilligan's Island was by far the most complicated TV project I had ever attempted. There were more than a dozen locations required, at such diverse places as a ranch, a dry dock, a college, a marina, a mansion; with production problems involving tugboats, helicopters, and hundreds of extras. It was a far cry from my usual three or four sets on a stage or two at a Hollywood lot, with seven or eight people in the cast. That's the norm for a writer/producer of half-hour situation comedies.

With all those production problems facing me, I had to start pre-production on the project at once. I had promised a September delivery of the film to N.B.C.

I would co-write the script and be the executive producer. My son, Lloyd, would be the producer. We had worked together for ten years by this time on many projects, and he had proven himself a very talented writer and producer. Then I hired Val Taylor as my associate producer. Val had considerable experience in physical production and accounting. Frawley Becker was highly recommended as location manager by many of my associates. Stan Jolley's reputation as production designer was impeccable in the industry.

Frawley and Stan started work at once based on the outline. Waiting for the script would have delayed them several weeks.

At the same time, I brought in the three writers who had done the most work on the original *Gilligan's Island* series to write the script with me: David Harmon, who had written several episodes and was the script editor for almost two years; my brother Elroy, who had written many episodes and was the script editor during the third year of the series; and my brother Al, who had written many of the episodes.

Obviously, a director had to be set as soon as possible to work with Stan Jolley and Frawley Becker, as well as with the writers.

Leslie Martinson had never directed a *Gilligan's Island* episode, but he had directed a number of episodes of *The Brady Bunch* for me. Of equal importance, he had directed many shows with difficult production problems like *Mission: Impossible* and *Swiss Family Robinson*. In addition, he had directed several theatrical motion pictures, among them *Batman* and *P.T. 109*. *Batman*, of course, was broad adventure comedy, and *P.T. 109*, the story of John F. Kennedy's experience in World War II, required many ocean sequences.

All in all, Les Martinson seemed like an ideal choice for *Rescue from Gilligan's Island*. Fortunately, he was available, and soon he was hard at work in preproduction with Lloyd, Stan, Frawley, Val and me.

While I was involved in all this physical preparation, I was also writing the script with David, Elroy, and Al.

Legal pre-production was also underway. Attorneys and business affairs were trying to hammer out their negotiations and arrive at a license fee. Meanwhile, Val Taylor was preparing a budget based on the information that was gradually being accumulated.

About this time, Bart Farber arrived from New York. At that point, the license fee being discussed for *Rescue* was one million dollars, a little below average for two-hour TV shows in 1978. The best estimate on the budget was $1,200,000. Mr. Farber wasn't thrilled at the idea of a $200,000 deficit on behalf of United Artists. He didn't say no, but on the other hand, he didn't say yes. He promised to talk it over with his management in New York.

It was my hope that the network would raise the license fee. It was also my hope that we could lower the budget. During the next few weeks my first hope was realized: The license fee was increased to $1,100,000. However, the budget went from $1,200,000 to $1,300,000, leaving the same $200,000 deficit. Still, I was confident United Artists would participate. I was wrong.

On Mr. Farber's next visit to the West Coast he told me it was foolish for United Artists to undertake a deficit of that size. Particularly because there was no assurance the deficit might not increase. Most budgets don't contract; they expand.

Looking at it strictly as a business venture, United Artists was right. No

Two Castaways pictures taken fifteen years apart, with Judy Baldwin as Ginger in the lower photo in place of Tina Louise.

matter who undertook the deficit, United Artists and Gladasya would still be paid a rights fee as the result of our 1974 agreement, and they would also participate in any eventual profits. So why undertake the risk of deficit? It made no financial sense, from their view.

This decision on the part of United Artists left me between the proverbial rock and a hard place. I could either risk the deficit financing myself, or I could drop the project, losing the monies I had already invested. With script costs and pre-production costs, that amounted to well over two hundred thousand dollars.

If I stopped now, that large sum of money would simply be a dead loss. At least, if I produced the film, there was a chance to recoup that money if

I could control the budget. And maybe, just maybe, I could raise the network license fee.

I decided two things. First, I would continue the project. Second, I would explain my predicament to the network and throw myself on the mercy of N.B.C. That was like throwing myself at the mercy of Attila the Hun.

Let me tell you the N.B.C. response: The network said they didn't ask for all those production values. They didn't ask me to film the hurricane and the Castaways' huts floating in from the ocean. They didn't ask for helicopters, and the Coast Guard and all those locations. As far as they were concerned, they could get a good rating if those seven Castaways discussed all those unseen adventures while sitting around their huts.

If you're smart, they told me, you can make this two-hour film for $800,000 and put $300,000 in your own pocket.

I was furious. What a disappointment this would be to the millions of people who would tune in to see *Rescue from Gilligan's Island* after fifteen years! They would watch some pleasant dialogue among the Castaways instead of an exciting film in which the Castaways are actually rescued in a dramatic adventure. What a cheat that would be! What a misrepresentation the title itself would become! Under no conditions would I try to turn *Rescue from Gilligan's Island* into a drawing-room comedy!

This film needed big production, big scenes, big action, big physical gags, and—now—a big bank loan. Or, at least a promise of one if it became necessary.

Fortunately, I have a good relationship with Phil Freeman, Jr., a senior vice president at my bank. He is aware of my continuing profit participation in two highly successful syndicated series. They are very tangible assets and make me a good risk. On several occasions he and his bank have been very helpful to me. This was one of them.

Against everybody's better judgment, including my own, I decided to go ahead with *Rescue from Gilligan's Island* as a personal venture. I knew the $200,000 deficit would escalate. However, I also knew the syndication rights to the two-hour film would be worth quite a bit because the *Gilligan* series was known worldwide. I doubted that there would ever be a profit, but I wanted to protect the money I had already spent in pre-production. And I believed *Rescue from Gilligan's Island* would add a little more fuel to the syndication fires on the original series.

Besides, I could provide an answer to all those TV viewers with all those questions to all those TV editors in all those cities.

Thus began my first brisk walk across the quicksand of deficit financing. I had no studio overhead to claim. I couldn't charge a distribution fee because I had no distribution to offer. I had no heads of departments to amortize. Etc. There was no place for me to perform creative bookkeeping, even if I were so inclined. My deficit was to be very real. And would get bigger and bigger, like a snowball rolling downhill.

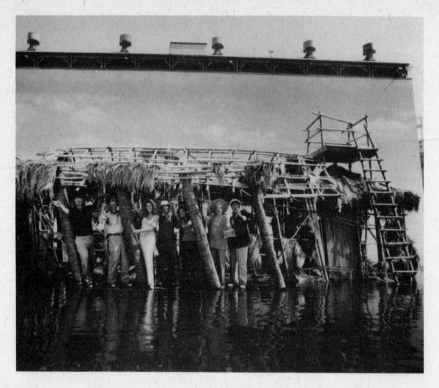

Hollywood make-believe magic: part of Rescue from Gilligan's Island *was filmed in a flooded parking lot, with a blue sky backing to complete the illusion the huts were far out at sea. (Photo by Jimmy McHugh.)*

As far as the casting was concerned, the only stipulation I made to N.B.C. was that I would provide a minimum of six of the seven original Castaways. I refused to guarantee all seven. As I've already mentioned, ever since the original series had stopped production, Tina Louise had complained about the detrimental effect playing "Ginger" had upon her career.

Negotiating with the rest of the cast wasn't easy either. Each of the Castaways knew I was trying to assemble the original group, and quite naturally they wanted to be well paid for their services. I couldn't blame them for that, but I was faced, personally, with a swelling budget and a ballooning deficit. Eventually, however, Bob Denver, Alan Hale, Jim Backus, Natalie Schafer, Russ Johnson, and Dawn Wells all signed contracts.

Tina was even more of a problem than I anticipated. That's because she *wasn't* as adamant as I thought she would be. First, she said she might do it after all. Then she changed her mind and refused to play Ginger under any conditions. Then she changed her mind again. And again. And again.

Finally, she said she would agree to do Ginger if I made her an offer that she couldn't refuse. The Godfather sum she mentioned was one-tenth of the budget of the entire show. It was far more than any of the other performers were being paid.

It was out of the question. I would have to renegotiate all the other deals if I gave Tina what she asked for. I would have been left with seven Castaways and no money to do the show.

By the time Tina made that decision it was around July 1. The first day of shooting was to be July 10. Under normal casting conditions, it would take two or three weeks to arrive at a decision for an important role like Ginger. We had five actual working days to get our new Ginger ready for wardrobe.

During those few days, we were fortunate: Millie Gussie, our casting director, found Judy Baldwin, a beautiful, tall, redhead who had ample proportions where Tina Louise had ample proportions. Judy became Ginger for *Rescue from Gilligan's Island,* and our Castaways were now complete.

On Saturday, July 8, I had lunch with Bob Primes, our director of photography, and we went over to Paramount to look at a parking lot exterior area. This area was located in front of a high sky "cyc." The cyc was to be the sky backing for a sequence in which we would flood the parking lot. Then we planned to float the Castaways' huts to make it appear they were far out at sea.

It was an important sequence in the film and would require a lot of coverage. Bob Primes was a rather young cinematographer with whom I had never worked before. He had been highly recommended, but I felt I should spend some time discussing this particular sequence in the film with him.

Bob and I walked around the lot searching for proper angles to get the most value out of certain scenes. In a situation like this the camera angles are limited because you're constantly in danger of shooting off the "set" and destroying the illusion that the huts are floating at sea.

There was a cement wall circling the parking lot. This wall would hold the water when we flooded the area. In attempting to get a certain look from a certain angle, I leaped up onto the top of the cement wall, a ledge about six inches wide. I wanted to stand there, so I turned my right foot as I landed. I heard a funny noise. In my right knee.

An hour later, I was telling the story to my orthopaedist, Dr. Harvard Ellman, in Century City. A half hour after that, my right leg was in a cast. Torn cartilage.

July 10, the first day of shooting, Mildred drove me to the studio. I was in the back, my right leg in the cast, stretched across the back seat. I also had a cane.

Mike Sheppard, our transportation captain, took one look and said, "Thanks, Mrs. Schwartz, but that's our job from now on."

Mike assigned a permanent driver to me. Over my objections, I must admit. Mike said he'd been through this with other producers who had been incapacitated in one way or another. He found from experience that producers become frustrated and miserable if they can't be close to the shooting. The

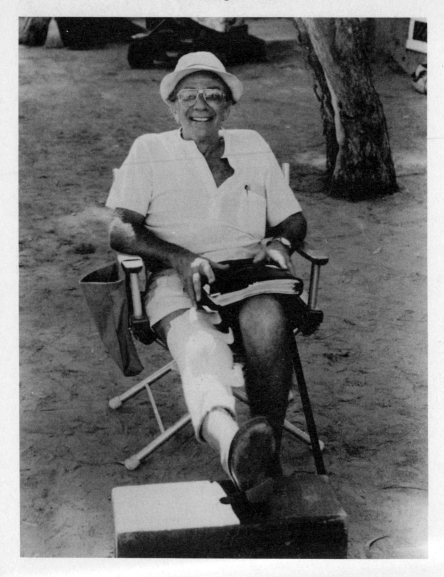

The producer (that's me), torn cartilage and all, keeping an eye on the filming of Rescue from Gilligan's Island.

only solution is a car at their disposal. He also insisted that the driver be the prettiest, youngest, brightest, female Teamster he could locate. That, he said, would also help keep my spirits up.

Mike was right on all counts. Having a car nearby to move me from place to place as the scenes were shot was wonderful. I remained part of the team, part of the action, making whatever helpful suggestions I could. And Claudia, my driver, was pretty, cheerful, gentle, and sympathetic. I didn't know they had Teamsters like her. She almost made me glad I tore my cartilage.

Getting my right leg in a cast just before we started shooting wasn't exactly an auspicious start. But that's the only serious problem that occurred during filming.

There were the usual difficulties that always occur. Mostly unexpected delays. For instance, in the "shark" sequence at Marina del Rey, divers were supposed to swim under the surface holding "shark fins" above the water. However, the waves beyond the breakers were too rough for the divers to control the fins. As a result, we lost a lot of time and finally filmed part of that sequence in the tank at Paramount.

There was filming on a dock involving Gilligan and some foreign spies. A barrel was supposed to roll down a ramp toward the spies. We tried it time after time with several matching barrels. None of them would roll straight down the ramp. They kept rolling off to one side or another. We were delayed over four hours shooting a relatively simple scene that should have taken twenty minutes.

In the ticker tape parade for the Castaways, which we filmed at Paramount, it was an overcast day. In order to make it cheery and sunny, we started the sequence using big bright arcs. The overcast got worse and worse. The arcs got bigger and brighter. In close shots, the actors almost melted. Hours were lost while we relit the same scene with banks of small merc lights, which achieved the same results without blistering the actors.

I could enumerate a multitude of these "normal" problems. But they happen to every film company, even on stages, where there's much better control. For the most part, filming *Rescue from Gilligan's Island* was really smooth. Much of the credit for that goes to my son Lloyd. With my right leg in a cast I was simply not as mobile as I usually am during shooting.

Lloyd was in constant touch with director Les Martinson, in constant touch with the actors, in constant touch with Val Taylor, in constant touch with Frawley Becker, and in constant touch with me. He seemed to be in all places at all times, and that's what held the whole production together.

Among things I will never forget is the day we shot at the marina. That was the sequence in which the Castaways, in their huts, were being towed into the harbor.

Coast Guard helicopters were flying overhead. Fire boats' hoses were spraying water high in the air, giving the Castaways a real heroes' welcome. Tugboats towing the huts into the harbor were blowing their horns. Extras we had hired as spectators along the marina were waving and cheering as the Castaways approached.

Hundreds, perhaps thousands, of the tourists who visit Marina del Rey daily to shop at the many stores and have lunch at the many restaurants were attracted by all the tumult and cheering and action. They came running to see what was happening. Then they joined the extras and began cheering and

The welcoming ticker tape parade in Rescue from Gilligan's Island. *Top:* Gilligan tries desperately to spell his name for some autograph seekers. *Bottom: "How vulgar! Throwing streamers instead of money!"*

yelling themselves. Somehow the tourists thought it was a real welcome for the Castaways who were actually being rescued.

It was another example of the reality power of television. People who had been watching these actors on television for years were cheering their "rescue" from that fictitious desert isle.

And if you want the ultimate suspension of disbelief, three of the Castaways started to cry. They confessed to me later that the crowds and the brass-band welcome made *them* believe they were actually being rescued. As the bands played and the people cheered, the Castaways climbed up the gangplank from their huts with tears in their eyes, overcome with real emotion. At that moment, a TV show had become reality not only to the people who were watching, but to the actors themselves.

I believe we captured those feelings on film. Some day, when *Rescue from Gilligan's Island* reruns again, look for that marina rescue sequence. You will see for yourself the reaction of the crowd and the reaction of the Castaways. They were all involved. They believed it.

Other than my torn cartilage, the only truly worrisome problem in shooting *Rescue* was the budget, which swelled even more than my knee. Maybe United Artists was right. But I don't think so—because of what happened on October 14, 1978.

On that night, Saturday, 9 p.m. on N.B.C., *Rescue from Gilligan's Island* got a 52 share with a rating of 30.2 on the National Nielsens. That remains one of the highest ratings of all time for a TV movie.

Unfortunately, Fred Silverman, who was then head of programming for N.B.C., had insisted that the two-hour film, originally scheduled from 8 to 10 p.m., be cut into two separate hours and shown on consecutive Saturdays, from 9 to 10. And the second hour of *Rescue from Gilligan's Island* didn't get as high a rating as the first hour. Indeed, many viewers, we learned later, thought it was a repeat of the previous week's show since it had the same title.

In any event, *Love Boat* on A.B.C. lost first place position for the first time in its TV history to a show on another network; not once, but twice in a row to the two separate hours of *Rescue from Gilligan's Island*.

In my opinion, if *Rescue* had been broadcast as originally planned, from 8 to 10, Saturday, October 14, it would have had over a 60 share, and would have ranked third or fourth as the highest-rated TV movie of all time.

Incidentally, or perhaps not incidentally at all, a few words about network interference on this particular project.

Paul Klein, during that phone call to me on March 16 confirming N.B.C.'s desire to make a deal on *Rescue from Gilligan's Island*, asked me to contact Deanne Barkley at N.B.C. Burbank about the project. She was Vice President TV Two-Hour Films, and *Rescue* came under her jurisdiction.

On April 6, Mike Rollens, Lloyd, and I went to Deanne Barkley's office for that meeting. I left a copy of the five-page outline with Deanne, and since

The author watching the heroes' welcome of the castaways in filming Rescue from
Gilligan's Island.

we had never worked together before, I asked her how she liked to work. Did
she want to see the first draft of the script? The second draft? The final?

Deanne said, "Bring me the film."

I didn't quite understand. "You mean, the rough cut? The next cut?
What?"

"The film," she answered.

I couldn't believe she meant the final film, but that's what she said.

The entire meeting couldn't have lasted more than five minutes. We
never discussed the story, the locations, the casting, or anything else.

Maybe this reflected the fact that she had no interest in the project. That
was possible, because Deanne dealt mainly in drama, and pretty heavy drama

at that. Many of her projects involved novels, biographies, and prominent works by well-known authors. I doubt that working with *Rescue from Gilligan's Island* filled her with pride and joy. At least, that's my opinion.

On the other hand, it's conceivable Ms. Barkley felt there was little point making recommendations or suggestions to the man who created, wrote, and produced the *Gilligan* series. She might have said to herself, he probably knows what he's doing, so why interfere? That's conceivable. But unlikely.

At any rate, after that preliminary five-minute meeting during which nothing creative about the project was even mentioned, I never saw Deanne Barkley again (until I met her at Universal, eight years later).

Despite her request to see only "the film," I sent Ms. Barkley and her department copies of all scripts, from first draft to final polish. In response, I never received a single note or memo from Ms. Barkley or anybody in her department. I invited her and/or someone from her staff to the *Rescue from Gilligan's Island* dailies each and every day. Nobody ever came. I invited her and/or someone from her staff to every screening from the first rough cut to the final version, edited to broadcast format. Nobody ever came.

Finally, two weeks before air date, I realized N.B.C. would be telecasting a two-hour film that *nobody* at the network had ever seen. Not a single frame of film had been viewed by any department at N.B.C.

I knew, from long experience, that Broadcast Standards and Program Practices at networks *have* to see every film on their network before it airs. It's an absolute regulation, because the network is responsible to the F.C.C.

I trust my own judgment so far as taste is concerned. I've never had problems with censors about sex, violence, or vulgarity in any show I've ever produced, including several hundred TV shows. I'm also fully aware of regulations regarding commercial products and advertising within the body of the show, as well as the format: time limits on credits, main titles, production logos, station breaks, promos, bumpers, etc. These are in the domain of Program Practices, and must be "adhered to without variation." Nevertheless, it was possible I might have violated some new regulation of which I was unaware. It was also possible I might have inadvertently violated an old regulation.

Since my memos and phone calls to Ms. Barkley had gone unheeded thus far, I myself placed an emergency call, instead of using my secretary, to advise Ms. Barkley's secretary that it was an extremely urgent situation. That finally got her attention.

I told Ms. Barkley my two-hour show, *Rescue from Gilligan's Island,* was about to be telecast and nobody at N.B.C. had seen the final film, or any part of it.

"You mean, Broadcast Standards hasn't seen it?" asked Ms. Barkley, alarmed.

"That's right," I answered.

"Program Practices hasn't seen it either?" she exclaimed, even more alarmed.

THOMAS WOLFE WAS WRONG
YOU <u>CAN</u> GO HOME AGAIN!

Part I
Number One Entertainment Program
Week Ending Oct. 15, 1978
National Nielsen: 30.2 Rating, 52 Share

SHERWOOD SCHWARTZ
REDWOOD PRODUCTIONS, INC.

Rescue from Gilligan's Island *still ranks as one of the highest-rated TV movies of all time.*

"That's right."

"And nobody from my department?"

"That's right, too."

How dare I broadcast a show on N.B.C. with no approvals, Ms. Barkley wanted to know.

I explained that for weeks I had been trying to get her, or someone in her department, to take a look at the film. My secretary had a list of the phone calls we had made, if she'd care to see them. We also had copies of all the memos we had sent.

"Under no conditions can that show be telecast until our departments have a chance to approve it," said Ms. Barkley firmly.

AHOY!

FIRST HOUR A BOFFO 52 SHARE!

Yes, we know it's overdue, but the Minnow's back in port(z).
We thank you for the "rescue" which we owe to
SHERWOOD SCHWARTZ
and

Producer: Lloyd Schwartz　　　　　　Director: Leslie H. Martinson
Writers: Elroy Schwartz,　　　　Albert Schwartz,　　David Harmon
Casting: Millie Gusse

and to all the cast and crew . . . we love you all!

BOB DENVER, ALAN HALE, JIM BACKUS, NATALIE SCHAFER,

RUSSELL JOHNSON, DAWN WELLS, JUDITH BALDWIN

Sat., Oct. 21, 9 P.M.　　　　　NBC-TV

A tribute to the producer, director, writers, casting director, the crew, and the other cast members, from the seven Castaways in Rescue from Gilligan's Island.

"I know the rules, Ms. Barkley. That's why I've been trying to reach you." Then I added, "The film's on footage now."

"On footage" meant the film had been cut to N.B.C. format, allowing time for commercials, local spots, network identification, news allocation, etc. Any changes in the film would be extremely difficult at this late date, because it would change the exact footage.

A few hours later, after my phone call with Ms. Barkley, Lloyd and I were in a screening room at N.B.C. in Burbank with Fenton Coe from Program Practices, Jack Petry from Broadcast Standards, and someone from Current Programming. We viewed *Rescue from Gilligan's Island*.

There was some laughter from the small group. When it was over, there were nice comments about the film, but very little in the way of criticism. I had, as I suspected, violated no rules that would upset Program Practices. There were no dialogue or visual problems to bother Broadcast Standards. Except for one tiny request.

Almost apologetically, Jack Petry from Broadcast Standards (the censor) said, "Sherwood, I even feel funny about raising this, and I wouldn't on any other show. But any *Gilligan's Island* show has so many youngsters viewing, there's one little thing I wish we could avoid."

"What's that?" I asked.

"You know that scene at the end, where Ginger and the other Castaways climb out of the lagoon and onto the beach?"

"Yes."

"Well, the camera is kind of high and Ginger's dress is kind of low and she's pretty well-built, and there's some cleavage." He hastened to add, "I know you can see more cleavage than that on every show on TV, but for *Gilligan's Island* and its audience—"

"Okay," I interrupted. "There's another angle on the group that's filmed from behind as they climb out of the water. I can use that one, without changing footage."

"Fine," Jack said, somewhat relieved.

"However, it's only fair to tell you that as Ginger climbs out of the water, and we see her from the rear, that dress is wet and it clings very tightly. You see cleavage, only it's behind instead of in front."

"No, no, no! Let's not have that shot," Jack said quickly. "Isn't there any other coverage on Ginger? A lower angle so we're not looking down her dress?"

"As a matter of fact, there is a low shot," I answered. "It's closer on the group and it's not as wide."

"Good," he said, again relieved.

"However, it's only fair to tell you that Ginger's wet dress that clings behind, also clings in front. It sort of outlines her crotch."

"Oh, God!" Jack exclaimed. "I'll settle for the boobs!"

Actually, it was a very innocent shot of Ginger, Judy Baldwin, with very little cleavage. By today's standards, it was mid–Victorian. And I was being very honest with the censor about the other two angles. They were far more suggestive than the shot I used in the film.

*

By the way, for those who think elegant offices decorated with thick carpets, hand-painted wallpaper, hand-carved desks, custom-built bars, Early American furnishings and Oriental accessories are necessary for a producer to film a successful movie, let me describe the *Rescue from Gilligan's Island* production building.

Our entire staff was housed in one plywood and aluminum trailer parked outside Stage 2 at C.B.S. Studio Center. It was a nice trailer, but that's all it was: a trailer. In this one trailer were four desks: one for Val Taylor, the associate producer; one for Shelley Friedman, now Shelley LaFleur, his production assistant; one desk for Marla Liebling Sawyer, the executive secretary/production assistant for Lloyd and me; and the last desk, separated from the rest of the trailer by a half-partition, was a desk shared by Lloyd and me, the producer and the executive producer.

In this humble home, a two-hour film was born that created quite a stir in television. In fact, its remarkably high rating led to quite a list of two-hour "reunion shows"; from *Leave It to Beaver,* to *Perry Mason,* to *I Dream of Jeannie,* to *The Andy Griffith Show,* among others. And even my own *The Brady Girls Get Married.*

All of them had high ratings. One of them led to a new syndicated series, a few of them led to more two-hour movies, including *Gilligan's Island.* But none of them came even close to matching that incredible 52 share rating.

31

The "Castaways" Hotel and the Globetrotters

"How about those ratings!" exclaimed Lloyd.

"The phone hasn't stopped ringing!" screamed Marla.

"It's a madhouse!" yelled Shelley.

"Wow!" said Val, raising his voice ever so slightly. For quiet-spoken Val, this was practically a shout.

"What's going on?" I asked, mystified by all the excitement.

It was about 4:00 p.m. when I opened the door to the "Rescue" trailer. I had been gone most of that Tuesday, October 17, 1978. I was returning from Long Beach, where I had given a lecture to a television class at California State University at Long Beach.

My daughter, Hope, was attending that class. She had spoken to Professor Finney about my work in television, and he had written to me several weeks earlier. He wanted a TV producer to speak to his class on the subject of sex and violence in television.

I told him I was hardly an authority on that subject, having spent some ten or eleven years writing and producing *Gilligan's Island* and *The Brady Bunch*. The only violence was in *Gilligan's Island* when the Skipper occasionally hit Gilligan with his captain's hat. The only sex was in *The Brady Bunch* where the six kids were living proof of same.

I had agreed to speak to Professor Finney's class on October 17. That Tuesday date, of no special significance to me at that time, had been determined several weeks in advance. Students and Professor alike seemed delighted with my remarks and my discussion with the class. About 3 p.m. I left Long Beach and started back to Los Angeles and C.B.S. Studio Center.

That's when I entered our trailer and was greeted with all that excitement from Lloyd, Marla, Shelley, and Val. "A 52 share! A 52 share!" they shouted.

Marla showed me the telephone lists. It didn't seem possible she could have logged that many phone calls in one day. There were three and a half pages, about 150 phone calls. People I hadn't seen or spoken to in years had called to congratulate me about the 52 share Nielsen rating of *Rescue from Gilligan's Island*.

There were phone calls from writers, producers, actors, and executives, not only at N.B.C., but A.B.C. and C.B.S. as well. Many were long-distance calls. What a day to be out of town! I answered as many of the calls as I could that afternoon, and spent the next day or two answering the rest.

Events then began to move rapidly, in the wake of that astounding rating. Paul Klein phoned from New York to discuss reactivating *Gilligan's Island* as an hour series. I.C.M. immediately pressed me to work out a deal. N.B.C. was talking about a firm thirteen-week commitment, so very heavy currency was involved. Ten percent of very heavy currency is very heavy currency, too. So Mike Rollens, on behalf of I.C.M., was very anxious for me to say "yes" to Paul Klein. Why was I dragging my feet, N.B.C., I.C.M. and United Artists (my partner) wanted to know?

Like anybody else, I have no objection to heavy currency. But there were several things to consider. After all, in the intervening fifteen years, *Gilligan's Island* had become a cult series with an incredibly loyal following. As proof, what else could have inspired that remarkable rating for the two-hour *Rescue from Gilligan's Island?* Would it be "fair" to that original syndicated series to follow it, after all those years, with the same kinds of stories and humor? I didn't honestly think I could do *Gilligan's Island* any better. It was possible I might not do it as well.

What about the cast? Was that original cast, with or without Tina Louise, physically capable of doing a new *Gilligan's Island*—especially an hour show—on a weekly basis? Would it be possible to do those big physical gags and special effects with that cast? Could viewers suspend their disbelief watching the older Castaways, with the "original" Castaways rerunning on TV every day?

And what about the characters of the Castaways? Would Gilligan retain his ingenuous boyish innocence? Or would he seem like a case of arrested development, eliciting sympathy rather than laughter? Would the Professor begin to seem ridiculous, still attempting rescues after fifteen years on the island? The other characters, too—would they remain acceptable to the viewers?

Might not a new *Gilligan's Island* series possibly have a negative effect on the syndication of the original series? That was a serious consideration, too.

Nobody else seemed to be worried about these things.

My original intention, if *Rescue* proved successful, was to do another two-hour film the following year. Sort of *Rescue II*. I wanted the Castaways to be rescued again, and then end the story with them shipwrecked on that same island again.

In fact, I wanted to do a series of two-hour films, with them always back where they started from, on "Gilligan's Island." It would be a funny, ironic series of films, I thought. And one that was physically possible for the original Castaways, on a one-a-year basis.

Now I was afraid *Rescue* had proven *too* successful. If N.B.C. thought my horse could win a race every week, they might not be satisfied to let me run it once a year. I was right. When I suggested my plan, N.B.C. thought it was insufficient. So did I.C.M. and so did United Artists. I wasn't giving enough *Gilligan* to the public.

Then I remembered the idea I had back in 1966, in case the ratings started to falter. That idea was to build a resort hotel on "Gilligan's Island," using Thurston Howell III's multi-billions. The hotel would be in the form of tropical huts, much like the huts the Castaways lived in, but beautifully decorated, with modern facilities, and superb dining. It would be a luxury retreat for vacationers who wanted to get away from it all. No TV or radios or newspapers to let the outside world intrude. The Howells would be the owners and the host and hostess. The other Castaways would function in logical positions of responsibility in running the hotel.

The new series would be done as an hour show, with a cast of guests, bringing two or three plots to the hotel in each episode. In form it would be something like *Love Boat*.

This idea removed my objections to doing a new version of *Gilligan's Island*. We would be doing very different stories from those we had done in the original series. Using guest stars would physically take the pressure off the original Castaways. It would not look like the original series, because there would be beautiful huts—elegantly furnished, luxurious accommodations.

Lee Gabler, Vice President of Television Packaging for I.C.M., thought this was a brilliant solution to everybody's problems. Lee and I flew back to New York to discuss this hour hotel format with Paul Klein. Paul was very pleased by this approach. In fact, he wanted me to do seven hour-shows based on this concept to start airing on N.B.C. in early February.

That was very little lead time: less than three months. I didn't think it was possible to gear up properly for production on an hour-long series in that time. What I wanted instead was to do an hour special to establish the hotel on "Gilligan's Island." This would, in effect, be the pilot film for the new series.

I.C.M. felt it was risky. We had a bird in the hand. What if the new hour special didn't get the same kind of rating as *Rescue?* I might very well lose the seven-hour-show commitment.

I knew it was risky. But I refused to start preparing seven hour-shows without enough time for pre-production. Preparing one film is very different from beginning a continuing series. If we could start the series the following September, we'd have the luxury of six months to prepare and polish the hour-long shows.

Finally everyone agreed to my plan: an hour pilot now, and an option for the seven hours in the fall. I worked out the story and outline for the pilot. Then I wrote the script with my two brothers, Al and Elroy, who had worked on the other *Gilligan's Island* shows.

Filming *The "Castaways" on Gilligan's Island* was a wonderful experience in almost every way. Tom Bosley, a truly consummate actor, was our major guest star. Marcia Wallace, an excellent comedienne, played his wife. They were the first two guests at the hotel on "Gilligan's Island," called the "Castaways."

This *Gilligan* film required a great deal of physical action. There was an old airplane the Castaways found on the island that had to be repaired. There was stunt work involved getting the plane off the ground, as well as second unit shooting with stunt doubles for a matching plane. In one scene Gilligan falls out of the plane, and matching problems were very difficult because the Castaways themselves had ostensibly fixed the old airplane they found.

Early Bellamy, a director with whom I had worked many times before, was particularly adept with the kind of physical production we needed. We were fortunate he was available to direct *The "Castaways" on Gilligan's Island*.

In retrospect, the most fascinating thing about the new *Gilligan* special occurred during business affairs negotiations, before production even started. It had to do with the old saying, "Everybody loves a winner" — to which *Rescue from Gilligan's Island* was no exception. While I had personally financed *Rescue,* because United Artists backed away, I had plenty of willing partners for the next *Gilligan* special. Everyone knew it was a pilot film for an hour series already under option by N.B.C.

Lloyd and I toured the facilities of the major production companies: Universal, Paramount, Warner Brothers, Fox, M.G.M. We needed a good-sized "lagoon" area with a "shoreline" large enough for a mooring dock and one or two good-sized buildings to establish the "Castaways" hotel.

We were very familiar with the lagoon at C.B.S. Studio Center, and that wasn't large enough for our purposes. In fact, the only studio that really fulfilled the lagoon requirement was Falls Lake at Universal. So the deal for *"Castaways,"* logically, should be with Universal.

I spoke with Don Sipes, then President of Universal Television, and he was delighted to participate in this project. His business affairs people started negotiations with Alan Levine, a partner in Barry Hirsch's law firm, which represented me.

As they were discussing contractual arrangements, I got a phone call from Dick Reisberg at Viacom, the company that had bought the syndication rights to *Rescue from Gilligan's Island* from me. Up to that time, Viacom was primarily, if not exclusively, in the syndication business. At that point in time they were becoming interested in entering production themselves. Since they already had the syndication rights to *Rescue,* Dick Reisberg felt this was a perfect opportunity to get into first-run product with this second *Gilligan* film. Particularly because he knew it was a pilot for a possible series.

Dick took me to lunch at LaSerre to discuss a partnership with Viacom in the new *Gilligan* special. "Lunch at LaSerre" was a sure sign that he was very interested. LaSerre is a very expensive restaurant in the Valley.

At lunch, I explained to Dick Reisberg it was very difficult to talk a deal with Viacom, which had no production facilities. I told him quite frankly the only film company with the proper lagoon area was Universal. Dick said Viacom would find one. I assured him Lloyd and I had examined all possible local locations, and nothing else was appropriate. Dick assured me Viacom would *make* some other location appropriate, even if they had to dredge part of Lake Sherwood, one of the potential locations Lloyd and I had seen and discarded.

I told Dick that would be too expensive. It would make the project prohibitive. But he persisted. He felt Viacom could make it work. I told him negotiations were already under way with Universal. Dick said, "We'll not only meet, we'll beat any deal Universal wants to make with you." Wouldn't I think it over, he asked, and have another meeting with him? I promised I would think it over.

I told Alan Levine, my attorney, about my conversation with Dick Reisberg, including the fact that Dick, for Viacom, had offered to meet and beat any offer Universal made. I also told Alan I had promised Dick I would think it over. But in all honesty, I told Alan, I didn't see how we could shoot the film anywhere but Universal.

Armed with this information, Alan went back to Universal for another meeting with Business Affairs. And that's when I got the weirdest phone call I've ever received, including the one from that lady in Kansas City.

"Hello," I said when I picked up the phone. That's all I say when I answer the phone. You would never think I'm a comedy writer.

"Hi. This is Alan. Alan Levine."

"Hi. Alan, what's going on?"

"Well," said Alan, "it's kind of bizarre. I'm locked in a room here, and I'm only allowed one phone call."

That certainly sounded bizarre, all right.

"Where are you calling from, jail?"

"No. I'm over at Universal. They won't let me out of the building."

"Alan, whatever you took, put it back," I advised him.

"I know this sounds strange, Sherwood, but they put me in this room and said I could make one phone call. To you."

"Alan, you better tell me what this is all about."

"Here's the story," said Alan. "I told them about Viacom, and I told them you're supposed to meet again with Dick Reisberg. They made a new offer, which I'm supposed to give you on the phone. If you don't accept this offer now, and you proceed with another meeting with Viacom, this offer will be withdrawn. That doesn't mean they'll break off negotiations. It just means this particular offer won't be there if you meet with Dick. Tomorrow they might even give you a better offer, but this one is off the table if you have further contact with Viacom. Is that clear?"

"Yes," I answered, "It's clear, but. . ."

I had heard crazy Hollywood stories about deals like this, but it always involved important stars, or famous novels, or directors of twenty-million-dollar pictures. What was I doing in the middle of this kind of a negotiation? With a one-hour *Gilligan's Island* special?

Actually, I had been giving more thought to Viacom and Dick Reisberg, and I had already decided their participation was impossible. The *only* place we could shoot this was at Universal. After these weird negotiations with Alan, Universal would certainly not allow Viacom to shoot this show on their lot. I really had no choice.

"You want a simple yes or no answer?" I asked Alan.

"Don't you want to know the terms of Universal's new offer?" asked Alan.

"Not really," I said. "I assume it's better than their last one, and I thought that one was very fair. So my answer is yes. Take the deal."

"It entails some future commitments, too."

"Fine. Now tell them they can take off your handcuffs, call off the guard dogs, and open the cell door. Besides, I think your three minutes are up."

Alan chuckled. "It's not as bad as all that," he said, "but this has never happened to me before. They really wouldn't let me out of the building and they just gave me this line for one phone call."

Recently, Alan and I laughed about that incident. He admitted it was the most peculiar phone call he ever had to make to a client.

I guess no film could be as fascinating as that negotiation—and *The "Castaways" on Gilligan's Island* wasn't. Not in the ratings, anyway.

I don't like excuses. I don't like to get them, and I don't like to give them. But I think it's only fair to state certain facts and circumstances.

The "Castaways" on Gilligan's Island was scheduled to be broadcast on N.B.C. 8:30 to 10:00 p.m., Friday, May 11. (The network had asked me to make the film 90 minutes instead of an hour.) Three weeks before that date, the network suddenly rescheduled it 8:30 to 10:00 p.m, Thursday, May 3, eight days *earlier*.

I was furious. All the publicity had been released with the May 11 date. Even TV Guide had that date and there was no way to change it. If the broadcast had been *delayed* a week or two, we could have managed. But it had been *advanced*. There was no way to change the publicity and promotion for the show. The boat had sailed.

In addition, the film had been moved from a Friday night to a Thursday night. This was a crucial blow to a show which was sure to have a huge audience of youngsters. There was no school Saturday. But there was school Friday. That would cost us several share points in the ratings.

Besides, at 8:00 p.m., Thursday, May 3, A.B.C. had scheduled *two* episodes of *Mork and Mindy,* the hottest show in television. That was its first year on TV and it was a phenomenon, averaging over a 50 share every week. It was the number one show with children, and teenagers. *The "Castaways" on Gilligan's Island* was now scheduled to start *between* those two *Mork and Mindy* episodes.

The "Castaways" Hotel, a tropical paradise without phones and TV. That's what makes it a paradise.

Our lead-in was virtually hopeless. At 8:00, against the first *Mork and Mindy,* N.B.C. had scheduled a show called *Highcliffe Manor.* That show gave *"Castaways"* the lowest lead-in of any show on any network that week, a 12 share.

Following the hour of *Mork and Mindy,* A.B.C. had scheduled *Ike,* the story of Eisenhower, the most heavily publicized mini-series that entire year. So *"Castaways"* was against the second *Mork and Mindy* and against the first hour of *Ike,* with no chance for publicity or promotion for our changed air date. As a famous dry cleaner once said, "I wouldn't wish that spot on a 50-cent tie."

Nevertheless, against those odds, *The "Castaways" on Gilligan's Island* raised its 12 share lead-in to a 26 share. And against all shows on all networks, we were thirty-second in the Nielsen ratings.

However, the bloom was off the rose. A 26 share for *"Castaways"* was a far cry from a 52 share for *Rescue.* The television industry wants to know the "bottom line." It's not interested in how, what, when, why, or where. And the "bottom line" on the *Gilligan* scorecard was *Rescue* 52–*"Castaways"* 26.

All talk about the hotel concept and seven hour-long "Gilligan" shows for the fall stopped. Along with any thought of a series. I was sure that was the end of the line for new projects from *Gilligan's Island.* I should have known better.

In 1980 I got a phone call from Brandon Tartikoff, President of Programming for N.B.C. under Fred Silverman.

"Fred has an idea about the Dallas Cowboys Cheerleaders on Gilligan's Island. Do you think you can work out some kind of story?"

"You mean, a two-hour special?" I asked.

"Yes," said Brandon. "Fred thinks that combination, all those good-looking gals in that island setting, would look great."

I thought to myself, maybe this would give me an opportunity to redeem *Gilligan* after the *"Castaways"* experience. Maybe the air date wouldn't be changed this time. Maybe the opposition wouldn't be impossible. Besides, the Dallas Cowboys Cheerleaders had done a network special which got a very high rating. They might add some share points. The Dallas Cowboys Cheerleaders might be just the remedy.

"Brandon, are you talking about the hotel concept on the island? With the Cowboys Cheerleaders as guests at the 'Castaways' Hotel?"

"Fred just wants to know if it sounds like there's a show there."

"Sure," I answered. "I think those cheerleaders will add viewers to the regular *Gilligan's Island* audience. It should get a good rating."

"Fine," said Brandon. "We can make this part of our Universal deal with you. Okay?"

"Okay."

While negotiations proceeded on this third *Gilligan's Island* special, I began to work on a plot involving the Dallas Cowboys Cheerleaders. Business Affairs finalized our arrangement, and I was still working on the story for the two-hour film when I got another call from Brandon.

"We just found out the Dallas Cowboys Cheerleaders are out."

"What happened?"

"They're unavailable. They're doing another special that would conflict with our schedule. Fred wants to know if you can do the same story with the Harlem Globetrotters."

"Why not?" I answered. "They look a lot alike."

"I'm serious. Fred wants to do another *Gilligan's Island* special, and the Harlem Globetrotters are very popular."

"I know," I answered. "I love 'em myself."

"They might give you some rating points, too." Brandon said.

"Right," I answered. "The Dallas Cowgirls and the Harlem Globetrotters both give you T and A. In the case of the Globetrotters, though, T and A stands for Tall and Agile."

Brandon laughed. Then, "You have no problems with this change?"

"No. I'm sure I can write a story for them. I'll get back to you."

I worked out a new story. Then I wrote the script with two of my old stand-bys, David Harmon and my brother Al. I added Gordon Mitchell, a good writer and a resident basketball expert, to our staff. And we wrote *The Harlem Globetrotters on Gilligan's Island*.

Then came the actors' strike. Production in Hollywood was shut down for several months.

The Harlem Globetrotters, with Gilligan, and guest stars Barbara Bain and Martin Landau of The Harlem Globetrotters on Gilligan's Island.

When the strike was over, there were scheduling complications with the Harlem Globetrotters. The Trotters travel the year round to countries all over the world. We had to fit our schedule to their open dates, and it became quite complicated. But somehow we managed to find five consecutive days for the Trotters.

Meanwhile, we had signed Martin Landau, Barbara Bain, and Scatman Crothers as guest stars. Connie Forslund was our new Ginger for this special. Dreama Denver, Bob's wife and a fine comedienne, was also in the cast.

As we prepared to film, Jim Backus became ill. That's when we brought in David Ruprecht as Thurston Howell IV, and he was excellent. As I've mentioned, Jim was able to come back for a short scene at the end.

Again, I was fortunate with directors. Peter Baldwin was available, and we had worked together many times before. In addition, Peter's an ardent basketball fan, so *The Harlem Globetrotters on Gilligan's Island* was a slam-dunk for him. And the Trotters were a delight to work with, off and on the court.

That show was broadcast Friday, May 15, 1981, 8:00 to 10:00 p.m. on N.B.C.

The huge rating of *Rescue* hadn't surprised me. The mediocre rating of *Castaways* hadn't surprised me either, because of the rescheduling. This time, however, I was surprised by the rating.

The opposition on the other networks was standard Friday night programming. I thought the Trotters would add several share points. I even hoped Martin Landau and Barbara Bain would add a point or two. But the rating of *The Harlem Globetrotters on Gilligan's Island* was the same as *"Castaways."*

It was a disappointment to me. Not that a 26 share is anything to be ashamed of. We still were higher than most of the other shows that week. But I was sure we'd have a share somewhere in the mid 30s.

Perhaps my biggest disappointment of all is that I've never done the special I've wanted to do for several years: *Murder on Gilligan's Island.* It would be a two-hour film in which one of the Castaways is supposedly murdered. A group of famous detectives would come to the hotel on the island to solve the mystery. I wanted to use four or five famous detectives from literature, or four or five famous TV detectives. That's not a likely special anymore.

On the other hand, with *Gilligan's Island,* you never know.

Priceless Rewards

"Pat, I'd like you to meet Mildred and Sherwood Schwartz," said Berle Adams.

Mildred and I exchanged greetings with Pat Diroll. Pat was one of the hostesses at a fund raising affair for K.C.E.T., the public television channel in Los Angeles. The party was on their stages on Sunset Boulevard near Vermont.

Berle and Lucy Adams support K.C.E.T., as do Mildred and I, and many other people in the entertainment field. Berle is a member of the K.C.E.T. board.

Berle and Lucy have been good friends of ours for many years. Berle distributes films and TV shows in foreign countries. In fact, it was Berle who helped me erase some of the red ink from my *Rescue from Gilligan's Island* deficit. He arranged for the sale of my film to Canada and Australia, before I worked out my syndication deal with Viacom.

We were nibbling on some refreshments at this K.C.E.T. fund raising event, when Berle introduced Mildred and me to Pat Diroll.

"Sherwood Schwartz!" exclaimed Pat Diroll suddenly. "Are you the Sherwood Schwartz who produced *Gilligan's Island?*"

"Produced it?!" exclaimed Berle. "He created it! He wrote it! He produced it! He's the real Gilligan!"

"I was going to play the title role," I said, "but I was the wrong size."

Mrs. Diroll looked at me, puzzled. "The wrong size?"

"Too big to be Gilligan, and too small to be the island."

Everyone laughed politely. People are nice.

"I've been wanting to meet you for a long time," said Mrs. Diroll. "Ever since my daughter Courtney was five years old."

"How old is she now?" I asked.

"Twenty-one. She's back East at Smith College."

"Well," observed Berle, "you're only sixteen years late."

"Isn't it awful," said Mrs. Diroll. "So often we mean to do things and we don't get around to them. But I finally met you," she said to me, "and I'm going to tell you what happened."

When Courtney was five years old, Mrs. Diroll told us, she developed a

BIZARRO   By DAN PIRARO

Jerry Bittle watches Gilligan's Island. *Dan Piraro watches* Gilligan's Island.

WATCHING THE DEMOCRATS IS LIKE WATCHING GILLIGAN'S ISLAND... YOU WONDER IF THEY'LL EVER GET OFF THAT REEF.

STAHLER.

PRESIDENTIAL DEBATES AGAIN

© 1986 The Cincinnati Post. Reprinted with permission.

Stahler watches Gilligan's Island.

terrible earache. It was the middle of the night, and Mrs. Diroll became alarmed at the amount of pain and also at the little girl's temperature, which was rapidly escalating. She awakened her husband, Richard, who himself is a doctor, an anesthesiologist. He had many doctor friends, among them a very well-known ear specialist, Dr. Fordyce Johnson. Richard was reluctant to phone him at 3:00 in the morning, but little Courtney was in obvious agony. So he phoned Dr. Johnson, who did something that was rare even back in 1964. He made a house call.

When the specialist examined Courtney's ear, he found a large abscess. Little Courtney was in such pain that Dr. Johnson didn't want to take the time to get her to a hospital. He wanted to relieve the pressure of the abscess immediately with a procedure called a myringotomy.

Mrs. Diroll told us the doctor asked Courtney what her favorite television show was. Through her tears, Courtney replied, *"Gilligan's Island."*

"Fine. Is there one particular episode that you liked the best?"

"Yes," replied Courtney, still sobbing, "The one with the gorilla in it."

"Good. I want you to tell me the whole story of that episode while I look in your ear. Meanwhile, keep looking at this watch."

Mrs. Diroll told us Dr. Johnson had an old-fashioned gold pocket watch on a chain. He swung it in front of little Courtney, hypnotizing her. Under his spell, she started telling the story of that episode of *Gilligan's Island* to the doctor. Meanwhile, he probed her ear.

As the child spoke about *Gilligan's Island*, her tears stopped flowing, and her sobbing ceased. Aided by the hypnotic effect of the gold watch, she was so absorbed in the story, she actually became animated as she described Gilligan, the Skipper, the other Castaways, and the gorilla.

Garry Trudeau watches Gilligan's Island. *Berke Breathed watches* Gilligan's Island.

Courtney didn't even wince, Mrs. Diroll said, when the doctor punctured and drained the abscess. She just kept telling him the story. Dr. and Mrs. Diroll watched in amazement as their daughter seemed completely relieved of pain during this process.

The next morning their daughter was fine. Mrs. Diroll asked Courtney about the experience the night before. The child remembered no pain, but repeated the whole story of that episode of *Gilligan's Island* again.

Mrs. Diroll said to me, "Ever since you did that for my daughter, I've wanted to give you a great big kiss."

"Never too late," I said.

I offered my cheek, and sixteen years after the fact, I got my reward.

Actually, of course, my reward was the knowledge that my show not only entertained that child, but helped her through the agony that night. It's a priceless reward that accompanies work in the entertainment field. Performers get it more directly from the public. But people behind the scenes sometimes hear about these rewards too.

One day, in 1964, I walked down the driveway from my house to collect the mail. As I opened the mailbox and took out the letters, there was a screech of brakes directly behind me in the street. I looked around and saw a station wagon. A young woman was driving. I didn't see anything in the road and I wondered why she had braked to this sudden stop.

Fagan watches Gilligan's Island.

"Mr. Schwartz?" she asked.

"Yes," I answered.

"Can you tell me the first word a child should learn to say?"

I was puzzled by the question. I didn't really know the young woman, but I had seen her before. She lived up the street, about two blocks away.

"What is the first word a child should say?" I repeated.

"Yes."

"Well, I'm not an expert in the field, but I'd say it's probably 'mommy' or 'daddy'."

"Then how come my little boy's first words are 'Gyagin Iyend'?"

"You're kidding," I said, chuckling.

'No, I'm not," she laughed. "He's fascinated by your show and those are his first two words."

"Sorry about that," I said. "Sorry, mommy."

"I thought you'd get a kick out of it," my neighbor said. Then she flashed me a smile and continued on down the street.

Another example: the daughter of some friends of ours, Lael Horowitz, was teaching a class of disturbed children in Santa Monica. She phoned me one day in 1965 and said the favorite TV show of her class was *Gilligan's Island*. She asked if I might come to her school and talk to the children.

Indeed I might. I drove out to Santa Monica and spent an hour talking to a group of children with a variety of learning problems. Some were hyperkinetic, others emotionally disturbed. Yet, somehow, during that entire hour, they were completely attentive. Even the most hyperkinetic participated courteously in the discussion.

I answered question after question. Some of the questions were about specific episodes and specific lines of dialogue. The youngsters wanted to know why Mary Ann said this, or the Professor said that. They had apparently

Tom K. Ryan watches Gilligan's Island. *Johnny Hart watches* Gilligan's Island.

memorized the episodes and knew the details better than I myself. Lael told me afterward that the children talked about my visit for weeks.

There were very few things that made those troubled youngsters happy. *Gilligan's Island* was one of them. That kind of reward has no price tag.

I got a letter from a Mr. Martin in 1965 who had a ten-year-old daughter named Jennifer. "Jennifer's favorite show is *Gilligan's Island!*" he wrote. "In fact, Jennifer has changed her name to 'Gilligan's Island.' She refuses to answer to any other name. She won't even come in to dinner unless we call her 'Gilligan's Island'."

Her distraught father pleaded with me to help him find a solution to his problem. He said he and his wife didn't know what to do about their daughter. They were embarrassed trying to explain the problem, when they introduced her to their friends as "Gilligan's Island."

I sympathized with Mr. Martin, but I explained there was nothing I could do about it. I couldn't change the name of my show to *Jennifer's Island*. "On the other hand," I said, "just be happy her favorite show isn't *Please Don't Eat the Daisies.*"

Mr. Martin's letter was written by a man who obviously had a sense of humor, because after he signed it, he added a P.S. "Aside from this one problem, we're delighted she likes your show, because it's good clean wholesome entertainment. We enjoy watching it ourselves."

I hope Jennifer has grown out of her problem by now. Otherwise she

"Whenever I go out, it Betamaxes a 'Gilligan's Island.'"

Even the people who read The New Yorker *watch* Gilligan's Island.

might have a couple of kids who have to introduce their mother as "my mom, Gilligan's Island'."

One of my daughters-in-law, Don's wife, Betty, was teaching school some years ago. It was a fourth grade class, and they were studying geography. They were learning about countries and oceans and islands. During the class discussion, Betty asked, "Who can tell me the name of an island?"

Every hand in the class shot up in the air. Everybody knew the same island. "Gilligan's Island."

Betty told me, "Dad, you put islands on the map!"

In 1966, there was a horse named "Gilligan" who won seven blue ribbons in steeplechase jumping contests.

In 1971, there was a German shepherd named "Gilligan's Island,"

New shows are in capital letters. Larry Tritten has prepared the schedule below
for the 2000-2001 TV season by employing the wisdom of satirical foresight. Wait
and see.

2000-01 TV SEASON SCHEDULE

MONDAY

7:30 P.M.	8:00 P.M.	8:30 P.M.	9:00 P.M.	9:30 P.M.	10:00 P.M.	10:30 P.M.	
Blue Genes	Morgue Janitor	Usherette	How the West Was Bought				ABC
Pagan Bridesmaid	Junk Male	Mutant Tennis	GAY COMPUTER	Plaguegirl	Telikinettiquette		CBS
Penthouse Voyeur	DRAG QUEEN DRUG KING		A Telekinetic Yankee in King Arthur's Court				NBC

TUESDAY

Last Meal Chef	San Diego Zoo Monkey Shoot		Family Rumble	Kahn and Kant	Little House in the Ruins		ABC
SLUMLORD	COUSINS IN LOVE		STOCKS AND BONDAGE MARKET UPDATE				CBS
Swineherd	Drinking for Dollars		Color Tease (Prem: St. Louis Blues vs. Chinese Reds)				NBC

WEDNESDAY

Ghetto Florist	INTERDIMENSIONAL FRISBEE		Championship Snake Punching		The Hitchhooker		ABC
Tinkerbull	Tumbling Maid	Fourplay	PSYCHODELICATESSEN				CBS
PRISON NURSE	Cat Toss	Reno Wino	Name That Rash		Dr. Jekyll and Ms. Hyde		NBC

THURSDAY

Quartz	All in the Closet	The Claustrophile	Yes Man	WONDERPIMP	Lawyers in Leather		ABC
Pintz	Star of Goliath		Mr. Disco Attorney		YOU BET YOUR PANTS		CBS
Gilligan's Island	FREE LANCE SURGEON		Honeymoon Photographer		Mobius Stripper		NBC

FRIDAY

The Sperm Bankers	Praying for Prizes		LOW GRAVITY PLANET SEXUAL OLYMPICS				ABC
Horse Meet	The Wuxtraterrestrials		The Mistress and the Moron		AUNTY VIVESECTIONIST		CBS
Ten in a Tub	ANN DROGYNOUS & ANN DROID		Celebrity Lobotomy		Pardon My Lesion		NBC

SATURDAY

The Fuhrer's Goose	Bellvue Revue	Automom	MUSKY & STENCH		Masochists' Masque		ABC
What's My Pudding?	Wax & Wayne	CoCaine Mutiny	MR. & MS. CONCEPTION		Sadists' Soiree		CBS
Hollywood Wouldn't	Test Tube Midwife		SHACK UP ON STAR 101				NBC

SUNDAY

TROJAN HORSEWIFE		Cohn & Clone	Down and Out on Uppers				ABC
The Streets of San Souci		Micro Drunk	Goldwater & Silverfish		Meals to the Suite		CBS
Paramecium Elysium		Punk Rock Nanny	Back Seat Bartender		Dancing on Downers		NBC

SUNDAY, SEPTEMBER 17, 197?   *CALENDAR*

By permission of Larry Tritten.

By permission of Bob Gorrell.

Top: *According to Larry Tritten,* Gilligan's Island *will be the only "current" series still on the air in the 2000–01 TV season.* Bottom: *In the final analysis,* Gilligan's Island *may outlast all future technologies.*

owned by Danny Dwier, who took 21 first prizes, the last one at Emmaus, Pennsylvania, which had a record 1,747 dogs competing. But "Gilligan's Island" came through with another victory.

As I was writing this book, a cat won $5,000 and the honor of endorsing a certain cat food. The name of the cat? "Gilligan."

A few years ago, I received a letter from Robert Rankin, a young man in Salt Lake City. He had graduated college and wanted to get a master's degree in theatre arts. However, he lacked the funds and was trying to win a scholarship.

He wrote me that a scholarship was being offered for the best exhibit based on some TV series. Robert was an ardent *Gilligan's Island* fan and wanted as much material as I could give him for a *Gilligan's Island* exhibit. His letter seemed very sincere. So I collected various items I thought would be useful: a copy of the original presentation of the show, the "bible" of characters, many photos of the cast, plus copies of other information I was able to assemble from my files.

About six months later I got a wonderful letter from Robert. His *Gilligan's Island* exhibit had taken second place in the scholarship contest. First place, and the scholarship, had gone to a *M*A*S*H* exhibit. However, some businessman in Salt Lake City had been so impressed by Robert's *Gilligan's Island* exhibit that he funded a second scholarship. Robert Rankin was now able to enroll for his master's degree.

Another priceless reward.

Some years ago, a candidate was running for the governorship of Ohio. His name was John J. Gilligan. He wrote to me asking permission to use *Gilligan's Island* as an endorsement for his candidacy.

Actually, the publicity would have been good for my show as well as for Mr. Gilligan. However, I didn't feel it was fair for *Gilligan's Island* to take sides in an election, whether Mr. Gilligan was a Democrat or a Republican. I reluctantly turned down the request.

Mr. Gilligan won the election without any help from our "island." However, you may be sure, if our Castaways could have cast absentee ballots adrift in bottles, they'd have voted for a Mr. Gilligan.

For the past few years I've participated in a seminar at the University of California at Los Angeles. It's a seminar for advanced students in film and television conducted each year by Michael Berk and Douglas Schwartz. Doug is my nephew, my brother Al's son. He and Michael are writer/producers who have worked in television for about ten years, in both two-hour films and weekly series.

The group of students attending the seminar this past year, some 150 or more, was surprisingly mixed. There were undergraduates at U.C.L.A., as well as men and women working on their master's degrees.

Most of the two-hour period was devoted to questions and answers. The group asked specific questions of specific panelists who might be best qualified to answer. As usual, many of the questions directed to me concerend *Gilligan's Island:* "How did you manage to sell such an off-beat idea?" "Was it particularly hard to write and produce because it was so confined?" "Do you think you could sell the same kind of show today?"

The answers to these questions, all of which I've been asked before, are, first, in those years it was easier to sell inventive, original, off-beat ideas. Second, it was not a difficult show to write and produce— it *seemed* confined because it took place in one locale, but it was based on character interrelationships, and story ideas based on seven backgrounds are plentiful. And third, no, I don't think there's much chance of selling a similar series today, because the nature of comedy in television has changed dramatically. Imagination and creativity are out, reality and one-liners are in. Optimistic humor has been replaced by pessimistic humor, positive replaced by negative.

After the question and answer period, the seminar students were given fifteen or twenty minutes to chat with the panelists. Three or four people spoke to me, mostly asking questions about the best way to sell situation comedy series ideas they had written.

A tall young man, who seemed to be about 22 or 23, shook my hand and told me he was especially happy he had an opportunity to meet me personally. I thanked him and asked why.

"Because," he said, "I just finished my film for my master's thesis."

"Congratulations. Is it a comedy?" I asked, knowing the odds were at least ten to one against it. I've talked with many graduate school filmmakers about the films they write, direct and produce for their master's degrees. The films are almost always dramatic and usually enigmatic, hardly ever humorous. Many student films take place in heaven or in hell.

"No," replied the young man. "It's a dramatic film. And you'd never guess where it takes place."

"Where does it take place?" I asked him.

"It's at the gates of Heaven," answered the young man.

"An interesting background," I observed.

"It's mainly a discussion between St. Peter and God, as new arrivals appear at the gates of Heaven. They await their fate. They wonder whether they'll be sent to Heaven or to Hell."

"For some, the pearly gates open. For others they remain closed, I presume," I said, still wondering why he had been so delighted to meet me personally.

"That's right," he said, "and you're in my film."

"Me?" I said, in some surprise. "I went for my annual checkup recently. The doctor says I'm fine."

"No, no, no!" exclaimed the young man seriously. "This is allegory. You don't have to be dead to appear at the gates of Heaven."

"That's reassuring. But we've never met before. How do I happen to be in your film?"

MR. BOFFO   JOE MARTIN

Reprinted by permission: Tribune Media Services.

Joe Martin watches Gilligan's Island.

"Not physically," he answered. "St. Peter says to God, 'Here comes the man who created *Gilligan's Island*.' You're not dead. It's just symbolic."

"I see," I said, a little uneasy. "I'm not sure I want to hear the rest of this."

The young man was too intense to appreciate my humor.

"I think you'll be very happy, Mr. Schwartz," he said. "God loves your show."

I didn't know what to say. The young man was so fervently earnest, any response seemed either flippant, sacrilegious, or ungrateful. I settled for a simple "good."

Other men and women crowded in for my attention. The tall, thin graduate student with the serious expression disappeared into the group. I never even got his name.

Don't misunderstand: I make no claim that God loves *Gilligan's Island*. But I'm certainly happy that people do.

That series has made friends for me everywhere I go. Nobody recognizes me by sight, because viewers don't know what people behind the cameras look like. But they recognize my name. It has appeared thousands of times in TV credits on various shows. In the reruns of *Gilligan's Island* alone, it has been on screen more than 10,000 times. My name is like a product people have seen over and over again in commercials.

Naturally, my name is also printed on my credit cards. In a restaurant, department store, or gas station, I give my card to the waiters, salespeople, or attendants. Very often when they return with the statement for me to sign, he or she will ask, "Are you the Sherwood Schwartz connected with *Gilligan's Island?*" In fact, it occurs with such regularity that when they begin to ask, "Are you—," my wife says, "Yes, he is."

Recently, we were having dinner with a group of friends in a restaurant where I had never dined before. At the end of the meal, I gave the waiter my American Express card. When the waiter returned with my card, he dispensed with the usual preliminaries. He simply handed me the charge slip to sign and said, "You know my favorite episode? It was the one with Phil Silvers, when he was the Hollywood producer who landed on the island."

I told him my own personal favorite was the one with Nehemiah Persoff, in which he plays the exiled dictator who takes over as ruler of the island. The waiter told me I was wrong; the Phil Silvers episode was better. I left him a tip anyway.

Another time, I stopped for gas at a Union Oil station some distance from Los Angeles. I gave my credit card to the attendant. When he returned with the slip for me to sign, he didn't say a word; he just whistled the first two bars of the *Gilligan's Island* theme. Then he asked, "Right?"

"Right," I answered, with a laugh.

A friend of mine recently returned from a trip to Europe. He told me about an incident that had occurred during a long all-day bus tour. To pass the time, the driver suggested that the passengers, many of them from different countries, should sing some popular song from their own country. In that situation, people usually sing some patriotic tune. That's exactly what most of the passengers did when called upon.

Much to my friend's surprise, some American youngster, instead of the usual "Home on the Range" or "America the Beautiful," sang the entire lyric to "The Ballad of Gilligan's Isle." Much to my friend's further surprise, people from a few other countries joined him, singing the same lyric in their own native tongue.

These are just a few of the priceless rewards I've received from creating *Gilligan's Island*. Over the years I've received hundreds of letters and phone calls from people of every age, color, religion, economic, and intellectual level, who find enjoyment in *Gilligan's Island*. Interestingly enough, almost everybody has a different favorite episode.

Cartoonists in magazines and newspapers have recognized the household-name acceptance of *Gilligan's Island*. The sophisticated *New Yorker* magazine, and highly acclaimed cartoon strips such as Garry Trudeau's "Doonesbury" and Johnny Hart's "B.C.," among others reprinted in this book, are proof that tropical desert isle has become part of the American scene.

In the Calendar section of the *Los Angeles Times,* Sunday, September 17, 1978, there was a future program schedule of television in the year 2000–2001, prepared by Larry Tritten. In that fictitious future schedule, every single series was a satiric title based on some past TV show. With one exception. That series is expected to continue, according to Mr. Tritten, as simply *Gilligan's Island*.

It wouldn't surprise me if those two words, "Gilligan's Island," are included in some future *Webster's Dictionary*.

33

Present Mirth Hath Present Laughter

As William Shakespeare said to me: "Fortunate indeed thou art, my friend/that thou created *Gilligan* when thou didst."

Obviously, that was an imaginary conversation. But I'm sure that's what Shakespeare would have said, because he knew everything there was to know about comedy as well as drama.

Bill was certainly aware that fashions in comedy undergo constant change. The broad farces of the old comedy of Aristophanes many centuries earlier had long ago given way to middle comedy, and then the so-called new comedy of the fourth century B.C. There followed periods of low comedy, high comedy, mime comedy, jesters, strolling minstrels, puppets, and even domestic comedy, as in the Shrovetide plays in the early 1500s.

As a particular point of reference to *Gilligan's Island,* there was the *commedia del l'arte* of the Middle Ages. In this type of comedy play, the actors were prototypes rather than specific individuals. In *commedia del l'arte* they even carried masks in front of their faces to hide identities and preserve the general nature of their characterizations.

There were other cycles of comedies that came and went after Shakespeare's day: restoration comedy, the comedy of manners, sentimental comedy, and, as time passed, combined forms of comedy which carried remnants of several others.

What was true about the changing styles in comedy in those years is even truer in this day and age. Fashions in art, dance, music, dress, and even general behavior are compressed into shorter and shorter time periods.

In television, comedy cycles come and go with great regularity. And each cycle tends to be very self-exclusive. It's much easier for a new show to join an existing trend than to start a new one.

In the beginning of commercial television, roughly 1949, the first TV comedy cycle was the variety show. The highest-rated programs from 1949 through most of the 1950s were variety shows: Milton Berle's *Texaco Star Theater,* Ed Sullivan's *Toast of the Town,* Sid Caesar/Imogene Coca's *Your Show of Shows, The Jackie Gleason Show, Arthur Godfrey's Talent Scouts, The Colgate Comedy Hour,* and *The Red Skelton Show.* (I myself was part of that variety cycle, having spent most of the 1950s writing *The Red Skelton*

Show.) This weekly variety comedy cycle peaked in the 1950s, gradually fell from favor in the 1960s, and finally vanished in 1971, with one major exception: *The Carol Burnett Show,* which ran through 1979.

Obviously, shows in a cycle don't screech to a halt, to be replaced by the next comedy cycle. Traditionally, as one cycle gradually fades away, another cycle phases in to replace it. In the case of the variety shows, as their number decreased, domestic family comedies, which gained popularity in the 1950s, moved into the top ratings in the 1960s. Programs like *Leave It to Beaver, Father Knows Best, I Love Lucy, The Danny Thomas Show, My Three Sons, The Adventures of Ozzie and Harriet, The Life of Riley, The Donna Reed Show, Dennis the Menace,* and *The Dick Van Dyke Show* became the mainstays of prime time.

Within this large domestic comedy cycle were two smaller cycles which were also very successful. One of these was the imaginative comedy show. These programs appeared on all three networks during the 1960s and were extremely popular. *Bewitched, I Dream of Jeannie, My Favorite Martian, The Munsters, Hogan's Heroes, Mr. Ed, The Addams Family, Batman, Get Smart,* and *Gilligan's Island* were part of this cycle within the cycle.

It's interesting to note that after this hefty serving of comedy fantasy, the appetite of the America viewer was apparently sated, and that particular cycle has never been repeated. In fact, there have been relatively few attempts to revive that form. Only one of these, *Mork and Mindy* was a major hit, albeit short-lived. In the past several years in prime time only one comedy fantasy show, *Alf,* has been high in the ratings.

The other, smaller cycle within the large domestic comedy cycle was the 1960s rural comedies: *Andy Griffith, The Real McCoys, The Beverly Hillbillies, Petticoat Junction,* and *Green Acres.* When that rural cycle died, it never revived either. However, rural comedies didn't fade away gradually, like fantasy comedies. They died a sudden death. In 1971. For a very specific reason.

In 1970 there was an important survey of the buying habits of TV viewers by an authoritative advertising publication. This survey revealed a tremendous difference in the buying power of urban viewers versus viewers in rural areas. Consumers in large metropolitan cities spent twice what their country cousins did, and were far more important for sponsors, and, therefore, to the networks who served them.

As a result of that survey, Bob Wood, Programming Chief at C.B.S., cancelled all the rural situation comedies on his network, four of which were in the top twenty in the Nielsen ratings. The inside joke in the industry that year was that Bob Wood had "cancelled every show with a tree in it." It was a bitter joke for the creators, writers, producers, directors, and actors of those shows, who were on top one minute and off the air the next.

While that economic survey was crucial in a negative way for the rural shows, it was equally crucial in a positive way, for an entirely new cycle that dominated the 1970s: the reality comedies.

Gilligan, the Skipper, Mary Ann and the Professor appeared on the N.B.C. show Alf, *in September 1987, and provided that series with its highest rating ever. It's appropriate that the Castaways, who were part of the comedy fantasy cycle of the 1960s, made this appearance on the only hit comedy fantasy show of the 1980s.*

The year 1971 ushered in Norman Lear's *All in the Family* at C.B.S., a show that changed the nature of TV comedy forever. It was the first of the hard-nosed reality comedies, and it was a huge success, particularly in metropolitan areas. As a result, it was especially welcomed by sponsors and advertising agencies, based on the 1970 survey of viewers' spending habits.

Here's the Skipper with Alf and Gilligan on the recent N.B.C. show Alf. *The Skipper is undoubtedly trying to figure out whether Alf or Gilligan is the creature from outer space.*

Lighthearted situation comedies were virtually eliminated from the television tube. They were replaced by the cynicism of the 70s. Imagination disappeared. Insult comedy and one-liners, long the staple of radio comedy, invaded television. Scripts became more like legitimate plays and less like motion picture scripts. Reality comedies accented character and dialogue and minimized movement.

This, in turn, led to a different mode of production. One-camera film comedies, long the staple form, were slowly but surely outnumbered by multiple-camera shows, film or video tape, with a minimum number of stages and sets. Comedy shows became living rooms, kitchens, bedrooms, and an office where Dad worked.

The subject matter of comedy shows also changed. Viewers were offered stories concerned with death, vasectomies, abortion, dope, mastectomies, rape, etc. — subjects never before touched in situation comedy. Reality comedies like *M*A*S*H, Maude, The Jeffersons, Barney Miller, Welcome Back, Kotter, Taxi, Sanford and Son, Chico and the Man, One Day at a Time, The Mary Tyler Moore Show, Bob Newhart, The Facts of Life, Rhoda,* and *Alice* took over from the simpler, good-humored domestic comedies of the 50s and 60s.

The only escapist comedies in the 1970s that maintained hit status with the viewers were *Happy Days* and *Laverne & Shirley*. It may be significant that neither one of those 1970s hits *took place* in the 1970s. The background for both was the 1950s, which were indeed "happy days" in terms of lighthearted comedy fare.

There's another type of situation comedy that's formed an important part of television fare. It's not exactly a cycle, because it has continued to accompany other, more clearly defined, comedy cycles. It's a family comedy in which the "family" is formed of unrelated people who either work together in a particular background or live together because of some mutual interest. In the 50s there was *Our Miss Brooks*, where teachers and children were the family; and *Private Secretary*, Phil Silvers' *You'll Never Get Rich*, *The Many Loves of Dobie Gillis*, among others. In the 60s, there were *McHale's Navy*, *F Troop*, *Family Affair*, and *That Girl*. In the 70s there were *The Mary Tyler Moore Show*, *M*A*S*H*, *Room 222*, *Rhoda*, *Welcome Back, Kotter*, *Three's Company*, *Taxi*, *Barney Miller*, *Alice*, and *The Odd Couple*. And in the 1980s there are *The Golden Girls*, *227*, *Newhart*, *Who's the Boss?*, *Cheers*, *Night Court*, and *Amen*.

But what about the 1980s? Is there a new comedy cycle in the 80s?

Many half-hour comedies arrived on TV in 1981, 1982 and 1983 on all three networks. The only thing they had in common was immediate cancellation. One after another, they were treated by the viewer with monumental disinterest. Some managed to last thirteen weeks, but many were cancelled in six weeks, and some in four.

Then, as often happens, one single show announced the arrival of the coming cycle: *Kate & Allie* appeared on C.B.S. in 1983. It was an immediate hit, the only half-hour comedy in the top ten in the Nielsen ratings that year.

Why did *Kate & Allie* succeed while so many half-hour domestic comedies had been failing? The answer to that question provides the answer to the latest comedy fashion—the 1980s cycle.

Kate & Allie is a *contemporary* version of the domestic family comedy series. It's about two divorced ladies, Allie with two children, and Kate with one. It's a reflection of what's happening in current society. Divorces are epidemic today, and so are single women raising children.

Television comedy is really a mirror. It reflects the society that's familiar to the viewer. As the mores and attitudes of the public change, the comedy changes with them.

Network programming executives got the message very quickly. Domestic comedy series had to show something different from the old nuclear families. New family units had to be changed in some way to reflect our changing social structure.

The Cosby Show is different because it's an upwardly mobile, educated black family. It bears little resemblance to earlier black series like *Sanford and Son*, *The Jeffersons*, and *Good Times*.

Gilligan and the Skipper, guest stars of a recent episode of the New Gidget *series, starring Caryn Richman (right) and Dean Butler (left).*

Family Ties is another variation on the traditional nuclear family. It's mom and dad and three kids, but there's a liberal/conservative role reversal between the youngsters and their parents that dominates the relationships and the stories.

In *Growing Pains,* the husband, who is a psychiatrist, has an office at home. It's his wife who leaves for work every morning. *Who's the Boss?* has a young male housekeeper running the family.

These television families are reflecting radical changes in family life in America. With broken marriages rampant, fathers abandoning families, and mothers abandoning families, the traditional "mom and dad and the kids" is fast becoming an endangered species. In current TV comedy, there seem to be more widows raising children, widowers raising children, and friends raising children, than there are parents raising children. Deviation from the norm has become the norm.

In retrospect, one of my own shows, *The Brady Bunch,* based upon a marriage where the wife and husband each had children from a previous marriage, was merely a mild forerunner of things to come.

In some ways, this is a healthy trend because it brings fresh approaches to the typical domestic family comedies. But in one important way, it's unfortunate. While television programs are mirrors reflecting our changing social reality, it's important to remember that the picture tube is a *two-way* mirror. As such, those TV reflections reinforce the viewer belief that the damaged family unit is the way things *should* be. In a sense, fiction becomes the truth because it's on television.

Does television have a responsibility to be more than simply a reflection? I believe it does. Otherwise, it's a wasted opportunity.

Television is such a pervasive force in modern life that it's more than an entertainment medium; more than an educational tool; more than a business. Television has become, in many ways, responsible for viewers' behavior patterns. As such, TV programs have a chance to provide some answers to people's problems.

Situation comedy series once helped bring the family unit closer together, with the kind of positive social reality that predominated in the households in this country. It was in half-hour comedies that stories featured the value of people's relationships, the importance of truth, love, learning, integrity, etc. *Gilligan's Island,* along with other situation comedies, always stressed these nobler attributes in the human condition.

The Fonz, in an episode of *Happy Days,* emphasized the importance of reading. The following week more than 300,000 new library cards were issued to young people all over the United States.

Episodes of *The Brady Bunch* dealing with typical family issues — the special problems of the middle child, the question of teenage smoking, the importance of women's liberation — always elicited hundreds of letters. They came from both youngsters and parents in households where we had touched a nerve and started family discussions.

Unfortunately, the number of family comedy series where this kind of modern miracle can be accomplished has been dwindling. In the past twenty years, the number of domestic comedies on television has gone steadily down. Meanwhile, the number of shows with stories focusing on the seamy side of life has gone steadily up. In this same twenty-year period, cops and robbers and private eye shows, devoted to drug busts, mad bombers, mafia activities, robberies, murders, prostitution and assorted mayhem, have gone from six hours on TV to twenty-six hours. Positive role models have given way to negative role models.

Twenty-six hours of violent hour series constitute almost 50 percent of all series programming on all three networks. To make matters worse, eight hours of violence, almost a third of the twenty-six hours, are in the 8 p.m. time period, which used to be reserved for family programming.

Studies and research by Drs. Dorothy Singer and Jerry Singer at Yale University, Dr. Aletha Huston at the University of Kansas, and Dr. George Gerber at the University of Pennsylvania have all reached conclusions which confirm a 1982 report by the National Institute of Mental Health: "Violence on television leads to aggressive behavior by children and teenagers who watch the program." This report, in turn, was a confirmation of earlier conclusions reached by a U.S. Surgeon General's panel studying this same problem.

Hopefully, this cycle of violence is now at its zenith, and will soon begin to decline. There are very encouraging signs that the number of family shows is in the midst of a strong comeback.

In the 1984/85 TV year, family situation comedies had fallen to their lowest number ever, thirteen half-hours on all three networks. Thanks in large part to the incredible success of *The Cosby Show*, which premiered that year, the number of domestic comedies in the 1987/88 TV season has increased to twenty-eight half-hours. That's more than a 100 percent increase in two years. If the networks continue that kind of scheduling, television will once again reflect life in America, rather than death in America.

The Three Musketeers

D'Artagnan, Porthos, and Aramis are gone, and life will never be the same.

For over thirty-five years, the broadcasting media, radio and television, had been under the stewardship of three men; William Paley at C.B.S., David Sarnoff at N.B.C., and Leonard Goldenson at A.B.C.

In the time I have been writing this book, there has been a complete and revolutionary change in the ownership of all three networks. Laurence Tisch, of Loew's Corporation, is now at the helm of C.B.S., Robert Wright of General Electric is the chief executive at N.B.C., and Thomas Murphy of Capital Cities Broadcasting is the new head of A.B.C.

What makes it such a stunning upheaval is that the previous administrations at the networks had given the broadcasting medium a feeling of security and relative calm over the years. There were shakeups from time to time at all three networks, usually in programming executives as a result of ratings problems, but the overall management had great stability in leadership.

In the space of eighteen months, all Three Musketeers, who had served among them over one hundred years, were replaced, virtually overnight. And three networks, all formerly independent, are now part of multi-billion dollar conglomerates.

Most observers, particularly in the media, were concerned about the effect this would have on the news departments. And, in fact, with all three new chief executives very cost-conscious, the effect on the news departments at all three networks became evident at once. Belt-tightening measures forced removal of many overseas network correspondents. Indeed, in some countries, networks simply picked up their equipment and left. Several hundred personnel in news departments domestically also lost their jobs at each of the networks.

Less attention was paid by the media to the effect the change in networks' ownership would have on the entertainment area of programming. Here, too, however, there has been cost-cutting, in both drama and comedy series, as well as the longer forms. Most of these economy measures have been passed on to the production companies. They have had to absorb tightened license fees as part of deficit financing. Since high profits in syndication remain the carrot at

Alan Hale, Jim Backus, Natalie Schafer, Russ Johnson, and Dawn Wells, representing the Castaways Family as contestants on the game show Family Feud.

the end of the stick, most production companies have grudgingly accepted the added financial burden.

However, there's an expense in entertainment programming at the network itself, where belt-tightening has had a direct effect: the development departments. It's in this arena that cuts in budget will have a profound consequence, particularly long-range.

Development departments at networks are the life force of future series. Economies practiced here result in fewer script commitments, and fewer pilot commitments. This has an obvious effect in limiting choices for the next television season. Hitting the bullseye is difficult at best, and now the target is getting smaller and smaller.

Money cut from development has already had an effect on current comedy programs. The poor quality of pilot films and the narrowed selection this last year has resulted in the renewal of a number of series languishing in the lowest 25 rated programs. In past years, these series wouldn't have had a chance for another season. But there simply weren't any replacements available that were any better than the disasters that have been renewed.

Unfortunately for the networks, this is occurring at a time when cable systems, video cassettes, first-run syndication, pay-per-view television, and original local channel programming are all biting large chunks of viewers out of the networks' hide. For example, in 1980, cable reached 30 percent of all homes. By 1987, it was up to 50 percent. The number of independent stations rose from 120 in 1980 to 285 in 1988. And where it counts most, in the pocket-book, network advertising revenues dropped from 45 percent of total TV revenues in 1980 to 38 percent in 1987. According to most estimates, each 1 percent loss of network viewers represents approximately 42 million dollars a year in lost advertising revenues. Losing 7 percent is almost 300 million dollars! Per year! That's a lot of money, even to Thurston Howell III.

As recently as 1975, in Nielsen ratings, the three networks had approximately 90 percent of the audience. That percentage dropped to approximately 71 percent in 1987. One week in 1987 it went as low as 45 percent *for the first time in history!* Network programming chiefs, who usually tend to dismiss negative news as aberrations, have openly voiced alarm at the continuing erosion of their share of audience, which dropped another 8 percent in 1988.

To add to their problems, this is the period during which all three networks have passed into the hands of new chief executives — three conglomerate businessmen who have had no experience whatsoever in program scheduling, development, or in any other creative phase of television. Yet they now can exercise final judgment in any or all of these areas.

The nuts and bolts of broadcasting, financially speaking, are no great mystery for capable executives. Businessmen understand profits and losses and budgets, no matter what their corporate background. They can quickly comprehend time charges for advertising revenue and sets in use and viewers per thousand, etc. Those are the same kinds of raw numbers faced by executives in any business.

But television isn't just any business. It's a very special business. The risks are very great, and so are the rewards. The pot of gold at the end of the broadcasting rainbow is original programming, especially the weekly series — particularly those in the 8 p.m. time period, which starts prime-time.

In 1981, N.B.C. had exactly one series which won its time period in the ratings: *Harper Valley P.T.A.*, Friday at 8 p.m. Just four years later, N.B.C. was king of the hill, with twenty-one series winning their time periods, and eleven shows in the top twenty. What happened during those four years?

What happened was *The Cosby Show.* Not only was it an immediate enormous 1984/1985 N.B.C. hit, its lead-in elevated the 8:30 show which followed, *Family Ties*, into an enormous hit. And *Family Ties* elevated *Cheers*, which, in turn, elevated *Night Court.* It's the television version of the domino theory.

The following year, *The Golden Girls* was also an instant N.B.C. hit. Its lead-in helped raise the show which followed, *227*, to hit status, and when that show was replaced by *Amen*, *The Golden Girls* lead-in turned *Amen* into a success.

As a direct result of the clever scheduling of several successful half-hour situation comedies, N.B.C. went from third place in 1983 to runaway first place in 1985.

That's all it usually takes: a few early-hour situation comedies. They can put a network in first place and keep it there for years.

N.B.C. was the clear leader in ratings in the early 50s. But along came *I Love Lucy*, *The Danny Thomas Show*, *The Red Skelton Show*, *The Andy Griffith Show*, and *Dennis the Menace*, and C.B.S. was soon in first place. Half-hour situation comedies kept them there for a remarkably long time, through 1975.

It was the half-hour situation comedies which brought a different network into first place. *Happy Days*, *Laverne & Shirley*, *Barney Miller*, *Three's Company* and *Taxi* put A.B.C. at the top for the first time in its history.

A.B.C. remained there for about four years when C.B.S. recaptured first place in the ratings with a new group of half-hour comedies: *M*A*S*H*, *Alice*, *The Jeffersons*, *One Day at a Time*, and *Newhart*.

The C.B.S. return to power was shorter lived this time, thanks to the appearance of *The Cosby Show*. And it returned N.B.C. to number one status for the first time in almost thirty years.

Does this mean that hour shows like *Dallas*, *Falcon Crest*, *Marcus Welby*, *Medical Center*, *Ironside*, *Kojak*, *The Love Boat*, *Charlie's Angels*, *Hawaii 5-0*, *The Rockford Files*, *Hart to Hart*, *Dynasty*, *Hotel*, *Cagney and Lacey*, or *Knots Landing* were not important to the networks? Of course they were. Those shows, and other hit dramatic shows, are vitally important in the programming schedule. But a show that's on from 10 to 11, or even a program that's on from 9 to 10, can't give a network the lead-in value of an 8:00 hit. It's the 8 p.m. period which starts prime time and gives the network an opportunity to dominate an evening.

It's not a question of comedy being more *important* than drama. It's the lead-in value of an 8:00 hit to the succeeding shows which gives it an importance far beyond its own thirty minutes. Historically, the 8:00 time period has been the home of situation comedies. That's the reason they have played such a key role in elevating a network into first place.

Programs at 9 and 10 p.m. have never had the impact on the overall ratings race that the early evening shows have had. And it's more than likely that when N.B.C.'s current reign is over, it will be two or three situation comedies on another network that will have toppled it from its throne.

Brandon Tartikoff, who programmed *The Cosby Show* and *The Golden Girls* into a sequence of hits that moved N.B.C. from third place to first place, has been in programming his entire executive life. He first served as Vice President of Programming at A.B.C. under Fred Silverman. Silverman had spent his own executive life in programming also, first at C.B.S., then at A.B.C., and later at N.B.C. Grant Tinker, who succeeded Fred Silverman at N.B.C., had been in development and programming for many years, at networks as well as production companies.

President of Programming is a very difficult position. It requires a special combination of instinct and experience. The instinct is a natural talent for sensing what viewers want to see, but it must be accompanied by training in programming. The schedule must take into account many things: the demographics for a given hour for a given night, audience flow, lead-in from a compatible program and lead-out to a compatible program. The head of programming also needs an understanding of television history in terms of past schedules on various nights, and he must also have more than a passing knowledge of the opposition on the other networks.

It's hardly a place for on-the-job training for the New Musketeers. Mr. Paley had always prided himself on his full participation in all programming decisions on the C.B.S. schedule. In fact, out of respect for Mr. Paley's well-known expertise in this area, one of Laurence Tisch's first acts, as the new chief executive at C.B.S., was to bring Mr. Paley, age 86, out of retirement to help a beleaguered C.B.S. schedule. 1988 is the first year C.B.S. has finished in third place in its entire history. Robert Wright will probably leave well enough alone at N.B.C., since Tartikoff and his programs are riding the crest. Nobody seems to know what Thomas Murphy plans to do at A.B.C. Although A.B.C. finished 1988 in second place, it was mainly due to the collapse of C.B.S. programming.

Of course, two or three 8 p.m. hits could change all this. It's happened before, and it will happen again. But will the New Musketeers, from the land of the conglomerates, be able to seize the moment like their predecessors who had spent so many years at the programming helm? With their eyes on cost controls and slashed budgets, will they spend the money needed to discover that occasional diamond that may glitter in their line-up? Will they have the wisdom to recognize that glitter? And will they spend the additional funds to turn that solitary diamond into a necklace of hits?

Unfortunately, it doesn't seem probable. Usually, the bigger the company, the more conservative their thinking. And conglomerates are the biggest companies of all. How likely is it that they'll take a chance on a unique program, a show that's a real departure? Like *Gilligan's Island*, for example; or *All in the Family*, or *Mission Impossible*, or *Laugh-In*, or *Sixty Minutes*, or *Candid Camera*, or *The Fugitive*, or *Hawaii 5-0?* Each of these shows, in one way or another, was a break-out concept, an unusual idea in television history, new and innovative.

Conglomerates, consumed with bottom-line economics, are generally the most cautious and least daring. Whether the main business of a conglomerate is soap, automobiles, or breakfast cereals, the changes they make in their products are invariably slight, usually preceded by the words "New and Improved." Radical changes are generally effected by smaller companies, where newer thinking is necessary to compete in the marketplace. If the New Musketeers carry a cautious philosophy into television, the new programming will likely stick to the tried and true. It's a lot safer to program a police show starring a young cop and an old cop, or a female cop and a male cop, or a black cop and a white cop, or a group of cops of assorted combinations, because a hardcore percentage of viewers will see *any* law and order show simply because they like to watch action and adventure on the tube.

The same variations on the theme that apply to dramatic shows will probably apply to comedy as well. A cautious approach will bring more "new and improved" deviations, rather than bold departures.

In addition, the new owners have inherited networks that are in disarray because of the loss of viewers. In spite of that fact, they have become more dictatorial than ever. They trust producers less and less, yet their increasingly arrogant behavior has produced fewer and fewer hit shows in recent years. Since 1961, when Newton Minow told the networks to get their act together, and gave them virtually complete authority, their use of power has continued to expand year after year.

Sponsors have lost their influence. The charge for network time has escalated to such an extent that most sponsors buy a thirty-second spot on one show, a fifteen-second spot on another, etc. Thanks to this "magazine concept" of broadcasting, sponsors, except in very rare instances (e.g. Hallmark), have little, if anything, to say about the program itself.

Advertising agencies, which in the early days of television were the dominant force in developing new programming for their clients, have relinquished any sort of creation or control. Their concern has become the commercial itself, not the program.

Producers and writers, who formerly dealt with the advertising agencies and sometimes the sponsors themselves, now have to present their ideas directly to the networks. The major concern of the networks is programs that suit their own need for certain time periods, not the public's need for entertainment.

Instead of "independent" production by "independent" producers, it has become "dependent" production. Production companies, producers, and writers, big and small alike, resemble waiters at a table ready to take orders from the networks. And if the specialties of the house don't interest the diner, they're ready to prepare whatever dish the network wants, whether they have the ingredients or not. Or even fire the chef if that pleases the customer. The only thing that matters is the network's desire to shore up a particularly weak link in its schedule.

With all the new technologies available to the public, with a multitude of choices ready and waiting on their dials, and with new channels continually appearing, there has never been a better time for the viewers to determine the kinds of programs they wish to see. By simply flipping the switch from one channel to another—from network, to cable, to local programming—they can indicate their favorites. Or by simply shutting off the set, they can show their displeasure for the entire medium.

Writing letters to the networks sometimes helps. It has kept a few shows on the air long enough to turn them into hits. *Cagney and Lacey* is an example. But those cases are very rare. The simplest way to express an opinion is to turn the dial.

Even before remote controls made it easier to change channels, viewers were able to express their opinions. Back in the early 60s there was one Sunday evening when an N.B.C. program was in fourth place in the ratings. Another N.B.C. show half an hour later was in first place. They were separated by a show that was in seventy-third place. Can you imagine how many millions of people got up from comfortable chairs to tune away from N.B.C., and then got up to tune back to N.B.C. again half an hour later?

But turning the dial worked. That program was quickly cancelled. It was a case of democracy in action.

So don't become a couch potato. Don't lie there and accept flickering images because you're too lazy to look for something you really like. Turn that dial! Change that channel! Pull that plug! It's the best way to let "them" know what you think.

The hand that rocks the cradle can also rock the schedules!

The public always gets what it wants, *as long as it exercises its right to vote*.

Gilligan's Island Sings and Dances

In 1980, I saw the musical *Annie* in New York. It was the third year of its run, and every performance was sold out. Actually, *Annie* was on its way to becoming the eighth longest-running musical in Broadway history, outlasting shows like *Oklahoma, South Pacific, The King and I, Guys and Dolls, Annie Get Your Gun, Cabaret, The Music Man,* and when it closed, Sandy was nipping at the heels of *My Fair Lady*.

With all due respect to *Annie*, which I found to be a pleasant, funny, and sentimental entertainment, it only had one truly memorable musical number, "Tomorrow." Compare that, if you will, with seven major song hits in *My Fair Lady*, six major hits in *Annie Get Your Gun*, and at least that many in *South Pacific, Oklahoma,* and *Guys and Dolls*. Was there some other magic at work in *Annie?*

I decided there was. And the magic element wasn't just little orphaned Annie herself, or Daddy Warbucks, or even Sandy. The magic, it seemed to me, was the Little Orphan Annie comic strip. It had been syndicated every day for thirty or forty years in newspapers nationwide. Three generations of children had grown up amused and captivated by the adventures of Little Orphan Annie. As those children got older, they read the strip with their own children. And, indeed, with their grandchildren. After all those years, Little Orphan Annie had become an extended member of their own family.

Meanwhile, the parents and grandparents were now old enough and affluent enough to afford Broadway ticket prices; affluent enough to pay for their kids and/or grandkids. And *Annie*, above and beyond anything else, was a true "family" show.

As I thought about this, it occurred to me that *Gilligan's Island* was starting to go through the same metamorphosis. The series had been on TV since 1964, and in daily syndication since 1967. By 1980 youngsters had been watching those episodes every day—sometimes twice a day—for thirteen years. In fact, *Gilligan's Island,* in syndication, was getting stronger and stronger, and *Gilligan,* like *Annie*, would soon become familiar to two or three generations of viewers. The seven Castaways were

becoming extended members of their families. I also felt the island
background was a very natural setting for a stage musical.

I approached United Artists, who had originally financed the series,
to see if they were interested in a musical version of *Gilligan's Island* for
Broadway. Unfortunately, United Artists had bankrolled two Broadway
plays the previous season, and both investments had proven disastrous. To
them the Great White Way had become the Great Red Ink. I tried to
explain the comparison with *Annie,* but to no avail.

At the same time, there was sudden interest by Paramount and
N.B.C. in a two-hour television film I had written with my son Lloyd. It
was a reunion show of sorts, *The Brady Girls Get Married.* Well, as the old
saying goes, "A bird in the hand is worth more than an empty nest."
Instead of beating on the Broadway door with *Gilligan's Island: The Musical,*
I headed back toward my usual habitat, television.

After this television interlude, my mind went back again to the play.
This time I discussed it with my son Lloyd. He was just as enthusiastic as
I was about a *Gilligan's Island* musical. What appealed to him, especially,
was the historic possibility of turning a TV series into a live stage musical;
something that had never been done before. Lloyd produced all three
Gilligan TV films with me, and knew the characters as well as I did.
However, neither of us knew the *Gilligan* episodes as well as millions of
true *Gilligan* fanatics, who have memorized every line of dialogue and
every move the Castaways made in every show. If Lloyd and/or I would
enter a trivia contest involving *Gilligan's Island,* we would lose to real
Gilligan buffs. It reminds me of the time Charlie Chaplin entered a Charlie
Chaplin Look-Alike Contest and came in second.

As luck and nepotism would have it, my son-in-law, Laurence Juber,
is a world-class guitarist. Laurence was, among other things, the lead
guitarist for Paul McCartney's group Wings. He is also a composer of
note—pun intended. My daughter, Hope, his wife, is a very talented
lyricist. So *Gilligan's Island: The Musical* quickly became a family affair.

As Lloyd and I worked on the book, Laurence and Hope worked on
the score. It was a very close collaboration; sometimes it was hard to draw
the line on who was contributing what. But that didn't matter, as long as
we liked the result.

It took about a year of concentrated effort before *Gilligan's Island: The
Musical* was ready for workshop performances. Since it was a musical, there
were a number of new and important considerations. In addition to finding
actors who could play comedy, and who resembled the original cast of the
Gilligan's Island series, the new Castaways had to be able to sing and dance.
Lloyd and I knew some good young actors, who fit the roles. We also knew
Patti Colombo, a wonderful choreographer. They were all eager to devote
their time and energies. There's something about starting a new musical
that's absolutely fascinating, almost mystical.

We rehearsed for two weeks. Then we gave three performances at The Main Stage, a small theater in North Hollywood. We learned a great deal about the play. And we spent the next six months rewriting scenes, removing scenes, adding scenes, eliminating songs, adding songs, and repositioning songs. A musical is a living, breathing organism, constantly changing, sometimes radically.

At the same time, all of us were busy on other projects, for television, films, and recording. One of these projects was *A Very Brady Christmas,* for which Lloyd and I had written the two-hour teleplay. When that was okayed by Paramount and C.B.S., we produced the film, and Laurence did the musical score. *A Very Brady Christmas* became the highest-rated TV film of 1988.

However, that resulted once again in *Gilligan's Island: The Musical* interruptus. Despite our love for the musical, it was television that paid the freight.

Meanwhile, coincidence had reared its sometimes beautiful head.

Steve Rothman attended one of the workshop performances at the Main Stage Theater. Steve was a stage/TV director, a friend of mine, and a close friend of Lloyd, and he had directed two of Lloyd's earlier plays. He loved *Gilligan's Island: The Musical,* and discussed it with Robin Farquhar, the artistic director/producer of the Flat Rock Playhouse, the state theater of North Carolina. Steve had directed several plays there. Robin was intrigued with the idea of moving an American TV icon to live theater, especially after he heard the score and read the book.

Robin and I quickly arranged to have the world premiere of *Gilligan's Island: The Musical* at the Flat Rock Playhouse in June 1992.

Flat Rock, North Carolina suited us perfectly. We wanted *Gilligan's Island: The Musical* to open far removed from New York, Chicago, Los Angeles, or any other large metropolitan area. If there were problems, we wanted to solve them before opening in a major city.

The musical was cast with two principals from the North Carolina area, Scott.Treadway as Gilligan and Janie Bushway as Mrs. Howell; three from New York, Steve Pudenz as Mr. Howell, Anthony Cummings as the Professor, and Rachel Jones as Mary Ann; and the Skipper and Ginger, Matt Kimbrough and Cathryn Hartt from Los Angeles.

Thanks in large part to the gifted Robin Farquhar and the great creative production team he had assembled at the Flat Rock Playhouse, the play was in wonderful hands. The audience loved it, and so did the critics. Critical acclaim and I are practically total strangers, and I guess it went to my head. I immediately arranged to produce *Gilligan's Island: The Musical* myself in Chicago with the same castaways.

We opened at the Organic Theater in Chicago in November. That experience taught me how truly gifted Robin Farquhar was, what a terrific production team he had at Flat Rock, and how important it is to be

familiar with a particular theater. The Flat Rock Playhouse was a prosce-
nium theater, and it was perfect for the musical. The Organic Theater was
sort of horseshoe shaped, and imperfect for *Gilligan's Island: The Musical.*
A great many other things were imperfect as well. I could write an entire
book about imperfections during my four months in Chicago; about
financial imperfections, design imperfections, lighting imperfections,
sound imperfections, etc.

However, during the Chicago run, a well-known Broadway producer,
Eric Krebs, who was intrigued with the idea of a musical version of
Gilligan's Island, made a trip to Chicago to see the play. He liked what he
saw, and had many suggestions to improve it. He wanted to produce it at
the John Houseman Theater, Off-Broadway on 42nd Street, a theater which
he owns and where he had produced many successful shows, among them
Driving Miss Daisy. I was delighted to put the show in the hands of a
veteran theatrical producer, particularly one who had produced many shows
in that precise venue.

Besides, *The Brady Bunch* beckoned again. This time it was a theatrical
feature. Lloyd and I had written a screenplay, *The Brady Bunch Movie,*
which we sold to Paramount. With pre-production, production, and post-
production, that would take eight or nine months. In addition, I had
another play, *Rockers,* being produced by Robin Farquhar at Flat Rock in
June. So, for many reasons, I was delighted Eric Krebs would be producing
Gilligan's Island: The Musical in New York.

Eric and I, and Lloyd, and Hope and Laurence, were fascinated by an
idea that developed in disucssion among us; multi-ethnic casting. When
Gilligan's Island first arrived on television, TV was white, There were no
blacks, or any other minorities, on the tube in continuing roles. But
American television, in 1993, reflected the changing colors of America's
population. Afro-Americans, Asians, Hispanics were represented on TV
now. President Clinton said he wanted his government to reflect the new
social face of the country. He wanted his cabinet, and his appointments in
general, to mirror this growing ethnicity.

Why couldn't *Gilligan's Island: The Musical* also reflect this changing
population of America? Are the all-white Castaways so engrained on the
TV audience that they wouldn't accept a black Skipper, or an Asian
Professor, or an Hispanic Ginger, or any other ethnic mixture? We decided
to hold color-blind casting. The best singing, dancing combination of
actors would get the roles as the Castaways, regardless of their race, color,
or ethnic backgrounds.

Our own sensibilities would be the first test. How would *we,* the
writers, directors, producer, choreographer react to this new look? Would
it be too distracting? Disturbing? Unsettling? Confusing? And above all,

would it hurt *Gilligan's Island: The Musical*? Or would it help? After all, the *characters* would remain the same, regardless of multi-ethnic casting. Actually, there might be an all-black cast some day, or an all-Hispanic cast, or an all-Japanese cast, etc.

Besides, even if *we* could accept it, could the *audience*? This was a major question, a critical question, and we knew our best answer would merely be a judgment call, nothing more.

The answer to this question, right or wrong, would hopefully come during casting in mid-June in New York.

After testing two hundred fifty or more performers for the roles of the Castaways, the producer, Eric Krebs, the director, Sue Lawless, Hope and Laurence, Lloyd and I decided on the best combination of performers. The result was a white Gilligan, a black Skipper, white Howells, a white Ginger, an Hispanic Professor, and an Oriental Mary Ann.

Rehearsals will start February 1994, with previews scheduled during March, and an opening in April. At least that's the plan as I finish this last chapter of *Inside Gilligan's Island*. But in show business you not only can't plan the future, you can't even plan the past.

Epilogue

Ubiquitous *Gilligan's Island* has already been the basis of a prime-time television series, two different animated series, three TV film specials, continuous syndication since 1967, the pilot for an educational channel, the first TV series to become an original musical comedy for the stage, and, with this publication, it has become the subject of a book.

Is there any place else those Castaways can go?

Very likely!

While I was finishing the last chapter, negotiations were proceeding between Ted Turner Entertainment and a major Hollywood studio for a theatrical feature with star names as the Castaways. The screenplay for *Gilligan's Island: The Movie* has already been written by Lloyd Schwartz, Elroy Schwartz, and me. As soon as attorneys and business affairs people agree on a few outstanding points, the feature will go into production. *Gilligan's Island* will probably celebrate its thirtieth anniversary in your neighborhood theaters during the 1994 Christmas holiday season!

The movie will be a major production with enormous props, state-of-the-art visual effects, and super stunts. It will feature seven of Hollywood's biggest stars as the Castaways and one very special guest star.

Will that movie be the final chapter for *Gilligan's Island*?

Not by a long shot.

If the movie is successful, will there be a sequel?

Will the sun rise in the East tomorrow?

Recently a number of people in Japan, Italy, Mexico, Australia, and Turkey, have joined *Gilligan's Island* Fan Clubs, according to Bob Rankin, President of The Original Gilligan's Island Fan Club (with headquarters in Salt Lake City, P.O. Box 25311, Salt Lake City, Utah 84125-0311, U.S.A., for those interested in joining).

What does this mean, this sudden flood of new fans from far-off places? I looked in my crystal ball, and it said, "Consult your Ouija board." So your guess is as good as mine.

There's one thing I can predict: plans are in work for *Gilligan's Island* to emerge in a multitude of other areas, in all sorts of merchandising.

I'd be happy to be more specific, but I'm unable to because of ongoing contractual arrangements between Ted Turner Entertainment, the Phil Silvers Estate, and me. There are overlapping jurisdictions in our relationship which concern Copyright and Separation of Rights that will determine the future activities of *Gilligan's Island*.

And always, there's the possibility of *Inside Gilligan's Island II*.

277

Appendix 1: Episode Synopses

These synopses of the 98 episodes of *Gilligan's Island* are presented in the order in which they were telecast. Over my objections, C.B.S. insisted on airing a "typical" episode first, instead of the pilot film. As a result, the series started with an episode in which the Castaways were trying to rescue themselves from the island, instead of showing how they arrived there.

In order to relate the story of the shipwreck, I reworked most of the pilot film into the Christmas show the first year. Thanks to the use of flashback, I was able to show the viewer how *Gilligan's Island* actually began.

The first episode of *Gilligan's Island* was telecast September 26, 1964. The pilot film, or about 75 percent of it, was broadcast December 19, 1964, as the twelfth episode.

Gilligan's Island was never on at the same time or the same night in its three-year prime-time history. First year, 36 episodes, black and white, Saturday, 8:30 p.m., September 26, 1964–June 12, 1965; second year, 32 episodes, color, Thursday, 8:00 p.m., September 16, 1965–May 5, 1966; third year, 30 episodes, color, Monday, 7:30 p.m., September 12, 1966–April 17, 1967.

Two on a Raft. *Written by* Lawrence J. Cohen and Fred Freeman; *directed by* John Rich.

Gilligan and the Skipper set sail on a raft to find help. After a harrowing experience at sea with sharks which demolish their raft, Gilligan and the Skipper manage to reach shore on an island. The Castaways have heard of the savage Marubi tribe on nearby islands, and Gilligan and the Skipper are terrified when they hear sounds of voices. Meanwhile, Mr. and Mrs. Howell, Ginger, Mary Ann and the Professor are equally terrified when *they* hear voices. Each group assumes the others are the savage Marubis. *Theme: Imagined dangers are often worse than real dangers.*

(*Note:* Aside from the pilot film, which was shot in Hawaii, this episode was the most expensive one in the series because of the complicated mechanical sharks and the breakaway raft.)

Home Sweet Hut. *Written by* Bill Davenport and Charles Tannen; *directed by* Richard Donner.

The Professor predicts that a hurricane is on the way. They build one large hut strong enough so they can all survive. However, after two days of living in the same hut, they get on each others' nerves, and they decide to face the storm in their individual huts. Unfortunately, their individual huts collapse during the tropical storm. They realize they'll have to make allowances for each other, and they move back to the big hut to save their lives. *Theme: United we stand, divided we fall.*

278

The Skipper thinks his little buddy Gilligan has been voodooed into a chimp in the episode "Voodoo Something to Me."

Voodoo Something to Me. *Written by* Austin Kalish and Elroy Schwartz; *directed by* John Rich.

Several items have mysteriously vanished. The Skipper has heard about witch doctors and voodoo curses on the islands, and he believes it's caused by evil spirits. The others search the island to find the real reason. While Gilligan is searching, he falls into a mudhole. He washes his clothes and sets them by the shore to dry while he goes for a swim. A chimp, actually the culprit who has been stealing things, finds Gilligan's

Hans Conreid, as Wrongway Feldman, is being pressured to fly to the rescue by sexy Ginger.

clothes and puts them on. When the Skipper sees the chimp, he's convinced a voodoo spell has been cast on his buddy Gilligan. The Skipper tells the chimp how much he (Gilligan) really means to him. *Theme: Very often we wait until it's too late to tell others how much we love them.*

Goodnight Sweet Skipper. *Written by* Dick Conway and Roland MacLane; *directed by* Ida Lupino.

A round-the-world lady flyer is passing over "Gilligan's Island." The Skipper once turned a radio into a transmitter when he was in the Navy, but he's forgotten how. The Professor hypnotizes the Skipper in the hope he'll recall the procedure. The rest of the Castaways pretend they are shipmates of the Skipper in order to recreate the original background. The Skipper manages to make the transmitter and the Castaways are sure they're going to contact the flyer, and are all ready to be rescued. At the last moment, however, Gilligan smashes the transmitter. *Theme: Don't count your chickens before they're hatched.*

Wrongway Feldman. *Written by* Lawrence J. Cohen and Fred Freeman; *directed by* Ida Lupino; *guest star* Hans Conreid.

The Castaways discover an ancient plane on the other side of the island. Then they discover the pilot, Wrongway Feldman. Wrongway still has fuel, but he can't fly the plane to get help, because he's lost his nerve. He teaches Gilligan how to fly the plane, but then he realizes he'd be endangering Gilligan's life, and he himself flies back to civilization. Unfortunately, Wrongway's calculations about the island are so wrong the authorities have no idea where the Castaways are. *Theme: People who are consistently wrong are likely to be wrong again.*

(*Note:* Hans Conreid [Wrongway Feldman] was the first guest star on "Gilligan's Island." He reappeared in this same role in a later episode, **The Return of Wrongway Feldman.**)

President Gilligan. *Written by* Roland Wolpert; *directed by* Richard Donner.

The Skipper and Mr. Howell would each like to be the voice of authority on the island. The group decides to hold an election for President. Thanks to electioneering for votes by the Skipper and Mr. Howell, it's Gilligan who is elected President. Suddenly everybody's attitude toward Gilligan changes. The other Castaways flatter him and each takes a high-ranking job in his "administration." However, they're all so busy being political, it's Gilligan, the President himself, who has to do all the work. *Theme: As President Truman said, "The buck stops here."*

The Sound of Quacking. *Written by* Fred Freeman and Lawrence J. Cohen; *directed by* Thomas Montgomery.

A blight descends on the island, destroying all the fruits and plants, except for small tropical berry bushes which the Professor claims are deadly poison. The Castaways are quickly running out of food when a duck arrives on the island. The duck would make a delicious meal. But, with a message tied to his leg, he is a possible means of rescue. Gilligan has a dream (the first of a number of dream sequences) in which he is Sheriff Matt Dillon, protecting the duck against the Castaways. Meanwhile, the duck eats the berries and survives, proving they can eat the berries and also send the duck away with a message. *Theme: When we are faced with two difficult alternatives, sometimes we can find a third alternative that's better than both.*

(*Note:* The dream sequence was actually shot on the *Gunsmoke* stage.)

Goodbye Island. *Written by* Albert E. Lewin and Burt Styler; *directed by* John Rich.

A great coincidence! A high tide will soon occur that will reach the wrecked boat. At the same time, the Professor discovers that the "maple syrup" Gilligan has discovered in a tropical tree is actually an incredibly strong glue. All the Castaways work feverishly to glue the broken parts of the *Minnow* together so it will be ready to sail when the tide reaches it. Just before the Castaways climb aboard, Gilligan discovers that the marvelous glue only holds for a short time. When high tide reaches it, the *Minnow* falls apart again. *Theme: Inside every problem is a bigger problem waiting to get out.*

The Skipper, the Professor, and Gilligan have just discovered a watertight glue, which they will use to mend the S.S. Minnow *in the episode "Goodbye Island."*

The Big Gold Strike. *Written by* Roland Wolpert; *directed by* Stanley Z. Cherry.

Gilligan finds a gold mine on the island, and Mr. Howell has him working over-time mining the gold. Meanwhile, the Skipper discovers the *Minnow* life raft, which has washed ashore. The Castaways prepare the raft to float them to some nearby island for help. Everyone is told to leave unnecessarily weighty objects behind. However, Mr. Howell sneaks all his bags of gold aboard the raft and it sinks, ruining their chances for rescue. *Theme: Greed remains one of the seven deadly sins.*

Waiting for Watubi. *Written by* Lawrence J. Cohen and Fred Freeman; *directed by* Jack Arnold.

The Skipper digs up a statue of a sacred Tiki god which was buried by the Watubi tribe, and he believes it dooms him forever. He tries to get rid of it, but it keeps

In the episode "So Sorry, My Island Now," Vito Scotti plays a Japanese sailor who doesn't believe the Second World War is over.

reappearing. The Skipper believes only a Watubi witch doctor can remove the curse. Gilligan dresses up as a Watubi witch doctor and performs a ceremony releasing the Skipper from the spell, and the Skipper is cured. *Theme: Sometimes the remedy for one superstition is another superstition.*

Angel on the Island. *Written by* Herbert Finn and Alan Dinehart; *directed by* Jack Arnold.

Being shipwrecked has cost Ginger a leading role in a Broadway play. To cheer Ginger, Mr. Howell promises to back the play personally when they're rescued, and the Castaways decide to rehearse the script. However, Mrs. Howell demands that her husband give her the starring role of Cleopatra. Mr. Howell can't say "no" to his Lovey, and Ginger becomes more upset than ever. Gilligan makes an impassioned plea to Mrs. Howell, pointing out she has everything she wants, and the only thing Ginger wants is the lead role. Mrs. Howell pretends to have laryngitis so Ginger can have the lead role. *Theme: Compassion is an individual trait, the exclusive property of neither the poor nor the wealthy.*

Birds Gotta Fly, Fish Gotta Talk. *Written by* Sherwood Schwartz, Elroy Schwartz and Austin Kalish; *directed by* Rod Amateau.

It's Christmas, and the Castaways are depressed since they can't spend the holidays at home. As they talk about the fateful day they were shipwrecked, thanks to the use of flashback film from the pilot, we see what happened when the *Minnow* was wrecked; how Gilligan lost the transmitter; and how they were unable to get rescued. After reliving those events, the Castaways realize they're lucky to be alive. *Theme: Don't count your problems. Count your blessings.*

Three Million Dollars More or Less. *Written by* Bill Davenport and Charles Tannen; *directed by* Thomas Montgomery.

Mr. Howell is on the island "golf course" when he becomes involved in a putting contest with Gilligan. They start with a 25-cent bet, and it escalates over a two-day period into $3,000,000, which Gilligan wins from Mr. Howell. When Gilligan becomes a millionaire, all the other Castaways become his best friends. Then Mr. Howell talks Gilligan into exchanging the $3,000,000 for a worthless oil well and the other Castaways are disgusted with Gilligan. Then they hear on the radio that the oil well has hit a gusher, and they become his pals again. *Theme: Everybody loves a winner.*

Water Water Everywhere. *Written by* Tom and Frank Waldman; *directed by* Stanley Z. Cherry.

There's been no rain for months, and the island is parched. The remaining fresh water is gathered into a waterproof bag. Gilligan accidentally spills it all, and the others are furious with him. Gilligan is miserable and wanders off to be by himself. The others are very upset at the way they treated him. Meanwhile, Gilligan is telling his troubles to a frog, when he suddenly realizes where there's a frog there must be fresh water. Following the frog, Gilligan falls into an underground freshwater spring, which provides the Castaways with plenty of water. *Theme: Sometimes the smallest of creatures can help the biggest.*

So Sorry, My Island Now. *Written by* David P. Harmon; *directed by* Alan Crosland, Jr.; *guest star* Vito Scotti.

Gilligan tries to warn the other Castaways that a strange creature is in the lagoon. The others pay no attention because Gilligan is always reporting strange creatures. This time, however, the creature turns out to be a Japanese one-man submarine. The sailor's radio and transmitter have been broken since 1942 and he is unaware the war is over. The Japanese sailor captures all the Castaways, except for Gilligan and the Skipper. The Castaways try to convince him that the war is over, but he refuses to believe them. Gilligan and the Skipper manage to release the other Castaways. The Professor hopes to fix the sailor's transmitter so they can radio for help, but the submarine sails away, leaving the Castaways without hope of rescue again. *Theme: Always listen to the boy who cries wolf, because one day he may be right.*

(Note: On this particular episode we were criticized by TV critics for doing such a "ridiculous, far-fetched episode," because it was so many years after the end of the war. About a year later, a news story reported that sixteen Japanese soldiers on a remote South Pacific island captured a group of tourists, unaware the war was over. Very often, fiction is simply truth that has not yet happened. Vito Scotti, who played the Japanese sailor, was the second guest star on *Gilligan's Island.* He also reappeared in this same

role in **Diogenes, Won't You Please Go Home?** He also played mad Doctor Boris Balinkoff in **The Friendly Physician,** and in **Ring Around Gilligan.**)

Plant You Now, Dig You Later. *Written by* Elroy Schwartz and Oliver Crawford; *directed by* Lawrence Dobkin.

Mr. Howell hires Gilligan to dig a barbecue pit for him. In digging, Gilligan hits an ancient buried treasure chest. Speculation runs high as to the contents. Meanwhile, a legal battle develops over who owns it. The Skipper insists his buddy Gilligan found it, finders keepers. Mr. Howell insists he hired Gilligan to dig, therefore the chest belongs to him. The result is the first courtroom trial in the history of *Gilligan's Island.* Fearful of the outcome of the trial, Mr. Howell gives each of the Castaways $100,000 for an "out-of-court" settlement. When they open the treasure chest, it contains nothing but old cannon balls. *Theme: Not all treasure chests contain treasure.*

Little Island, Big Gun. *Written by* Dick Conway and Roland MacLane; *directed by* Abner Biberman; *guest star* Larry Storch.

Two gangsters, Jackson Farrell and his accomplice, arrive on a boat. They've robbed a bank, and plan to hide a large sack of money on this "uninhabited island" so they can return for it later when the heat is off. Jackson produces a gun to keep the Castaways away while he and his accomplice take their sack of money to a different island. As they leave, Gilligan tosses their anchor to them. It hits the sack of money, which falls under the boat, and all the hundred-dollar bills are chewed to pieces by the propeller. *Theme: As Gilligan would put it, cheaters never prosper.*

X Marks the Spot. *Written by* Sherwood Schwartz and Elroy Schwartz; *directed by* Jack Arnold.

The Castaways hear a special news bulletin from the United States Air Force: An experimental warhead will be dropped over their "uninhabited" area within the next twenty-four hours. Unbeknownst to them, however, the explosive in the warhead has been removed, rendering the missile harmless. Thinking they are facing the end, each Castaway changes his outlook on life and becomes super-nice to all the others. *Theme: Sometimes it takes a life-and-death situation to show us what's really important.*

Gilligan Meets Jungle Boy. *Written by* Al Schwartz, Howard Merrill and Howard Harris; *directed by* Lawrence Dobkin; *guest star* Kurt Russell.

Gilligan meets a young boy who was obviously left on the island when he was a small child. He`has never learned to speak any language. However, he shows the Castaways a hole on the other side of the island from which a gas escapes, like hydrogen or nitrogen. This gives the Professor an idea. The Castaways seal the sleeves of their rain-coats and sew them together. The gas can make the strange-looking balloon rise, and one of them can float to a nearby island for help. Gilligan, who is the lightest member of the Castaways, is chosen to navigate. However, the jungle boy leaves in the balloon, while the others delay Gilligan's departure. *Theme: Strike while the iron is hot, or you might not be able to strike at all.*

(*Note:* Once again *Gilligan's Island* was hit by TV critics for airing a "ridiculous" episode. About ten years later, a group of Communist dissidents successfully defected to the West by sewing several raincoats together, sealing the sleeves, and filling the "balloon" with helium.)

St. Gilligan and the Dragon. *Written by* Arnold and Lois Peyser; *directed by* Richard Donner.

For months on the island, the Skipper, the Professor, and Mr. Howell are the ones

Kurt Russell plays a junior Tarzan they find on the island in the episode "Gilligan Meets Jungle Boy." Yes, that's Kurt Russell, circa 1964.

who make the decisions. Finally, the women rebel. They move away and build huts of their own. The men each have a dream in which the women become their slaves. At night, a huge "monster" appears, and the men and women both run into each others' arms, seeking help, protection, and comfort. Actually, the huge monster turns out to be a lost United States Navy weather balloon, but it makes both sides realize how much they really need each other. *Theme: No man is an island, nor is any woman.*

Big Man on a Little Stick. *Written by* Charles Tannen, Lou Huston, and David P. Harmon; *directed by* Tony Leader; *guest star* Denny Scott Miller.

On a giant Tsunami tidal wave, a surfer, Duke Williams, rides his surfboard onto the island. Ginger and Mary Ann are captivated by this handsome hunk of a man. Meanwhile, the Professor, who has studied the action of the waves and the tides, predicts a reverse Tsunami wave in the very near future. If Duke can ride the wave out, he can bring help to the Castaways. However, Duke is basking in the adoration of two lovely ladies, and is in no hurry to rescue them. Ginger and Mary Ann make him jealous so he will leave the island by pretending mad infatuations with the Professor and Gilligan. The scheme works, and Duke leaves on the next Tsunami. Unfortunately, when he arrives in Hawaii, he hits his head, and has no memory for where he's been. *Theme: Jealousy gets results, but the results are often unpredictable.*

Diamonds Are an Ape's Best Friend. *Written by* Elroy Schwartz; *directed by* Jack Arnold.

Mrs. Howell's favorite diamond brooch disappears. Mr. Howell is suspicious of the other Castaways at first, but then Mrs. Howell herself disappears. They find Mrs. Howell, and her brooch, in a cave, where they are guarded by a huge ape. They finally learn it's Mrs. Howell's perfume that actually attracted him. The Castaways try various contraptions to capture the ape and set Mrs. Howell free, but the situation is saved by the appearance of a female ape. The male ape likes the female ape better than he likes the brooch, Mrs. Howell, or her perfume. *Theme: Birds of a feather flock together.*

How to Be a Hero. *Written by* Herbert Finn and Alan Dinehart; *directed by* Tony Leader.

Gilligan is unable to save Mary Ann from drowning, and the Skipper has to dive in and save them both. The other Castaways make a big fuss about the Skipper, and Gilligan feels miserable because he has failed. The Skipper understands this and tries several schemes to make it appear Gilligan has done something heroic. When a native headhunter lands on their island, Gilligan is convinced it's just another scheme to make him seem like a hero. As a result, Gilligan is fearless with the headhunter and forces him off the island. *Theme: Self-confidence is half the battle.*

The Return of Wrongway Feldman. *Written by* Lawrence J. Cohen and Fred Freeman; *directed by* Gene Nelson; *guest star* Hans Conreid.

Wrongway Feldman returns to "Gilligan's Island," but not to rescue the Castaways. He plans to make the island his home; never to return to the madness of civilization, with all its crowding, traffic, and building. The Castaways decide the only way to get Wrongway to go back home again so they can be rescued is to make life on the island more crowded and hectic than civilization. Their plan succeeds. But instead of returning to civilization, Wrongway simply flies to a nearby uninhabited island where he can live in peace. *Theme: Everyone has his own idea of paradise.*

The Matchmaker. *Written by* Joanna Lee; *directed by* Tony Leader.

Mrs. Howell, a confirmed matchmaker, decides to make a romantic match on the island: Gilligan and Mary Ann. She and Mr. Howell invite Gilligan and Mary Ann to dinner at the Howell hut. She wants to show the youngsters the joys of married life. During dinner she and Mr. Howell get into such a quarrel that they decide on a trial separation. It takes all the other Castaways to get the Howells back together again. *Theme: As Robert Burns said, "The best laid schemes o' mice and men gang aft a-gley."*

Music Hath Charms. *Written by* Al Schwartz and Howard Harris; *directed by* Jack Arnold.

Inspired by Gilligan beating a drum, Mrs. Howell gets the idea for a cultural activity: a Castaways symphony orchestra. With Mr. Howell as the conductor of the group, and the Castaways playing various island-made instruments, the "music" drifts to a nearby island. On that island, the natives react angrily to the "music," which they consider a war chant (subtitles explain this). The chief herds them into their war canoes to attack the "enemy." One look at the war paint on the natives and the Castaways hide in a cave. They try various ways to frighten the natives away, but nothing works. It's Gilligan who solves the problem, by organizing a joint symphony orchestra between the natives and the Castaways. *Theme: Enemies can become friends through a common bond.*

New Neighbor Sam. *Written by* Charles Tannen and George O'Hanlon; *directed by* Thomas Montgomery.

The Castaways are terrified when they hear the voices of several gangsters on the island. They are very relieved when the "gangsters" turn out to be a parrot, who was doing all the voices. The parrot also talks about a boat somewhere on the island. But how can you get information from a parrot? Reacting to key words, he leads them to a cave where they find a yellowed old newspaper. The gangsters he's imitating have robbed an art musuem, but it was back in 1906, according to a yellowed newspaper in the cave, and the boat is long since gone. *Theme: Parrots are like computers: The information you get out is only as good as the information you put in.*

They're Off and Running. *Written by* Walter Black; *directed by* Jack Arnold.

In a series of turtle races Mr. Howell wins everything the Skipper owns, including, finally, the services of his first mate, Gilligan. Gilligan has to go to work for the Howells instead of the Skipper. When the Howells see how miserable the Skipper is without Gilligan, and how much Gilligan misses the Skipper, Mr. Howell offers the Skipper a chance to win Gilligan back in another turtle race. Mr. Howell exchanges his champion turtle with the Skipper's loser. And he does it secretly, because he doesn't want anybody to know his generosity. *Theme: Virtue is its own reward.*

Three to Get Ready. *Written by* David P. Harmon; *directed by* Jack Arnold.

Gilligan finds a semi-precious stone which the Skipper insists is the "Eye of the Idol." The Skipper claims that the person who finds the Eye of the Idol is granted three wishes before sundown. Gilligan immediately wishes for a quart of ice cream, and a quart of ice cream floats into the lagoon. The Professor says it's a simple coincidence; the ice cream fell from an airplane or from an ocean liner. In trying to decide on another wish, Gilligan accidentally repeats his first wish. Another container of ice cream floats into the lagoon. Now all the Castaways are convinced about the power of the Eye of the Idol. They gather together as Gilligan makes the third and final wish. He wishes they were off the island. The weight of all the people gathered together at the lagoon makes the land slide into the water—and they are all "off the island." *Theme: Be careful what you wish, because you might get exactly what you wish for.*

Forget Me Not. *Written by* Herbert Margolis; *directed by* Jack Arnold.

The Skipper is accidentally hit on the head and gets amnesia. The Professor hypnotizes him in order to help him regain his memory. First he takes the Skipper back to his grammar school days. The Skipper visualizes the other Castaways as his classmates. Then he takes the Skipper back to the war years and he sees the other Castaways as Japanese soldiers. He captures the Castaways and forces them into a cave, convinced they are the enemy. In the resultant confusion, the Skipper hits his head on the side of the cave and the blow returns him to normal. *Theme: Sometimes the very thing that causes a problem, cures the problem.*

Diogenes, Won't You Please Go Home? *Written by* David P. Harmon; *directed by* Christian Nyby; *guest star* Vito Scotti.

The Skipper, suffering from a blow on the head, sees the Professor, Ginger and Gilligan as Japanese soldiers in the episode "Forget Me Not."

Gilligan writes a diary, which he keeps hidden from the other Castaways. He writes about their adventures on the island, including the incident with the Japanese sailor. When the other Castaways learn about Gilligan's dairy, they all write their own diaries to describe the same incident. Each one views himself as the hero, à la Rashamon. Actual footage from that episode with the Japanese sailor, "So Sorry My Island Now," is used in this episode. The incident is then repeated from the perspective of each of the Castaways. *Theme: We all have a tendency to view ourselves in a favorable light.*

Physical Fatness. *Written by* Herbert Finn and Alan Dinehart; *directed by* Gary Nelson.

The Professor manages to make yellow flourescent dye markers from chemicals on the island. Everyone is convinced a plane or a boat will see it and rescue them. They're all delighted, but the Skipper is concerned about his weight. The Navy regulations about weight mean he must lose 22 pounds if he wants to rejoin the Navy by the time they're rescued. They also find that Gilligan must gain five pounds by the time they're rescued. The other Castaways stuff Gilligan and starve the Skipper so they'll be ready. In eating and drinking everything in sight, Gilligan accidentally swallows the yellow dye the Professor made. *Theme: There's many a slip twixt the cup and the lip.*

It's Magic. *Written by* Al Schwartz and Bruce Howard; *directed by* Jack Arnold.

Gilligan is fishing in the lagoon and hooks a large magician's crate. It contains all kinds of magician's tricks: cards, flowers, canes, flags, handcuffs, and even a large cabinet to make people disappear. Gilligan tries tricks on the other Castaways, always with disastrous results, and everyone tells him he's a nuisance. Ginger uses Gilligan as the subject in the disappearing cabinet trick, and much to everyone's amazement, Gilligan really disappears. Actually, Gilligan is so hurt by the way the others treated him he goes to another part of the island to live in a cave by himself. The others realize why Gilligan has "disappeared." They each apologize to him, and Gilligan rejoins his old friends. *Theme: To err is human, to forgive divine.*

Goodbye Old Paint. *Written by* David P. Harmon; *directed by* Jack Arnold; *guest star* Harold J. Stone.

On the other side of the island the Castaways discover a famous artist, Alexandri Gregor Dubov. The critics hated his abstract paintings, so he left civilization to develop a style the world will love. The Castaways praise his paintings to convince him he's ready to bring his work back to civilization. If he goes, they can be rescued, too. Unfortunately, Gilligan gives their plan away. They try a second plan. They tell Dubov his paintings are so terrible, Gilligan's a better painter. They hope this terrible insult will drive him from the island and they can leave with him. Instead, Dubov sails away without them to some other island. *Theme: Art, like beauty, is in the eye of the beholder.*

My Fair Gilligan. *Written by* Joanna Lee; *directed by* Tony Leader.

Gilligan saves Mrs. Howell's life. As a reward, Mr. Howell adopts him as their son and heir. But when Gilligan joins them in their hut, the Howells begin to reconsider. They don't like his table manners, his clothes, his lack of understanding of money and stocks and bonds. By the same token, Gilligan isn't too happy as the Howell heir. While the other Castaways are having fun, Gilligan has to study Mr. Howell's financial publications. That night Gilligan dreams he's not only a millionaire, he's a king. And his dream becomes a nightmare. He has to guillotine several of his subjects. When Gilligan awakens he doesn't want to be Mr. Howell's heir any longer. *Theme: You shouldn't try to be something you're not.*

A Nose by Any Other Name. *Written by* Elroy Schwartz; *directed by* Hal Cooper.

Gilligan falls out of a tree, and it leaves him with a badly swollen nose. The Professor tries to assure him his nose is just bruised, but Gilligan is convinced it's broken. The other Castaways tell him he looks better with his new nose, but Gilligan is miserable, and he wants the Professor to operate. With the other Castaways acting as assistants and nurses, the Professor puts Gilligan to sleep and then "operates" on his nose. He orders Gilligan to wait five days before removing the bandages. When he does, Gilligan is delighted he's got his old nose back. The Professor did nothing during "surgery." He knew the swelling would be down by the end of five days. *Theme: Further proof that time heals all wounds.*

Gilligan's Mother-In-Law. *Written by* Budd Grossman; *directed by* Jack Arnold; *guest stars* Henny Backus, Russ Grieve, Mary Foran, Eddie Little Sky.

The native chief from a nearby island decides Gilligan is the perfect husband for his daughter, a particularly unattractive maiden. Gilligan resists, but the others convince Gilligan to marry her so they can all get to the other island and possible rescue. As part of a native custom, Gilligan must engage in a spear-throwing contest with his "bride's" former suitor—throwing spears at each other. Gilligan drops out of contention, and the native girl marries her former suitor. *Theme: Everyone should know when to fold his cards.*

Beauty Is As Beauty Does. *Written by* Joanna Lee; *directed by* Jack Arnold.

To settle an argument as to who's the most beautiful woman on the island, the Castaways have a Miss Deserted Island beauty contest. The Skipper is clearly for Ginger; Mr. Howell just as clearly for Mrs. Howell; and the Professor favors Mary Ann. Gilligan holds the deciding vote. To keep from hurting anyone's feelings, Gilligan chooses Gladys, a monkey who has become his friend, as Miss Deserted Island. His reason is simple: Gladys is the only true native on the island. *Theme: Sometimes using a technicality can help you avoid making a no-win decision.*

The Little Dictator. *Written by* Bob Rodgers and Sid Mandel; *directed by* Jack Arnold; *guest star* Nehemiah Persoff.

A firing squad takes pity on a deposed Central American dictator and leaves him on this "uninhabited" island instead of shooting him. When the Dictator finds the Castaways, he does the only thing he knows how to do: be a dictator. Especially because he has a gun. Gilligan has a dream in which the Dictator convinces Gilligan to be the dictator. But Gilligan is simply a puppet controlled by the Dictator. The Castaways, accustomed to a democracy, finally realize they have to fight for freedom, and they overthrow the Dictator. Meanwhile, there's a counterrevolution, and the firing squad comes back to the island to pick him up and return him to power. *Theme: Democracy and freedom are precious, and one must fight, if necessary, to preserve them.*

Smile, You're on Mars Camera. *Written by* Al Schwartz and Bruce Howard; *directed by* Jack Arnold; *guest stars* Booth Coleman, Arthur Peterson.

A United States Space Satellite with a TV camera lands on the island. The scientists on the mainland think they're making a TV space probe of the planet Mars. At this time Gilligan has collected a mass of multi-colored feathers, and the Castaways have become covered with them. The lens on the space probe camera sends back pictures of the Castaways covered with feathers, and the scientists think they've discovered chicken people on the planet Mars. *Theme: Things are not always what they seem.*

The Sweepstakes. *Written by* Walter Black; *directed by* Jack Arnold.

Before Gilligan left on the S.S. *Minnow,* he bought a sweepstakes ticket. The winning number is announced on the radio, and Gilligan has the lucky ticket. But Gilligan can't find it. Meanwhile, on the island, the Howells have created a private country club, and none of the other Castaways have the necessary membership fee. Mr. Howell has a dream in which he is a grizzled old prospector who strikes it rich in a gold mine, and he shares the wealth with his friends in the western town. When he awakens from his nightmare, Mr. Howell has learned a lesson about wealth. Even though Gilligan's sweepstakes ticket turns out to be worthless, Mr. Howell allows all the other Castaways into his "exclusive" county club. *Theme: True friendships are rarer and more valuable than gold.*

(*Note:* Again, we used the *Gunsmoke* stage for the dream sequence.)

Quick Before It Sinks. *Written by* Stan Burns and Mike Marmer; *directed by* George Cahan.

The Professor has been doing depth tests in the lagoon, and he believes the island is sinking fast. The men begin to build an ark in the event the island goes under water. At first they don't tell the women. But the women learn about the island sinking, and they help the men with "ark" tests; rocking the "ark" back and forth, simulating ocean currents. The ark falls apart. But happily, they learn the island isn't sinking after all. The Professor's measuring stick was being moved by Gilligan to deeper and deeper water. *Theme: Leaping to conclusions can be dangerous to your health.*

Castaways Pictures Presents. *Written by* Herbet Finn and Alan Dinehart; *directed by* Jack Arnold.

The Castaways find some crates that have washed ashore in their lagoon. They're filled with costumes, cameras, makeup, etc.—probably lost by a film company. The Castaways make a film to show their plight: how they were shipwrecked and cast adrift on this island. Due to differences among them, the film is a total mess, but they set it adrift anyway in hopes someone will find it and come to their rescue. Nobody believes it's a true-life documentary, but it wins a prize at the Cannes Film Festival. *Theme: Truth can sometimes be mistaken for fiction.*

Agonized Labor. *Written by* Roland MacLane; *directed by* Jack Arnold.

The Castaways hear on the radio that Howell Industries has collapsed and Mr. and Mrs. Howell's fortune has been wiped out. Mr. Howell is ready to kill himself when he hears the news, and the others try to convince the Howells, without success, that money isn't everything—especially on a desert island where money is meaningless. A new announcement on the radio indicates the previous announcement was erroneous. Mr. Howell is as rich as ever, and he becomes his old self again. *Theme: Real riches are in the mind, not in the bank.*

Nyet, Nyet—Not Yet. *Written by* Adele T. Strassfield and Robert Riordan; *directed by* Jack Arnold; *guest stars* Vincent Beck and Danny Klega.

Two Russian cosmonauts, Igor and Ivan, arrive on the island in a space capsule. They have landed there accidentally, but the Castaways believe they have ulterior motives. By the same token, the Russians think the Castaways haven't been shipwrecked, but have a secret mission. The Professor wants to use the transmitter in the space capsule to radio for help. Before he can do it, a Russian submarine arrives and rescues the two cosmonauts and the space capsule. *Theme: Trust is a two-way street; mistrust is a dead end.*

Hi-Fi Gilligan. *Written by* Mary McCall; *directed by* Jack Arnold.

Gilligan gets hit in the jaw, and when he opens his mouth, he has suddenly become a radio. The Professor explains it is the result of two different kinds of fillings in Gilligan's teeth, which have set up an electrical current. There's a typhoon headed for the island, and when the regular radio is broken, the only way they can get news about the typhoon is from Gilligan's mouth. Thanks to this odd source of information, the Castaways know when to seek shelter in a cave before the typhoon hits. *Theme: A negative event can sometimes have a positive effect.*

The Chain of Command. *Written by* Arnold and Lois Peyser; *directed by* Leslie Goodwins.

The Skipper is almost killed by a falling tree. This makes him realize somebody else should be ready to take his place—especially since there's evidence that savage natives from a nearby island may be on the warpath. The Skipper tries to prepare his first mate, Gilligan, for this role, but he seems hopeless as his replacement. So do the other Castaways. The Skipper sets up a test case, pretending he's been captured by the savages. In the resultant confusion among the Castaways, it's Gilligan who emerges as the person in command, thanks to the earlier training the Skipper had given him. *Theme: Sometimes it's the unlikeliest person who turns out to be the hero.*

Don't Bug the Mosquitos. *Written by* Brad Radnitz; *directed by* Steve Binder; *guest stars* Les Brown, Jr., and the Wellingtons (Ed Wade, George Patterson, Kirby Johnson).

A rock group, the Mosquitos, is left on this "deserted" island by their agent to get some rest and relaxation from their screaming fans. They plan to stay for a month. The Castaways want them to leave sooner and take them back to civilization. Their first plan is to act even worse than the regular screaming fans. When that plan fails, the four men form a group called "The Gnats," who volunteer to perform as a warm-up act for the Mosquitos. That plan fails because the Mosquitos think the men are awful. Then, as a third plan, the three ladies form a group called "The Honey Bees" to perform as a warm-up act. Unfortunately, the Mosquitos think the Honey Bees are so good they're afraid of the competition, and they leave the island by themselves. *Theme: Inside every failed plan is another failed plan waiting to be released.*

Gilligan Gets Bugged. *Written by* Jack Gross, Jr., and Mike Stein; *directed by* Gary Nelson.

Gilligan may have been bitten by an ugly tropical bug. Based on his book of tropical bugs, the Professor learns the bite of the mantis cane could be fatal within twenty-four hours. The Professor discovers there's an antidote, if the Castaways can round up the correct ingredients on the island. As the other Castaways search for the various elements, they are all bitten by the same kind of bug. Upon further study, the Professor discovers there are two types of mantis cane bugs, and they have been bitten by the non-poisonous type. *Theme: As Alexander Pope said, "A little learning is a dangerous thing."*

Mine Hero. *Written by* David Braverman and Bob Marcus; *directed by* Wilbur D'Arcy.

Gilligan is fishing in the lagoon, and he hauls in an old land mine from World War II. Unfortunately, Gilligan starts the land mine ticking. It will explode at whatever time the mechanism is set for. The Professor is unable to deactivate it. Gilligan feels this whole problem was his fault in the first place, and he tows it far out in the lagoon, where it explodes with no harm to the Castaways. *Theme: Once again, a heroic deed is done by the unlikeliest hero.*

Erika Tiffany Smith to the Rescue. *Written by* David P. Harmon; *directed by* Jack Arnold; *guest star* Zsa Zsa Gabor.

A yacht arrives near the island and a very rich socialite, Erika Tiffany Smith, comes ashore. She is searching for a tropical island to build an elegant resort hotel. She soon becomes more interested in the Professor than in the hotel. The other Castaways encourage a romantic relationship, thinking this will lead to their rescue. But the Professor is more at home with test tubes than he is with women. Nevertheless, Erika Tiffany Smith decides to build the hotel anyway. She returns to her yacht, promising to send for them. However, there's a bad storm, and she can't relocate the tiny island again. *Theme: It was Virgil who first said, "Love conquers all," but even Virgil can be wrong.*

Zsa Zsa Gabor, a wealthy widow, arrives to buy the island, but tries to buy a husband instead—the Professor.

Not Guilty. *Written by* Roland MacLane; *directed by* Stanley Z. Cherry.

Gilligan reels in a crate while fishing. It contains some old newspapers from Honolulu which indicate that someone who left Hawaii on the S.S. *Minnow* might be a murderer. It seems that they were each shopping in the same store the same day the man was murdered. The Castaways all begin to suspect each other. They reenact the scene in the store to determine who's guilty. In doing so, they learn it was an accident; slamming the door released the spear gun which killed the victim. *Theme: Murder will out, and so will a non-murder.*

You've Been Disconnected. *Written by* Elroy Schwartz; *directed by* Jack Arnold.

After a big storm, a loop of telephone cable is washed into the lagoon. The rest of the Castaways help the Professor cut into the cable to communicate with the outside world and call for help. Then they use a crude dial system to try to reach someone. But they have no place to put the coins the operator asks for. Before they can try again, another storm hits and carries the cable out to sea. When the cable repair crews come to fix it, they know they'll be rescued. But Gilligan sealed it back together so perfectly there's no need for a repair crew. *Theme: There are some people who never seem to do wrong, and there are some who never seem to do right.*

The Postman Cometh. *Written by* Herbert Finn and Alan Dinehart; *directed by* Leslie Goodwins.

For months Mary Ann has been writing to her boyfriend, putting the letters in bottles and tossing them out to sea. The Skipper and Gilligan hear on the radio that Mary

Ann's boyfriend has eloped with someone else. Mary Ann overhears them talking about "poor Mary Ann" and thinks she's going to die. That night Mary Ann has a dream: She's in the hospital with a fatal disease. The other Castaways are doctors and nurses in her dream. The next day, she learns about her "boyfriend's" elopement. She confesses she hardly knew him. She wanted the others to think someone was very much in love with her. *Theme: As Robert Frost said, "Love is an irresistible desire to be irresistibly desired."*

Seer Gilligan. *Written by* Elroy Schwartz; *directed by* Leslie Goodwins.

Gilligan discovers he can read minds. All the other Castaways are annoyed with him because he knows what they're thinking. Even more importantly, they want to find out how he does it. They track down Gilligan's newfound mind reading powers to a bush he found which produces certain rare berries. In answer to the other Castaways' pleas, Gilligan brings back enough berries for everyone. They eat the berries and then read each other's minds. This leads to arguments because each one knows exactly what the other one thinks of him/her. Gilligan burns the bush. *Theme: Some things are better left unsaid.*

Love Me, Love My Skipper. *Written by* Herbert Finn and Alan Dinehart; *directed by* Tony Leader.

Everyone, except the Skipper, receives an invitation to a party at the Howell hut. In retaliation, the other Castaways plan their own party the same night. The Howells are furious everyone is boycotting their party. Then Gilligan finds the lost invitation to the Skipper which had been sent by the Howells. This finally clears up the misunderstanding. All animosities are forgotten when the Howells and the other Castaways get together and have one big party. *Theme: For a happier life, turn misunderstandings into understandings.*

Gilligan's Living Doll. *Written by* Bob Stevens; *directed by* Leslie Goodwins.

Thanks to a parachute, a robot lands on the island, apparently missing its objective. The Castaways are delighted because they're positive a search party will be looking for the robot and they'll be rescued. Then they hear a radio report that the search for the robot is being abandoned. They try to get the robot itself to save them. Maybe he can walk to Hawaii on the ocean bottom. Amazingly, the robot is able to accomplish this feat. Unfortunately, Gilligan inserted a rabbit's foot in its mechanism for good luck and it garbled the message the Professor had programmed. *Theme: Unfortunately, high technology is at the mercy of low I.Q.s.*

Forward March. *Written by* Jack Raymond; *directed by* Jerry Hopper.

The Castaways are besieged by hand grenades and machine-gun fire. They finally track down the source. It's a gorilla who has discovered a cache of army supplies left over from World War II. Somehow they must remove the arsenal from the cave before the gorilla kills them. The other Castaways try various complicated ways to trick the animal. Gilligan, on the other hand, teaches the gorilla how to throw the grenades like a baseball pitcher, and the two of them toss the grenades into the lagoon, where their explosions are harmless. *Theme: The simplest approach is often the best.*

Ship Ahoax. *Written by* Charles Tannen and George O'Hanlon; *directed by* Leslie Goodwins.

Being shipwrecked for so long is starting to drive all the Castaways crazy. The Professor and Ginger concoct a scheme for Ginger to convince the others that she can foretell the future in her "crystal" ball. She puts on an act as a fortune teller and convinces them a ship is coming to rescue them. Just then there's an announcement on the radio that a fleet of ships is in search of a missing destroyer near their group of islands. They're convinced she's a real fortune teller. During her next seance, Ginger passes notes to the other Castaways telling each one her fortune telling is a fake and trusting each one to keep her secret from the others. *Theme: Hope for the future is necessary for survival.*

Feed the Kitty. *Written by* J.E. Selby and Dick Sanville; *directed by* Leslie Goodwins.

A crate washes into the lagoon containing a lion, which was headed for a zoo, but was obviously washed off the boat. With the lion loose on the island, all the Castaways are terrified. Gilligan takes a thorn out of the lion's paw, and they become friends. But when the lion runs out of food, he begins to eye the Castaways hungrily, and the Professor and Skipper cage the lion. Gilligan, terrified when he thinks the lion has eaten the Skipper, agrees with their action. The crated lion is on the shore of the lagoon when a huge wave floats him out to sea, where he is rescued. *Theme: You can never be sure you've taken the "wild" out of wild animals.*

Operation: Steam Heat. *Written by* Terence and Joan Maples; *directed by* Stanley Z. Cherry.

Gilligan is happy when he finds a hole in the ground which is spouting hot water. Unfortunately, the Professor determines it indicates a nearby volcano is about to erupt. The Professor makes a crude bomb from materials on the island. If they drop the bomb into the volcano, the force of the explosion will reverse the eruption. There are anxious moments when they believe Gilligan has swallowed the ingredients; more anxious moments when they believe Ginger has thrown herself into the volcano to save the others; more anxious moments when the fuse to the bomb becomes tangled on Gilligan's feet. But in the end, they drop the bomb, and it reverses the volcanic eruption. *Theme: Near misses don't count; the result does.*

Will the Real Mr. Howell Please Stand Up? *Written by* Budd Grossman; *directed by* Jack Arnold.

The Castaways hear on the radio that Thurston Howell III has returned to Wall Street. He's selling his companies and spending money like crazy. He's obviously an imposter. Mr. Howell, trapped on the island, is frantic at the loss of all his millions. Then they learn the imposter bought a yacht and is taking a cruise. The phony Mr. Howell is not only a swindler, but also a drunk. He falls off his yacht and swims ashore on the island. He knocks out the real Mr. Howell and pretends to be him. For awhile, he's able to fool the Castaways, even Mrs. Howell. But after he's exposed, he swims away from the island and is picked up by his yacht. Upon his return to the business world he's recognized as a fake. *Theme: Sometimes it's hard to tell the phony from the real thing.*

Ghost a-Go-Go. *Written by* Roland MacLane; *directed by* Leslie Goodwins; *guest star* Richard Kiel.

Gilligan sees a ghostly figure on the island. Ordinarily, nobody would believe him. But Mary Ann and Ginger see it, too. Then the "ghost" tells them they must leave the island immediately or suffer the consequences. He'll provide the boat. The Professor is suspicious of this gift. So the Castaways make dummies of themselves and set them adrift in a new boat. The boat explodes, blowing the dummies to pieces. The "ghost" reports to his superiors that he has destroyed the inhabitants and they're in control of the off-shore oil rights. The Castaways dress themselves in sheets, become "ghosts"

The episode of "V for Vitamins" features a dream sequence of "Jack and the Beanstalk," with the Skipper as the giant and Bob Denver's own son, Patrick, playing Gilligan.

themselves, and scare away the intruder "Ghost." *Theme: Here's to that old saying, "fight fire with fire"!*

Allergy Time. *Written by* Budd Grossman; *directed by* Jack Arnold.

The Skipper suddenly can't stop itching and sneezing. The Professor tests different things and finally determines the Skipper is allergic to Gilligan. Gilligan goes to sleep in the Professor's hut. But the Professor develops an allergic reaction to him also. So do the Howells, and Mary Ann and Ginger. Gilligan leaves, with a note saying he's moving to the other side of the island. The Professor develops a vaccine for the allergy to Gilligan and asks the Castaways to take the shots. It's a tough shot and a big needle, but they all agree to take it, for Gilligan's sake. Then Gilligan discovers he's allergic to himself. It's the coconut/papaya hair tonic he's been using. *Theme: A friend in need is a friend indeed.*

The Friendly Physician. *Written by* Elroy Schwartz; *directed by* Jack Arnold; *guest stars* Vito Scotti, Mike Mazurki.

A kindly doctor, Dr. Balinkoff, arrives on the island, and he says he'll help the Castaways get rescued. On his island, the Castaways find torture chambers, etc., and they learn about the doctor's experiments: changing the mind of one animal into another animal's body. Now the doctor wants to try it with people. He exchanges Gilligan's mind with Mr. Howell's body, Mrs. Howell's mind and the Skipper's body, Mary Ann and the Professor, and Ginger and Igor, his assistant. Then Ginger/Igor help them all return to their correct bodies and they escape back to their own island. *Theme: In spite of Tennessee Williams, one cannot always depend on the kindness of strangers.*

"V" for Vitamins. *Written by* Barney Slater; *directed by* Jack Arnold.

Because of the lack of citrus fruit, the Castaways become afflicted with a vitamin deficiency. It's Gilligan's job to guard the few remaining orange seeds, but he falls asleep and has a nightmare. In his dream Gilligan is Jack in "Jack and the Beanstalk." His mother (Mrs. Howell) sends him to the store to buy some oranges. On the way, he exchanges her jewels for some beans. The beans form a giant beanstalk leading to the Giant's castle, where the Giant is hoarding crates full of oranges. With the help of the other Castaways, who play various roles in the Giant's castle, Jack tries to elude the Giant. When Gilligan awakens from his nightmare, he learns the Professor has found a citrus grove on the other side of the island with oranges, grapefruits, and lemons. *Theme: People usually fail to appreciate important things in life until they're gone.*

(*Note:* In the dream sequence with the Giant, Bob Denver's own small son, Patrick Denver, played the part of Gilligan in the Giant's castle.)

Mr. and Mrs.? *Written by* Jack Gross, Jr. and Mike Stein; *directed by* Gary Nelson.

The Castaways hear on the radio that the minister who married Mr. and Mrs. Howell had not been ordained, and all his marriages are invalid. Mrs. Howell refuses to share the hut with Mr. Howell until they are properly married. Fortunately, the Captain of a ship can marry couples. So the Castaways arrange the wedding on a raft in the lagoon. However, the happy couple gets into an argument, and the wedding is off. But when a savage headhunter (the Skipper) appears, Mr. Howell dramatically leaps in front of his wife to protect her, and his brave act brings them together again. *Theme: It takes an occasional thorn to remind us that marriage is truly a bed of roses.*

Meet the Meteor. *Written by* Elroy Schwartz; *directed by* Jack Arnold.

A piece of a meteor lands on the island. The Professor warns them not to go near it; the fact that it glows indicates it has picked up cosmic rays in its path through the stratosphere. The meteor has an immediate effect on the trees around it, aging them fifty years within a week. If it speeds up the life process of the Castaways at the same rate, they'll all die of old age within two weeks. Gilligan has a dream, a nightmare in which all the Castaways are fifty years older, still on the island, gray, wrinkled, and bent. Fortunately, a lightning bolt hits the meteor and disintegrates it before the Castaways can be affected by its cosmic rays. *Theme: Growing old may not be an enjoyable prospect, but it's clearly better than the alternative.*

Up at Bat. *Written by* Ron Friedman; *directed by* Jerry Hopper.
Gilligan is exploring a cave when he's bitten on the neck by a bat. Having seen the Bela Lugosi pictures, Gilligan is positive he's going to turn into a vampire. He goes to the other side of the island to prevent himself from biting the other Castaways. A bat flies into the Skipper's hut and the Skipper is convinced his little buddy is, after all, a vampire. Meanwhile, Gilligan is having a nightmare: Transylvania in 1895. He's in a coffin, like Dracula, awaiting the arrival of guests at his castle; the other Castaways are servants, guests, etc. Finally, the Skipper awakes Gilligan from his nightmare with good news: The Professor has learned the bat that bit him is a harmless red fruit bat. *Theme: Belief in superstitions brings bad luck.*

Gilligan vs. Gilligan. *Written by* Joanna Lee; *directed by* Jerry Hopper.
A foreign power believes the Castaways are on the island for some secret military purpose. In order to discover this purpose, the foreign power makes up one of its spies to look exactly like Gilligan. He arrives on the island, captures Gilligan, puts him in a cave, ties his hands and feet. Then he acts exactly like Gilligan while he talks to the other Castaways to discover their real motives on this island. He reports everything to his superior on his miniaturized walkie-talkie. Gilligan finally unties himself, tries to convince the others that there's another Gilligan on the island. The spy, meanwhile, having failed at his mission, is recalled by his foreign government. *Theme: Governments, like people, are forever looking for hidden meanings, and very often there are none.*
(*Note:* This is the second episode in which one of the Castaways plays a dual role. Mr. Howell played one in **Will the Real Mr. Howell Please Stand Up?** and Ginger later played one in **All About Eva.**)

Pass the Vegetables Please. *Written by* Elroy Schwartz; *directed by* Leslie Goodwins.
A crate of vegetables is fished out of the lagoon by Gilligan. The Castaways are delighted because they haven't had real garden vegetables since they were shipwrecked, and they quickly plant the seeds. The Castaways are astounded at the speed at which the seeds sprout and turn into plants. After eating them they learn that the vegetables they've eaten come from "experimental radioactive seeds." They're afraid the radioactivity will kill them. Instead, the radioactivity has increased the power of the vegetables. Mary Ann, who ate carrots, can see things twenty miles away; Gilligan, who ate spinach, is able to lift tree trunks; Mrs. Howell, who ate sugar beets, is so full of energy she does everything at four times normal speed. *Theme: As ye sow, so shall ye reap.*

The Producer. *Written by* Gerald Gardner and Dee Caruso; *directed by* George M. Cahan and Ida Lupino; *guest star* Phil Silvers.
Harold Hecuba, a famous producer, scouting a location, crash-lands his plane and floats into the lagoon. Accustomed to giving orders, Hecuba treats the Castaways as his flunkies. The Castaways, feeling they'll be rescued when a search party locates Hecuba, accede to his every wish. The Castaways want to show off Ginger's talents for the producer, so they put on a musical. The only plays they have on the island are in the Professor's book of Shakespeare, so they do a musical *Hamlet*, fitting Shakespeare's words to various operatic themes. Hecuba thinks it's such a great idea, he leaves the island

Gilligan and Ginger as vampires in an episode appropriately titled "Up at Bat."

quietly so he can take sole credit for a musical *Hamlet* when he returns to Hollywood. *Theme: As Shakespeare himself said, "Love all, trust a few."*

Voodoo. *Written by* Herbert Finn and Alan Dinehart; *directed by* George M. Cahan; *guest star* Eddie Little Sky.

Gilligan discovers native artifacts in a cave. The Skipper, who believes in island superstitions and voodoo, doesn't want them touched. The other Castaways, particularly the Professor, laugh at the Skipper's fears and remove the artifacts. Soon afterward, the Castaways react in pain as a native witch doctor sticks pins in dolls he has made of each of them. When he turns the dolls, the Castaways turn; when he puts a flame under the dolls, their feet burn; when he tickles the dolls, they laugh, etc. Then he turns the Professor, the absolute non-believer in witchcraft, into a zombie. Gilligan finds the dolls the witch doctor made, and that breaks the voodoo spell. *Theme: Your lack of belief in certain things does not necessarily eliminate their existence.*

Phil Silvers, as a Hollywood producer, and his Castaways production of Hamlet, *with Mr. Howell as Claudius, Mrs. Howell as Gertrude, Mary Ann as Laertes, Skipper as Polonius, Gilligan as Hamlet, and Ginger as Ophelia. (The Professor was a one-man tech crew, behind the scenes.) The songs from this musical version — clever paraphrases of Shakespeare's lines, set to popular operatic themes — are well remembered by fans of the Bard and the Castaways alike.*

Where There's a Will. *Written by* Sid Mandel and Roy Kammerman; *directed by* Charles Norton.

Mr. Howell, feeling sickly, takes to his bed. All the other Castaways try to comfort him. Because they are so solicitous, Mr. Howell changes his will, leaving huge fortunes to each of them. Then he overhears part of a conversation in which they're planning to trap and kill a dangerous animal on the island. Mr. Howell thinks he's the target, now that they're going to share in his will. In order to confirm his suspicions, he pretends to fall into quicksand. As Mr. Howell watches his own funeral service, he sees that the Castaways are all genuinely grief-stricken, with no thought of their inheritance. *Theme: There's an old Chinese proverb, "He who is suspicious of his friends has a tiger by the tail."*

Man with a Net. *Written by* Budd Grossman; *directed by* Leslie Goodwins; *guest star* John McGiver.

Lord Beasley, a collector of rare butterflies, has reason to believe a Pussycat Swallowtail is on this island. He has a flare gun to signal the boat to pick him up after he catches it. The Castaways, hoping to be rescued with Lord Beasley, try to help him capture the rare butterfly, without success. Then the Castaways try to get Lord Beasley tipsy on some fermented island fruit so they can use his flare gun. Instead, they all pass

A native witch doctor (played by Eddie Little Sky) stuck pins in these dolls to cast a spell over their look-alike Castaways in the episode "Voodoo."

out while the brew has no effect on Lord Beasley. Just then, Lord Beasley captures the elusive Pussycat Swallowtail. He tries to rouse the Castaways, but they're all in a deep sleep, so he leaves without them. *Theme: Once again, the Castaways learn the truth of Shakespeare's words, as they are "hoist with their own petard."*

Hair Today, Gone Tomorrow. *Written by* Brad Radnitz; *directed by* Tony Leader.

One day Gilligan wakes up and finds all his hair has fallen out; he's completely bald. The others try to convince him he looks great, but he's ashamed, and hides in a cave. They make a wig for him, but he refuses to wear it. The Skipper berates Gilligan for making such an issue about being bald. Then the Skipper's hair falls out. He, too, is completely bald. And he's more upset than Gilligan was. The Professor finds that the homemade bleach they were using to do the laundry made their hair fall out. *Theme: Giving others advice is easy; taking it yourself is difficult.*

Ring Around Gilligan. *Written by* John Fenton Murray; *directed by* George M. Cahan; *guest star* Vito Scotti.

Doctor Balinkoff, the mad scientist, returns to the island to test a new invention. It's a ring which places the person wearing it under Balinkoff's control; they each become his robot doing his bidding. His eventual plan is to use the Castaways as robots to steal all the gold bars at Fort Knox. In the final rehearsal for the Fort Knox crime, using coconuts for gold bars, the Castaways accidentally smash the robot control box, which the mad scientist can never hope to duplicate. *Theme: How to succeed in the hero business without even trying.*

Topsy-Turvy. *Written by* Elroy Schwartz; *directed by* Gary Nelson; *guest stars* Eddie Little Sky, Allen Jaffe, Roman Gabriel.

An ominous drum beat indicates savage natives from a nearby island are on the warpath. As he attempts to collect branches to make spears and clubs for defense, Gilligan runs into a tree. The resultant blow to his head causes him to see the entire world upside down. The Professor says the only possible cure for Gilligan's strange

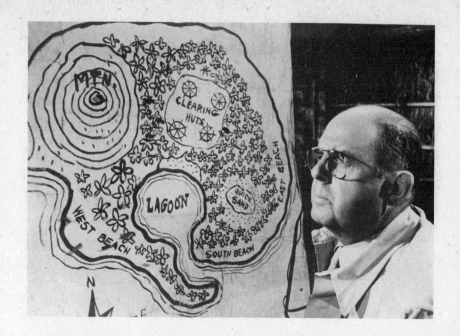

Top: *Lord Beasley (John McGiver), a world-famous butterfly collector, examining a crude map of "Gilligan's Island" for a likely place to find the rare Pussycat Swallowtail in the episode "Man with a Net."* Bottom: *Lord Beasley examines a butterfly. Skipper and Gilligan claim it is the Pussycat Swallowtail, but they have actually painted a common butterfly to resemble the rare species — note palette that Gilligan fails to conceal.*

Thanks to a strange allergy which makes Gilligan bald, the only thing on his head is the Skipper's lips in the episode "Hair Today, Gone Tomorrow."

condition is keptibora berries. Their brew does cure Gilligan of his topsy-turvy condition. Unfortunately, it has a side effect: it causes him to see everyone in multiples. This gives Gilligan an idea. He pretends the potion is delicious, and the invading natives quickly drink the rest. As a result, the natives see multiple Castaways in such large numbers that they believe themselves completely outnumbered. They dive into the lagoon and leave the island. *Theme: The darkest of clouds sometimes has a silver lining.*

The Invasion. *Written by* Sam Locke and Joel Rapp; *directed by* Leslie Goodwins.
    A battered, water-soaked leather attache case, with a dangling handcuff, is pulled from the lagoon. It's obviously top secret, bearing the legend, "Property of U.S. Government—Do Not Open!" The Professor says it must have been handcuffed to a secret agent, and Washington will spare no expense in tracking it down. Therefore, the

Top: *The episode "The Invasion" featured a spy dream sequence in which Gilligan is James Bondish and the Skipper is Motherish.* Bottom: *In the same dream sequence, Mr. and Mrs. Howell are the "Evil Agent Guys," determined to eliminate "Good Guy Gilligan."*

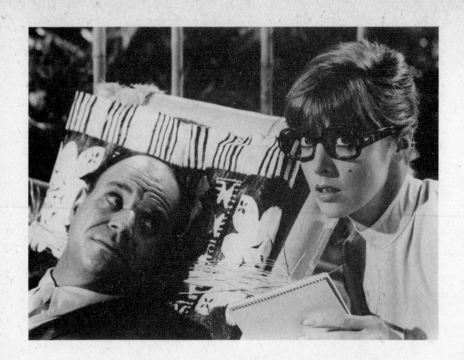

Top: *In the episode "The Kidnapper," Ginger tries her skill as an amateur psychiatrist to decriminalize Don Rickles, a professional thief. She's lucky he doesn't steal her couch.* Bottom: *Mrs. Howell's jewels are about to recriminalize Rickles again.*

Castaways will be found and rescued. Gilligan has a dream: he's Secret Agent Gilligan, Superspy. The other Castaways are agents of evil, trying to prevent Superspy Gilligan from delivering the attache case. His dream turns into a nightmare. After Gilligan awakens, the attache case breaks open, and the contents are revealed. They are United States secret defense plans, but from World War I. The case has been floating around in the ocean for over fifty years. *Theme: Wine may get more valuable with age, but not secret plans.*

The Kidnapper. *Written by* Ray Singer; *directed by* Jerry Hopper; *guest star* Don Rickles.
Mrs. Howell is kidnapped, and there's a ransom note demanding $10,000 for her safe return. Obviously, there's a stranger on the island. Mr. Howell pays the money, and Mrs. Howell is released. Then Mary Ann is kidnapped and the ransom note demands $20,000. Then Mary Ann is released and Ginger is kidnapped, for $30,000. Finally, the Skipper captures the kidnapper. He's a professional thief who deliberately left civilization to be on an uninhabited island where he wouldn't be tempted by crime. But once he saw people he got the itch again. The Castaways resolve to reform the criminal. After he seems cured, the Castaways hold a coming out party for him. During the party, the crook steals Mrs. Howell's jewels, Mr. Howell's wallet, everything else of value, and leaves the island in his motor launch. *Theme: It's hard to teach an old dog new tricks.*

And Then There Were None. *Written by* Ron Friedman; *directed by* Jerry Hopper.
One after another, the Castaways begin to disappear—first Mary Ann, then Ginger, then Mrs. Howell, then the Skipper. Gilligan has a nightmare in which he is Doctor Jekyll and Mr. Hyde, on trial in an English Victorian court. In the trial, Mary Ann is Eliza Doolittle; Mrs. Howell is Mary Poppins, and Ginger is the Lady in Red. They all testify against Doctor Gilligan, who becomes Mr. Hyde when the mention of various foods makes fangs and bushy evil eyebrows appear. When he awakens from his nightmare, Gilligan disappears, too. He falls into an underground munitions room built during World War II, and is reunited with the others. *Theme: When your imagination runs wild, don't go along for the ride.*

All About Eva. *Written by* Joanna Lee; *directed by* Jerry Hopper.
A motorboat pulls into the lagoon with Eva Grubb. Eva is tall, unattractive, with horned-rimmed glasses and a hopeless hairstyle. She's left civilization behind because men ignore her. She plans to live her life on a deserted island. She gives them the key to her motorboat if they promise to leave her there. The Castaways are afraid she might do away with herself. Instead, they decide to turn the ugly duckling into a beautiful swan, thanks to makeup, a new hairdo, etc. Then they can all leave the island together. With her newfound beauty, Eva is an exact duplicate of Ginger. Once she realizes this, Eva leaves by herself, returns to Hollywood and resumes Ginger's career. *Theme: Sometimes the reward you get for giving someone a pat on the back is a kick in the pants.*

Gilligan Goes Gung Ho. *Written by* Bruce Howard; *directed by* Robert Scheerer.
The Castaways believe there should be some form of law and order on the island. The Skipper is quickly named Sheriff, and Gilligan becomes his Deputy. Gilligan takes his new assignment very seriously. The Professor is collecting rock samples with a phosphorescent element, scheelite, which glows in the dark. With these rocks, a plane

Gilligan, as Mr. Hyde, in a dream sequence in which he believes he has murdered the other Castaways. From the episode "And Then There Were None."

might spot them. Meanwhile, Gilligan, the Deputy, is putting his newfound power to use. He arrests Mr. Howell for some infraction of the law, and puts him in jail, a hut with bars on it. Then he puts Ginger in jail, followed by Mary Ann, Mrs. Howell and the Professor. When the Skipper hears how Gilligan has abused his power as Deputy, he tries to get the key to the jail away from Gilligan. This puts the Skipper behind bars, too. Then Gilligan accidentally locks himself in with them. At this point the plane flies over the island but can't rescue them since Gilligan has put them all in jail. *Theme: As Sir Charles Percy Snow said, "No one is fit to be trusted with power."*

Take A Dare. *Written by* Roland MacLane; *directed by* Stanley Z. Cherry; *guest star* Strother Martin.

George Barkley, a contestant on a quiz show, *Take a Dare*, will get $10,000 if he can exist on a deserted island for one full week without help from anyone. Mr. Barkley does just fine on this particular "deserted" island, stealing food, cooking utensils, blankets, a hammock, etc., from the Castaways. Finally, the Castaways discover him. Mr. Howell offers him a million dollars if he will help rescue them, but Barkley refuses to believe the Howell money is real. Instead, he leaves the island without them and collects the $10,000 on *Take a Dare*. *Theme: Some people settle for hamburger when they could have filet mignon.*

Court Martial. *Written by* Roland MacLane; *directed by* Gary Nelson.

A radio broadcast indicates the Maritime Board of Inquiry has found the Skipper of the S.S. *Minnow* guilty of negligence in the shipwreck. The Skipper is so upset at this verdict he tries to do away with himself. The Castaways reenact the final hours of the storm aboard the ship to prove he was innocent. In doing so, they prove the shipwreck was Gilligan's fault. This causes Gilligan to have a nightmare in which he is Lord Admiral Gilligan storming a pirate ship in order to free the queen mother and her two lovely daughters. When Gilligan awakens, he hears the good news: an announcement on the radio absolving the Skipper and his crew of all blame. An incorrect weather report, failing to mention the storm, was responsible. *Theme: No one should blame himself for events beyond his control.*

The Hunter. *Written by* Ben Gershman and William Freedman; *directed by* Leslie Goodwins; *guest stars* Rory Calhoun, Harold Sakata.

A helicopter lands on the island carrying a famous hunter, Jonathan Kincaid, and his assistant, Ramoo. They've hunted big game all over the world. On this island Kincaid finds the biggest game of all—man! Which one of the Castaways will it be? Gilligan! If he can stay alive for twenty-four hours, Kincaid promises to rescue all the Castaways. They don't trust him, but Kincaid has the only rifle and all the ammunition, so the game is played by his rules. With help from the other Castaways, Gilligan manages to remain alive for the twenty-four hours. *Theme: Where there's life there's hope.*

Lovey's Secret Admirer. *Written by* Herbert Finn and Alan Dinehart; *directed by* David McDearmon.

Mrs. Howell receives a love letter from a secret admirer. She's flattered at receiving the note, and Mr. Howell is furious. Obviously, the note must have been written by the Skipper, the Professor, or Gilligan. The Professor rigs up a lie detector machine, and the secret admirer turns out to be Mr. Howell. The love notes were meant to add a little excitement to his wife's life. This causes Mrs. Howell to dream that she is Cinderella with two ugly sisters. The fairy Godfather, Gilligan, turns Cinderella into a beautiful princess. She goes to the ball with her two ugly sisters, where she meets Prince Howell, who prefers her to any other woman in the kingdom. *Theme: It's wonderful to appreciate others, and it's just as wonderful to be appreciated.*

Our Vines Have Tender Apes. *Written by* Sid Mandel and Roy Kammerman; *directed by* David McDearmon; *guest stars* Denny Scott Miller, Janos Prohaska.

The potential star of a new series of movies, "Tongo, The Ape Man," arrives on the island. The method actor has been dropped on this "uninhabited" island, to swing from trees, eat fruits, and live like Tarzan. When the Castaways discover the "ape man," it's a perfect way for Tongo to see how convincing he can be. The Castaways try to teach him how to behave like a human being. One day the ape man is captured by a gorilla. Then, all pretense at being an ape man disappears and he blubbers and cries, terrified of the gorilla, until the Castaways rescue him. They think the actor will, in turn, rescue them when the helicopter comes to pick him up. But that would reveal his cowardice

Top: *From the episode "The Hunter": Gilligan is terrified of guns, especially when they're in the hands of Rory Calhoun, a big game hunter who's planning to aim one at* him. Bottom: *Mr. and Mrs. Howell as Prince Charming and Cinderella in a dream sequence from the episode "Lovey's Secret Admirer."*

on the island. So he leaves them there. *Theme: At the risk of rewriting Shakespeare, "how sharper than a serpent's tooth is a thankless actor."*

Gilligan's Personal Magnetism. *Written by* Bruce Howard; *directed by* Hal Cooper.

Gilligan and the Skipper are bowling with a round rock when a tropical storm hits. Gilligan, holding the rock, is struck by lightning, and the iron content of the rock causes a molecular attraction between the metal and his hand so he can't release it. However, a second lightning bolt hits the magnetized rock, and the molecular viscosity makes Gilligan completely invisible. Because he's invisible, Gilligan tells the Skipper what he thinks of him; that he's sick of being browbeaten by someone just because he's bigger and fatter and stronger. Unfortunately for Gilligan, at this moment he becomes visible again. *Theme: "Gilligan's Island Law: Inside every misfortune is a bigger misfortune waiting to get out."*

Splashdown. *Written by* John Fenton Murray; *directed by* Jerry Hopper; *guest stars* Chick Hearn, George Neise, Scott Graham, Jim Spencer.

According to a radio report, a spacecraft with two astronauts has been launched to rendezvous with an unmanned spacecraft. However, the unmanned spacecraft goes out of control, and lands in the lagoon. The Castaways are delighted because Mission Control will be searching for it. Mr. and Mrs. Howell, Mary Ann and Ginger, anxious to be the first ones rescued, sneak aboard the spacecraft at night and stow away. When the four stowaways are discovered and leave the spacecraft, Gilligan fails to obey the Skipper's instruction to guard it, and it floats out into the lagoon. Mission Control, concerned top secret instruments aboard the unmanned spacecraft might fall into the hands of an unfriendly nation, blows it up. *Theme: Every now and then, disobeying an instruction can be the best instruction of all.*

High Man on the Totem Pole. *Written by* Brad Radnitz; *directed by* Herbert Coleman; *guest stars* Jim Lefebvre, Al Ferrara, Pete Sotos.

The Castaways come upon a totem pole on the island which was made by ferocious headhunters. Oddly enough, the carved head on the top of the totem pole looks exactly like Gilligan. As a result, Gilligan is convinced he has headhunter blood in him. The other Castaways try to convince him the resemblance is just a coincidence, but Gilligan is obsessed. To avoid looking at the head on the pole, Gilligan cuts it off. Three ferocious headhunters from that tribe arrive and find their totem pole disfigured. They swear to kill whoever is responsible. They capture the Howells, the Skipper, Ginger, and Mary Ann. The Professor convinces Gilligan to climb the totem pole, substituting his head for the head of the dead king, and the "wooden head" orders the headhunters to release the prisoners. The natives are terrified when their dead king speaks, and they leave the island. *Theme: Superstition is a two-way street.*

The Second Ginger Grant. *Written by* Ron Friedman; *directed by* Steve Binder.

Mary Ann, who has always admired Ginger's singing and dancing, falls and hits her head. When Mary Ann regains consciousness she believes she's Ginger. She starts wearing Ginger's dresses and acting sexy with all the men. The Professor decides the Castaways should put on a show introducing Mary Ann as Ginger Grant, to sing and dance as Ginger would. The shock might snap Mary Ann out of it. In trying to dance like Ginger, Mary Ann trips and falls, hitting her head. And Mary Ann is Mary Ann again. *Theme: As the soap opera says, each of us has "One Life to Live."*

The Secret of Gilligan's Island. *Written by* Bruce Howard, *story by* Bruce Howard and Arne Sultan; *directed by* Gary Nelson.

In one of the caves Gilligan finds some stone tablets covered with ancient hieroglyphics. The Professor believes these tablets are part of a larger stone slab used by some ancient civilization to record the tides and the winds. Gilligan has a dream: All the Castaways are cave people, living millions of years ago, and making the tablets which he has found. The dream turns into a nightmare when a dinosaur invades their cave. The Professor has his own nightmare: Instead of the tablets telling how to *leave* the island, he realizes the hieroglyphics indicate how to *get* there. *Theme: Reading is important, but it's even more important to understand what you're reading*.

Slave Girl. *Written by* Michael Fessier; *directed by* Wilbur D'Arcy; *guest stars* Midori; Michael Forest.
Kalani, a beautiful native girl, paddling into the lagoon, falls into the water, striking her head on the canoe. Gilligan dives into the lagoon and saves her life. She becomes his slave, which is the custom in her tribe. If Gilligan refuses, Kalani threatens to kill herself. Meanwhile, Mrs. Howell, Mary Ann, and Ginger are upset with the gorgeous Kalani, who distracts all the men. Kalani's native boyfriend arrives on the island, searching for Kalani. He learns she is Gilligan's slave and Ugandi wants to fight Gilligan to the death so he can reclaim Kalani. To solve this problem, the Professor uses a drug on Gilligan to make him appear dead. When Gilligan suddenly comes alive, it frightens Ugandi and the other natives, who quickly leave the island with Kalani. *Theme: Slavery anywhere has always caused problems.*

It's a Bird, It's a Plane, It's Gilligan. *Written by* Sam Locke and Joel Rapp; *directed by* Gary Nelson.
A one-man jetpack, manually operated, is being considered for official Air Force use. During a test, it is lost at sea, and the Castaways find it in the lagoon. The jetpack is filled with enough fuel to get to Hawaii. The Professor believes it's too dangerous for one of them, and he builds a dummy who will take a message. Gilligan accidentally starts the robot and it circles around the lagoon, using up most of the fuel. There's only enough left for Gilligan to stay aloft for fifteen minutes. That's sufficient if a search plane from the Air Force comes by at the right time. It does. But just then, Gilligan steers into a cloud and the Air Force misses him. *Theme: Man's most ingenious new inventions are at the mercy of man himself.*

The Pigeon. *Story by* Jack Raymond and Joel Hammil, *teleplay by* Brad Radnitz; *directed by* Michael J. Kane; *guest star* Sterling Holloway.
A carrier pigeon, blown off course by a storm, arrives on the island. After he's fit to fly again, he's sent off with a note from the Castaways explaining their predicament. Burt, his owner, is in prison. He receives the message, and thinks it's a joke from his ladyfriend with whom he communicates via the pigeon. The pigeon returns to the island with a note to Burt's ladyfriend saying he had gotten a good laugh out of her message. Notes go back and forth. Finally, they send a rolled-up photograph of themselves on the island to prove their story. Just as the pigeon arrives in Burt's cell, the warden gives Burt a pardon. Burt is free. And because he's free, he frees the pigeon, too, leaving the Castaways on the island. *Theme: Freedom for one sometimes leads to imprisonment for others.*

Bang! Bang! Bang! *Written by* Leonard Goldstein; *directed by* Charles Norton; *guest stars* Rudy LaRusso, Bartlett Robinson, Kirk Duncan.
The government has perfected a soft synthetic plastic which, when hardened, becomes a powerful explosive. A test crate of this material washes ashore on the island. The Castaways are delighted with this clay-like substance which can harden into plastic

dishes, golf balls, costume jewelry, etc. A monkey throws one of the golf balls, which explodes, blowing up a tree. The Castaways realize all these objects they've made from the plastic are actually explosives. The monkey continues to steal objects from the Castaways and throw them around the island, keeping the Castaways under continuous state of siege. Gilligan, who has a special friendly relationship with the monkey, goes to his cave to retrieve all the "explosives." This puts an end to the danger from seemingly harmless articles. *Theme: Innocent objects can sometimes turn out to be deadly weapons.*

Gilligan, the Goddess. *Written by* Jack Paritz and Bob Rodgers; *directed by* Gary Nelson; *guest star* Stanley Adams.

The native king of a nearby island arrives. Legend says Goddess Winomi will be found on this little island. Mrs. Howell, Ginger, and Mary Ann all are delighted at the prospect of becoming a goddess. That is, until they learn that the goddess must become the bride of the volcano. In order to save the women from this fate, Gilligan dresses as a woman, hoping to find some means of escape later. The king is so taken with "Gilliana" he wants her for himself instead of the volcano. However, during a romantic scene with the king, Gilligan's wig, high heels and grass skirt fall off, revealing Gilligan. The king and his entourage believe this goddess is evil and dash to their canoe and leave the island. *Theme: As Margaret Wolfe Hungerford said, "Beauty is in the eye of the beholder."*

Appendix 2: Synopses of *Gilligan's Island* Movies and Specials

Rescue from Gilligan's Island. *Air date:* October 14 and 21, 1978. *Written by* Sherwood Schwartz, Elroy Schwartz, Al Schwartz, and David P. Harmon; *directed by* Leslie Martinson; *guest stars* Judith Baldwin, Vincent Schiavelli, Art LaFleur, Barbara Mallory, John Wheeler, Norman Bartold, Mario Machado, Don Marshall, Robert Wood, Judd Laurence, Alex Rodine, Martin Rudy, June Whitley Taylor, Melvin Prestidge.

Gilligan finds a metal disc on the island made of some strange alloy. The Professor is able to use it as a barometer, and he learns that a tropical hurricane is headed their way which will cause a tidal wave. The Castaways tie themselves to the supports of the two main huts, and when the tidal wave hits, they are swept out to sea in their huts, which become rafts. They're rescued by the Coast Guard and given a heroes' welcome in Honolulu.

Meanwhile, two Russian spies have been sent to recover the metal disc that Gilligan wears on a leather thong around his neck as a good luck charm. It's part of a secret satellite which had gone off course, and which the Soviets had blown up.

The spies have trouble tracking down Gilligan. That's because Gilligan and the Skipper are visiting the other Castaways, who have each returned to their former ways of life. The Skipper needs their signatures on an insurance form so he can be repaid for the wreck of the S.S. *Minnow*. He needs the money to buy a new boat.

The Skipper and Gilligan visit Ginger in Hollywood, where she is disturbed at the kind of X- and R-rated movies now being made. Then they visit the Howells, who are very disturbed at the way their snobby friends treat Gilligan and the Skipper. Next they visit the Professor, and they learn he's disturbed because his new celebrity status has overshadowed his work as a scientist. Finally they visit Mary Ann, and they find she's disturbed because she's supposed to marry her boyfriend who's waited so many years, but she no longer loves him.

After the Skipper collects everybody's signatures on the insurance form, he's able to buy a new boat which he calls the S.S. *Minnow II*. He's so grateful, he invites all the Castaways for a Christmas cruise. Gilligan suggests that they look for the old island where they were shipwrecked for so many years.

Just before the Castaways leave, the Russian spies try to remove the metal disc from Gilligan's neck. But they have been tracked by some F.B.I. men, who seize them and recover the strange metal alloy for our government.

Then the Castaways shove off to look for their desert island. As luck would have it, another storm develops and the *Minnow II* meets the same fate that befell the first *Minnow*. The Castaways are once again cast away on the island from which the tidal wave had rescued them.

Top: *The Castaways return to civilization in* Rescue from Gilligan's Island. *(Judy Baldwin, second from right, replaced Tina Louise as Ginger.)* Bottom: *Mr. and Mrs. Thurston Howell III, traveling light—only one chauffeur—in* Rescue from Gilligan's Island.

Theme: When you return to the same place and the same people you once knew, things are seldom the way they were; the only thing that remains constant is change.

The "Castaways" on Gilligan's Island. *Air date:* March 3, 1979. *Written by* Sherwood Schwartz, Al Schwartz, Elroy Schwartz; *directed by* Earl Bellamy; *guest stars* Marcia Wallace, Tom Bosley, Mokihana, Judith Searle, Joan Roberts, Rod Browning, Peter MacLean, Judith Baldwin, Robbie Sloan, Robert Carlson, Sonny Craver, Denise Cheshire, Natasha Ryan, Maurice Hill, Ron Kuhlman (voice only).

Gilligan discovers two old semi-demolished World War II airplanes on the island. The Professor figures out a way to put the two broken planes together, and with the help of the other Castaways, makes one that can fly, à la *The Flight of the Phoenix.* They take off to fly to Hawaii, but to keep the shaky plane in the air, they have to throw all their belongings off the plane. In the process, Gilligan himself falls out of the plane along with the luggage. He parachutes down to the island, and the others return to pick him up. Meanwhile, the Air Force has spotted the plane while it was in the air, and they land on the island to come to the aid of the Castaways.

Happy about their rescue, the Howells build a hotel on the island called the "Castaways," a restful resort with no phones, no mail, no cars, no TV; a place for guests to get away from it all. The Howells are the managers of the "Castaways," and the other Castaways run the resort. Gilligan and the Skipper bring in guests from passing cruise ships with their motor launch; Ginger entertains in the Shipwreck Room; Mary Ann is in charge of the Exercise Hut; and the Professor is in charge of lectures and scientific studies.

Among the first guests are Myra Elliot and her husband, Henry, a workaholic businessman. Another "guest" on the island is a twelve-year old stowaway named Robbie. He has sneaked off the cruise ship with the Elliots' to get away from his parents. They want him to practice gymnastics eight hours a day so he can join the United States Gymnastics Team. The Skipper and Gilligan assume he is the Elliots' son, since he came ashore with them. But after Robbie arrives on the island, he disappears into the jungle area beyond the hotel, swinging easily from tree to tree on the vines.

Even on the island, Myra can't stop her workaholic husband from working. In spite of all the facilities at the "Castaways" for swimming, scuba diving, fishing, and relaxing, Henry refuses to put away his briefcase and papers. Even on this remote island he's consumed with arranging real estate deals.

When the Castaways learn the young boy is on the island, they alert his parents on the cruise ship, and they try to find him in the jungle. It's Gilligan who locates the young gymnast and gains his confidence. When the boy's parents from the cruise ship land on the island, they are reconciled with their son, thanks to Gilligan. Both sides recognize the other's point of view.

The same is true for Myra and Henry Elliot. Henry finally learns that all work and no play can be just as harmful as all play and no work. Thanks to Mary Ann's massages, and Ginger's hula dance, Henry puts away his briefcase and papers. Meanwhile, Myra is forced to acknowledge that without Henry's dedication to business affairs, they would never be able to afford vacations like this one.

At the same time, the Professor laughs at the fears of the assistant manager, a native Hawaiian, who believes a native mask will bring bad luck. The professor insists on using it as a decorative motif at the big luau to prove it is superstition. In the midst of the celebration there's an earthquake which rocks the island. Although no one is injured, the Professor is forced to admit the possibility of evil spirits.

Top: *Tom Bosley and Marcia Wallace, guest stars on* The "Castaways" on Gilligan's Island. Bottom: *Tom Bosley as a guest at the "Castaways," enjoying a massage from Mary Ann.*

Martin Landau and Barbara Bain played bad guys J.J. Pierson and Olga Smetna on The Harlem Globetrotters on Gilligan's Island.

Theme: Relationships among people, whether they are husbands and wives, parents and children, or Castaways, or, indeed, the nations of the world, remain one of the most difficult problems in society.

The Harlem Globetrotters on Gilligan's Island. *Air date:* May 15, 1981. *Written by* Sherwood Schwartz, Al Schwartz, David P. Harmon, Gordon Mitchell; *directed by* Peter Baldwin; *guest stars* Martin Landau, Barbara Bain, Constance Forslund, David Ruprecht, Dreama Denver, Scatman Crothers, The Harlem Globetrotters, Whitney Rydbeck, Rosalind Chao, Chick Hearn, Stu Nahan.

J.J. Pierson, a power-mad billionaire, and his science associate, Olga Smetna, former guests at Thurston Howell III's "Castaways" hotel, discover an incredible new element, Supremium, in one of the caves on the island. They are determined to frighten the Castaways off the island and own the world's supply of Supremium. Their robot, "George," does their dirty work for them. George puts deadly spiders in Gilligan and the Skipper's hut, and in Ginger and Mary Ann's hut. He also puts poison in an experiment the Professor is conducting, and then sends a huge boulder crashing down a hill toward the Howells.

When these attempts to frighten the Castaways off the island don't work, J.J. Pierson and Olga register at the hotel so J.J. can swindle them out of the island by getting all the Castaways to sign over the deed.

Meanwhile, the Harlem Globetrotters, on a world tour with their coach to play basketball with teams of various countries, are forced to ditch their plane. They're all saved in a life raft and drift ashore on "Gilligan's Island." While awaiting their rescue, they practice basketball, using coconuts. Gilligan discovers them and brings them to the hotel where the Howells make them honorary guests at the "Castaways."

J.J. Pierson gets Ginger to sign the deed to the island by tricking her into thinking it's a contract to do a film with his studio. Gilligan signs his name to the deed after a physical threat from George. Mary Ann signs after she is plied with charm and champagne by J.J. Pierson. The Skipper thinks he's signing a contract to be the captain of Pierson's new oceanliner. And Olga gets the Professor to sign what he believes is an application for the Pierson Prize for Island Research.

Pierson only needs the Howells' signatures to complete the deed to the island. He makes a bet with Thurston Howell IV: a basketball game between the Howells' team, the Harlem Globetrotters, and Pierson's team, the Invincibles, the winner to get the island. The Invincibles are computerized robots designed by Olga.

At the last moment, thanks to Gilligan, who physically accompanies the ball through the basket, the Harlem Globetrotters win the game.

J.J. Pierson, who always covers his bets no matter how sure, has stolen all the Supremium from the island and transferred it to his yacht. However, it turns out to be an unstable element, and it blows up Pierson's yacht and the entire world's supply of Supremium.

Theme: Devious and underhanded schemes rarely succeed; or as Gilligan would put it, "Cheaters never prosper."

Index

321